ARABIC   ASTRONOMY   BANKING   BEE-KEEPING   BIOLOGY
GANISATION   CALCULUS   CANASTA   CARPENTRY   CHEMISTRY
COMMERCIAL CORRESPONDENCE   COMMERCIAL TRAVELLING   TO
OKING   CRICKET   DRAWING   DRESSMAKING   DUTCH   DUTTON
ELECTRICITY IN THE HOUSE   ELOCUTIONIST   EMBROIDERY
ENGLISH RENASCENCE TO THE ROMANTIC REVIVAL   ROMANTIC
EVERYDAY FRENCH   TO EXPRE   FISHING   TO FLY
ASE BOOK   GARDENING   GA   O
IONARY   GERMAN GRAMMAR   OLI
GOOD FARM ACCOUNTING   INC
UIT FARMING   GOOD GRASSLA   MAL
GOOD POULTRY KEEPING   SOIL
BLE   HINDUSTANI   HISTORY :   TH
AU   CONSTANTINE   COOK   CRANMER   ERASM   AND
MILTON   PERICLES   PETER THE GREAT   PUSHKIN   RALEIGH   RICHELIEU
ODROW   EMENT
ALIAN   ETTER
ENGIN   · · · · AND HE WILL BE   ANICS
ODERN   ORINC
PHILOSO   HYSIC
PLUMBI   YET WISER Proverbs 9:9   PUBLIC
RECKO   USSIAN
X: ITS N   AND PURPOSE   SOCCER   SPANISH   SPE   AND
SWA   SWEDISH   TEACHING   THINKING   TRIG   METRY
BRITH   RAILWAYS FOR BOYS   CAMPING FOR BOYS AND GIRL
FOR GIRLS   MODELMAKING FOR BOYS   NEEDLEWORK FOR GIRLS
BOYS AND GIRLS   SAILING AND SMALL BOATS FOR BOYS AND GIRLS
ORK FOR BOYS   ADVERTISING & PUBLICITY   ALGEBRA   AMATEUR
PING   BIOLOGY   BOOK-KEEPING   BRICKWORK   BRINGING U
NTRY   CHEMISTRY   CHESS   CHINESE   COMMERCIAL ARITHMETIC
TRAVELLING   TO COMPOSE MUSIC   CONSTRUCTIONAL DETAIL
NG   DUTCH   DUTTON SPEEDWORDS   ECONOMIC GEOGRAPHY
ST   EMBROIDERY   ENGLISH GRAMMAR   LITERARY APPRECIATION
IVAL   ROMANTIC REVIVAL   VICTORIAN AGE   CONTEMPORARY
FISHING   TO FLY   FREELANCE WRITING   FRENCH   FRENCH
OUSE   GEOGRAPHY OF LIVING THINGS   GEOLOGY   GEOMETRY
ASE BOOK   GOLF   GOOD CONTROL OF INSECT PESTS   GOOD
FARM CROPS   GOOD FARMING   GOOD FARMING BY MACHIN
ND   GOOD AND HEALTHY ANIMALS   GOOD MARKET GARDENING
GOOD SHEEP FARMING   GOOD SOIL   GOOD ENGLISH   GREEK
ORY: ABRAHAM LINCOLN   ALEXANDER THE GREAT   BOLIVAR   BOTHA
CRANMER   ERASMUS   GLADSTONE AND LIBERALISM   HENRY V   JOAN O
EAT   PUSHKIN   RALEIGH   RICHELIEU   ROBESPIERRE   THOMAS JEFFERSON
HOME NURSING   HORSE MANAGEMENT   HOUSEHOLD DOCTOR
OURNALISM   LATIN   LAWN TENNIS   LETTER WRITER   MALAY
PONENTS   WORKSHOP PRACTICE   MECHANICS   MECHANICAL
MORE GERMAN   MOTHERCRAFT   MOTORING   MOTOR CYCLING
APHY   PHYSICAL GEOGRAPHY   PHYSICS   PHYSIOLOGY   PITMAN
UESE   PSYCHOLOGY   PUBLIC ADMINISTRATION   PUBLIC SPEAKING

THE TEACH YOURSELF BOOKS
EDITED BY LEONARD CUTTS

FRENCH

**Uniform with this volume
and in the same
series**

———————

TEACH YOURSELF

FRENCH

A BOOK OF SELF-INSTRUCTION IN FRENCH BASED
ON THE WORK BY SIR JOHN ADAMS, M.A., LL.D.,
COMPLETELY REVISED AND ENLARGED BY NORMAN
SCARLYN WILSON, M.A.

THE ENGLISH UNIVERSITIES PRESS LTD
102 NEWGATE STREET
LONDON, E.C.I

First published in this form April 1938
This impression 1960

Printed in Great Britain for the English Universities Press, Limited,
by Richard Clay and Company, Ltd., Bungay, Suffolk

PREFACE

NOT long ago a witty foreigner wrote a book called : *The English, are they Human ?* to which question he gave a qualified assent. Students learning French forty years back might equally well have entertained doubts of the human qualities of a nation which, to judge from the sentences provided for translation, displayed such inordinate interest in the whereabouts of the gardener's cat, and waxed so disputatious about the ownership of a pencil.

We have progressed since then. Such works as that brilliant anonymous volume *Brighter French* reveal very clearly the idiomatic raciness of the French language and the essential humanity of those that speak it. But there is a reservation to be borne in mind. The full title of that book is *Brighter French—for bright young people who already know some.*

Teach Yourself French is not intended for such readers. Those who use this book do not need any previous acquaintanceship with French. They do not even need to be particularly bright. But they will find it useful. It steers a middle course between the old fatuity and the modern slang. It contains all the essential points of grammar, which are illustrated by the sentences.

Anyone who studies it conscientiously should be able at the end to read any novel or newspaper, to write understandable French, though it won't be faultless, and to find his way about in France without choosing toothpicks on the menu instead of soup or telling an astonished waiter that he has an enormous wife, when he really means that he is very hungry.   In other words he will know quite a lot of French and something about France and be in a position to get to know a good deal more about both.   What more can he want?

N. SCARLYN WILSON.

INTRODUCTION

HOW TO USE THE BOOK

THE purpose of this book is to enable the student to learn French by using French, and that without any help other than that given in this book. Accordingly it is essential to begin dealing with French sentences at once, and to seek the shortest way to begin the reading of a bit of actual French. The book is not a Grammar, and therefore does not require to follow the formal arrangement that grammarians regard as essential. Yet it is not to be assumed that the following pages lack method because they are not formal. Each fact is presented as it is required in the process of preparing the student, in the smallest possible number of lessons, to begin to read a French author.

The book consists of two parts, which are complementary. Part I contains most of the actual instruction, and a series of exercises in turning French into English, and English into French. The French–English exercises are distinguished by the letter *a*, the English–French by the letter *b*. Part II contains a Key to all the exercises in Part I; but it is more than a Key, as it supplies by means of Notes a great deal of information, the need for which arises out of the difficulties of the different exercises. Help is always most appreciated where the need for it is most felt, therefore in Part I enough information is given to enable the student to work the exercises correctly; while in Part II additional information is given which throws light upon difficulties which can be properly appreciated only after the exercise has been attempted.

Parts I and II should be carried on abreast, for any given exercise in Part I implies a knowledge of everything in Part II before the Key to the given exercise.

The book should be worked through exercise by exercise. Thus Exercise 5a in Part I should be written out and corrected by means of the version of 5a in Part II, before 5b is attempted. Remember that you will learn more from a careful examination of the French–English exercises than from all the "instructions" that anyone can give you. Whenever you are in doubt as to how to turn an English sentence into French, turn back to preceding French–English sentences, and you will almost always find a model to supply the guidance you need.

Most students will find it desirable to revise after every five lessons. An excellent way of revising is to study each lesson in Part I, as in the first reading, but for exercises turn to Part II, and then use Part I as the Key to correct those exercises. This gives entirely fresh practice, for what was formerly English–French is now French–English, and *vice versa*.

To students who find great difficulty with the exercises, the following plan may be recommended. Study carefully each lesson; then translate the French into English, and compare it with Part II. Then, instead of turning back to Part I for the corresponding English–French, stay at Part II and do the French–English there and use Part I as the Key. Thus the student would write the English for 5a in Part I, and correct it by 5a in Part II; then he could write the English for 5b in Part II and correct it by 5b in Part I. In this way the student would go through the whole book without doing anything but French–English. The book could then be worked through a second time, this time in the regular way.

Students who find little difficulty in going through the

book in the regular way for the first time, might revise the whole by doing *all* the exercises in the form of English–French exercises.

It is clear that the book can be used in many ways according to the circumstances of each case—the important point being that however the student works it, he will find within the book itself all that he needs to test his work.

In keeping with the plan of the book, the Vocabulary at the end is entirely French–English. Give an Englishman one or two English equivalents for a French word in a given French sentence, and he can easily select the word which suits the English translation; but give him one or two French equivalents for an English word in a given English sentence, and he has great difficulty in choosing the word which suits the French version. If we wish a French equivalent for an English word, we ought to seek it in our memory, not in the dictionary; for whatever words we find in our memory are there *because we have used them*. We therefore know by experience what they mean in actual usage. A French equivalent borrowed from an English–French dictionary may be a total stranger to us, and may be quite wrongly used by us in perfect good faith.

Further, the Vocabulary has been made as short as is consistent with the satisfactory working of the exercises. This has been accomplished by the omission of all the little words that occur over and over again which the student cannot help knowing, articles, common conjunctions, pronouns, numerals. Proper names are also omitted.

A more startling omission is that of the Irregular Verbs. No class of words gives so much trouble as this, so it may seem strange to omit these verbs from the Vocabulary. But since there is an alphabetical list of the Irregular Verbs given immediately before the Vocabulary, the effect of the omission will be to drive the student to consult this list very frequently. By the time he comes to require the Vocabulary at all, he knows whether the word for the meaning of which he is hunting is a verb or not. If it is a verb, and is not to be found in the Vocabulary, he will be certain that it is an Irregular Verb, and will know where to find it. Familiarity with the Irregular Verbs is of the utmost importance in French, and any plan is to be commended which will make students work among them. While looking for one verb, the student will notice something about many other verbs.

The purpose of these omissions is not merely to make the Vocabulary more workable—though that is in itself a most desirable object. The student should be encouraged in every possible way to refer to what he has already done for information as to what he is now to do. If he is not sure of the meaning of a *ce qui* or a *ce que*, or an *au delà* or *de travers*, he ought to seek help rather in a previous exercise than in a Vocabulary. The Vocabulary is, after all, only a sort of museum where mummified words are to be found. In the exercises and translations the words are living and explain themselves. The main use of the Vocabulary is for the translation of French passages. You will find that the English–French exercises which follow these passages can be worked almost entirely with the words already used.

Further, since there is a worked-out version supplied for every exercise in the book, there is the less need for an elaborate Vocabulary. But here a warning is necessary. Never use the Key as a short cut to the meaning of a word. The exercises are so arranged that you can in every case find the meaning of every English and French word in them, either in the Vocabulary or in a previous exercise. If, however, any doubt arises as to a particular word, be sure that you write down *something* before you consult the Key. For while the student must depend ultimately on the Key for help, he must see to it that that help is legitimately worked for. He ought to make it an absolute rule never to consult the Key till he has made *some* version of a whole exercise. However difficult the exercise, the student can always at least write out something. The mere fact of facing a problem prepares the mind to understand and *enjoy* the solution, whereas if every difficulty is removed by at once turning to Part II to see how the thing is done, little impression is made on the mind, and there is little real progress.

CONTENTS

PART II

PART I

PART I

FRENCH PRONUNCIATION

IT is impossible to learn French pronunciation properly from a book. Yet we must say something about this subject, for if you learn French at all you must pronounce it somehow. If you wish to learn French for no other purpose than to read and write it, you might simply pronounce it as in English. But this would be an unreasonable limitation of the usefulness of the results of your study. This book cannot give you a good French accent, but it can give you such hints as may keep your French sounds within measurable distance of what they ought to be.

You can learn French sounds properly only by hearing French correctly spoken. Yet those of you who afterwards have the privilege of hearing good French speakers will, from your study of this chapter, know better what to listen for. You will know the difficult sounds, and will be able to correct your first impressions gained from this book by the actual sounds you hear. There is one method of becoming accustomed to French pronunciation within the reach of almost every student, and that is the radio. Make a habit of listening to the French stations, especially to the reading of French news. In London and other large towns, too, a student nowadays can see French films and hear the spoken word, while the English sub-titles afford a clue to what is going on.

In French the pronunciation is affected by the accents. Of these there are three : the *acute* ('), the *grave* (`), and the *circumflex* (ˆ). It is interesting to note that the circumflex is made up of a combination of the other two.

17

Having no accents in English, we are apt to pay little attention to them in French. This is a mistake, as they give a very real help in pronunciation. In the meantime it is enough to say that the *acute* when placed over a vowel sharpens the sound : the circumflex lengthens the sound. You will learn their use and importance much better from the examples which follow.

Vowels.—The French *vowels* are *a, e, i, o, u* and *y*.

a has two sounds in French :—

> (1) as in *fat*. Examples : *avoir* = to have, *année* = a year.
>
> (2) as in *father*. This sound is indicated by the circumflex, as in *âme* = soul and *âge* = age.

a never has the sound it has in the English *fame*.

e has four sounds :—

> (1) *e* mute : like the *u* in *cut* : as *de* = of.
>
> (2) *é* : a sound between the *e* in *lexicon* and the *ai* in *fair* : *opéra* = opera.
>
> (3) *è* : for this sound the tongue is more used, the *e* in *met* is near it : *très* = very.
>
> (4) *ê* : a sound between the first *e* in *there* and the *a* in *hate* : *bête* = beast.

i has two sounds—a short and a long, the long being marked by the circumflex. The foundation of both sounds is *ee* as in *seen*. The sound of the English *i* in *fire* is never given to the French *i*. In French *mire* sounds *meer*.

o has two sounds :—

> (1) like *o* in *not* : *sol* = the soil.
>
> (2) like *oa* in *foal* : *pôle* = pole.

u has nothing exactly like it in English. It is not the *u* sound in *few*, nor the *oo* sound in *poor*, but something between them. A rule sometimes given to produce the sound is : put your lips in the position of saying *u* and try to say *e*. The queer sound that results is not unlike the French *u*.

y (called in French *i grec*) has the same sound as *i*.

Consonants.—Of the French consonants the following behave exactly as in English : *b, d, f, k, m, n, p, q, r, t, v, z.*

c is always sounded like *k* unless it comes before *e, i,* or *y,* or has a cedilla under it.   *Car* is pronounced kar, *celle* and *maçon* are pronounced sell and masson.

g has the hard sound as in *gas,* except before *e, i* and *y,* where it sounds like the *s* in *pleasure.*

h is a troublesome letter which is sometimes sounded and sometimes not. It is never so strongly sounded as in English.

j sounds like the *s* in *pleasure.*

l has two sounds :—

    (1) exactly as in English.

    (2) a queer sound called *liquid,* of which we shall
        speak below.

s has two sounds :—

    (1) a hissing sound as in English *speak.*

    (2) a *z* sound when used between two vowels as in
        maison = a house.

x sounds as in English except when it begins a word, when it sounds like *gz* as in *Xerxes.*

Nasal Sounds.—These must be heard before they can be properly imitated. If you try to say *bang,* passing the sound through the nose as much as possible and snipping off the *g* just when it is to be sounded, you come to something a little like the French nasal *an.* The other nasals are *in, on* and *un.*

Though *m* occurs in the spelling of nasals, it is always sounded like *n.*

1. Nasals sounded like *an* are *am, em, en* and *ean.* *Ambassadeur* sounds *An*bassadeur, *Jean* sounds Jaṇ, the dot below the *n* indicating the nasal element.

2. Nasals sounded like *in* are *aim, ain, ein.* Thus *faim* = hunger, sounds exactly the same as *fin* = an end. In French poetry *main* (hand) and *frein* (a brake) rhyme.

3. *om* sounds the same as *on.* *Ombre* (shade) sounds *on*bre.

4. Like *un* are sounded *um* and *eun*.

A nasal ending followed by a vowel ceases to be nasal. *Fin* (fine) is pronounced through the nose. Add an *e* and the nasal sound disappears, the word *fine* being pronounced *feen*. The same effect is produced if the following word begins with a vowel. *Bon* (good) is nasal, but in the phrase *bon enfant* (good child), *bon* loses its nasal sound.

Important Combinations of Letters.—*ch* sounds *sh* except when it comes before a consonant; then it sounds *k*.

gn is a very troublesome sound. *Line* sounds like the English *lean*, except that the *ē* sound is a little longer. *Ligne* sounds the same, with the difference that the final *n* is prolonged in a peculiar way by raising the upper lip slightly. In order to stop this sound you are apt to make the word end in a little jerky sound like *yeh*—*lee-nnnyeh*. This *yeh* is to be repressed as much as possible. *ll* is another disagreeable combination. *gn* is called a liquid sound, and so is *ll*. A single *l* is sometimes liquid too, as in the word *pareil* (equal). The liquid *l* (or *ll*) has always an *i* before it. There are two ways of sounding this liquid. The correct way is to press the tongue against the palate and let the air escape at the sides. The incorrect way is to sound *ll* like a short *y* or like the *yeh* above. *Ailleurs* (besides) is thus sounded *a-year*. You should adopt the incorrect way. It is much easier—and what is good enough for Paris is good enough for us. The incorrect way is the usual one in Paris.

ph is sounded *f* as in English.

oi is sounded with a little explosion like *wa : bois* (wood) is sounded *bwa*—short and sharp. *oy*, *oe* and *oê* are sounded like *oi*.

ou is an easy, good-natured sound, exactly like the English *oo*. But English people are apt to presume upon its good nature, and apply its sound to other combinations, particularly to *eu*—a very serious blunder.

eu is sounded pretty much like the little sound we make at the back of our throats when we are tired and have drawn a long breath. It is sometimes compared with *e* in *her*, but is, if anything, a little longer than that sound. At all events you will do well to make it a little longer. You will get nearer the truth that way. Perhaps the sound is still better described as that of *ea* in *heard*. The importance of this difference in sound is easily seen when you find that when you mispronounce a word it not only does not mean what you want, but does mean something else. If you call *leur* (their) *loor*, a Frenchman thinks you mean *heavy*, for which the word is *lourd*. Every self-respecting teacher of French tells this story : Two Englishmen were staying in Paris in winter. One of them went out one evening, telling the waiter not to let out the fire. Now, the French for *fire* is *feu*, but this Englishman made the common mistake of calling it *fou*. Unfortunately, *fou* is the French for a *madman*. The waiter accordingly locked the door on the Englishman who remained; and then the fun began.

au and *eau* sound like the *o* in *go* : *mauvaise* sounds *movaise*, not *mawvaise*. The word *beau* is almost an English word now, yet keeps the French pronunciation.

You should practise the following six words; they are very instructive as to French sounds : *fille, faille, fauille, fouille, feuille, feille*. [Some of these are not actual words in French.]

The *ille* with which they all end sounds eeee-eh—a long-drawn-out *e* and a tired little *eh* at the end. *Fille* sounds feeee-eh.

Faille has three *separate* sounds : fa- (as in *father*) -eeee-eh; but these must be run together so as to make one continuous sound, as if the word were of one syllable.

Fauille, in the same way, must make into something like one syllable the three sounds foe- (as in English word *foe*) -eeee-eh. The *eh* you can easily find by practice is really the sound you cannot help making when you cease saying the long *eeee*.

Fouille is made up of foo-eeee-eh.

Feuille is made up of feu- (eu sounds like *ea* in heard) -eeee-eh.

Feille is made up of fe- (e like *u* in butter) -eeee-eh. The pronunciation of the three sounds is closer in *feille* than in any of the others, except, of course, *fille*. It *nearly* rhymes with *heigh* in *heigh-ho*, but has not so much of the long *i* sound.

As good a way as any for practising the sounds in single French words is to learn off the numerals from one up to twenty.

1.	un	sounded	un (nasal).
2.	deux	,,	deu (NOT *doo* nor *dew*).
3.	trois	,,	trwa.
4.	quatre	,,	kat'r (NOT *kat er*).
5.	cinq	,,	sank.
6.	six	,,	seece.
7.	sept	,,	set.
8.	huit	,,	weet (nearly; the sound is got by beginning to say *oo* and ending sharply with *eet*).
9.	neuf	,,	nuf.
10.	dix	,,	deece.
11.	onze	,,	onze [1] (nasal).
12.	douze	,,	dooze (NOT *dooce*).
13.	treize	,,	treze (NOT *trees*).
14.	quatorze	,,	katorze.
15.	quinze	,,	kanze (nasal).
16.	seize	,,	sez (NOT *sees*).
17.	dix-sept	,,	dees-set.
18.	dix-huit	,,	dees-weet.
19.	dix-neuf	,,	dees-nuf.
20.	vingt	,,	van (nasal).

[1] None of the final *e*'s in this list is sounded.

Taking it for granted that you have carefully studied the notes about the different sounds in French, let us suppose that we have a Frenchman reading to us a bit of French—we shall find certain peculiarities that we must carefully examine. In the following, the ordinary type is the French, the words in italics are to be sounded as if they were English words. Note that a dot below the line in our italic version means that the *m* or *n* above it has to have the nasal sound; while the diæresis means that the *u* over which it is placed is to have the troublesome *u* sound peculiar to French. The sign ～ over a letter *n* shows that it is to have the liquid sound.

Il était une fois un bûcheron et une bûcheronne qui
ee letey tuṇe fwa un büchroṇ ey üne büchrone kee
avaient sept enfants, tous garçons; l'aîné n'avait que
avey se [1] *tanfaṇ toos garsoṇ ; lāney navey kŭ*
dix ans, et le plus jeune n'en avait que sept. Ils étaient
dee zaṇ ey lŭ plü zheun naṇ avey kŭ set. Eel zetay
fort pauvres et leurs enfants les incommodaient beau-
for povre ey leur zanfan le [2] *sankommoday bo-*
coup, parce qu'aucun d'eux ne pouvait encore gagner sa
koo pars kokuṇ deu ne poovey tankor gañey sa
vie.
vee.

Liaison.—Probably the first thing that strikes you is the way in which certain letters are carried forward from the end of one word to the beginning of the next. This happens when one word ends with a consonant and the following word begins with a vowel. Thus in the first line *l* is carried from *il* to *était*, while the final *t* of *était* is in its turn carried forward to *une*. We must not think that this is peculiar to French. We do this sometimes ourselves. *N* is very frequently carried forward by us, so that young children are sometimes not quite sure

---

[1] Like *se* in *set*.   [2] Like *le* in *let*.

whether they are eating an *apple* or a *napple*, and have the impression that a hen lays *neggs*. *T* is also carried forward, as is proved by the contraction *'tis*. *S* is carried forward too. It is only by making an unusual pause between the words that we can make a distinction between *this table* and *this stable*. If we were teaching a Frenchman English, we might quite fairly give him the following two lines exactly as we have done with the French extract above :—

> it is arranged out of court
> *ĭ ti zarrange dou tof court.*

If there is any reason for keeping words distinct in English, we do not carry forward, as when we say *this stable*. It is the same in French. The *liaison*, as this joining-on is called, does not take place at a natural pause in the sense. Thus the *s* of *fois* in the first line of French is not carried forward to the *un*.

The *liaison* is much more marked in French than in English from another peculiarity which you will observe as soon as you hear a Frenchman reading French. This may be called :—

Evenness of intonation.—French reading flows much more smoothly than ours. In a way it is monotonous, though it is very pleasant to the ear. The French go on the principle of giving fair play to all the syllables in a word. In all our words one syllable gets much more importance than the others. In English we say *in-cap'-able*, in French they say *in-ca-pa-ble*, each of the four syllables being sounded with equal force, and both *a*'s sounded as in *father*. Sometimes it is said that in English the accent is thrown as near the beginning of the word as possible, in French as near the end. This is true about English, but in French the better statement is that the accent is equally distributed. What makes it appear that the final syllable gets a special accent is the force of contrast with English, where the final syllable often gets almost no attention at all. Take the English *respiratory* for example and the French *respiratoire* (res-pee-ra-twar), and the fact that the final *twar* gets fair play makes it appear to an English ear as if it got more than fair play.

Silent Letters.—Talking of fair play brings up another point that you cannot help noticing while listening to a Frenchman reading French. A great many letters, when they come at the end of a word, don't get fair play, and indeed are not sounded at all. Examining our French extract again, we find that the *s* at the end of *fois*, the *p* in *sept*, the *t* in *et*, the *t* and *s* in *enfants* and the *s* in *garçons*, in *ans*, in *plus* and in *ils*, the *t* in *fort*, the *p* in *beaucoup*, the *x* in *d'eux*, the *r* in *gagner* are all silent, while in a whole group of words *aient* is sounded simply as *ay*.

The letters that get fair play at the end of a word are *b, c, f, k, l, m, q,* and *r* (unless in the form *er* when *r* is usually silent). The letters that do not get fair play when they come at the end of words standing alone or at the end of a sentence are *d, g, h, p, r* (in form *er*), *s, t, x* and *z*.

grand (great or big) pronounced		grañ.
sang (blood)	,,	sañ.
ah ! (ah !)	,,	as in English.
coup (blow)	,,	koo.
porter (to carry)	,,	portey.
gros (big)	,,	grow.
toupet (cheek, impudence)	,,	tupey
dix (ten)	,,	deess
nez (nose)	,,	nay

Observe that it is only when the words ending with those letters stand alone, or are followed by a consonant, that they lose their power. If they are followed by a vowel they are carried forward : *fort* (very) sounds *for*, but *fort épaisse* (very thick) sounds *for tepaisse*. *d* is peculiar in this way : when it is carried forward it is sounded like *t*. *grand enfant* (big child) is sounded *graṇ tenfaṇ*.

One or two words of very common occurrence demand special attention. *Et* (and) is always sounded like *ey* (as in *whiskey*), and the *t* is *never* sounded or carried forward. *Est* is sounded longer than *et*, and has the *t* silent, but *always* carried forward when followed by a vowel. *Six* (six) and *dix* (ten) have three pronunciations : (1) Standing alone, seess, deess, (2) before a vowel, seeze, deeze, (3) before a consonant, sēē, dēē. *Neuf* (*nine* and also *new*), when followed by a vowel, changes the *f* into a *v*. *Neuf enfants* sounds *nu venfan*. *Cinq* and *huit* do not sound the final consonant before a consonant : *cinq francs*, *huit jours*, sound *saṇ fraṇ, oueee zhoor* (five francs, eight days).

There is one general hint well worth your attention in beginning French pronunciation : *Keep your eye on the e mute*; it usually belongs to the syllable *before* it. In English a word like Inverashley is pronounced In'-ver-ash'-ley : in French it would be sounded Inve-rash-ley—three syllables instead of four. The word *bachelier* (*bachelor*, in University sense) is very commonly mispronounced by beginners *bach-el'-i-er*, whereas it should be *bache-li-er*. So *savetier* (cobbler) and *cafetier* (one who keeps a coffee-house) are pronounced *save-ti-er* and *cafe-ti-er*. Even in the case of separate words the tendency is still to throw the *e* mute backwards. *Je ne suis pas* (I am not) may be correctly pronounced in four syllables, but in ordinary French speech the first two words are usually combined, by the *e* mute being thrown backwards, into *jin swee pa*.

A second important hint about *e* mute is to pronounce it always as lightly as possible; just let it be heard and no more. English people are strongly tempted to pronounce *sera* (will be) *serra*. Now, there is a French word *serra* (meaning *pressed* or *squeezed*), so that confusion is certain. The word should be pronounced nearly *s'ra*. It is better to cut the *e* out altogether than to over-pronounce it. Indeed, the final *e* mute is really cut out when followed by a vowel. *Pauvre animal* (poor animal) is very apt to be pronounced *pau ver animal* instead of the correct form *pauv-ranimal*, in which the *e* mute has disappeared.

To put into practice all the rules we have had, read over the following continuation of the passage with which we began :—

Ce qui les chagrinait encore, c'est que le plus jeune était
Sŭ kee le shagreeney taṇkor say kŭ lŭ plü zheun etey
fort délicat et ne disait mot, prenant pour bêtise ce
for deyleeka ey nŭ deezey mo, prenaṇ poor beyteese sŭ
qui était une marque de la bonté de son esprit. Il était
kee etey tüne mark dŭ la boṇtey dŭ son espree. Ee letey
fort petit, et, quand il vint au monde, il n'était guère
for p'tee, ey, kaṇ teel vaṇ tow monde, eel netey guerr
plus gros que le pouce, ce qui fit qu'on l'appela le petit
plü gro kŭ lŭ puss, sŭ kee fee koṇ lap'la lŭ p'tee
poucet.
puss-ey.

Those who wish to make a wider study of French Pronunciation, as private students, should get *Pronunciation of the French Language Simplified*, by A. Bernon (Hachette, 2s .od.).

LESSON I

VERBS AND PRONOUNS

The most fundamental difference between French and English is that French is fonder of indicating changes of meaning by changes in the endings of words. Take the English word *to carry*. The French equivalent is *porter*. Here the *er* at the end tells the Frenchman exactly the same thing as the *to* at the beginning tells the Englishman, *viz.*, that we are speaking merely of the idea of *carrying* in general with no reference to who is carrying, or when the carrying is done, or how it is done. This part of a verb which tells the idea of the verb and nothing more is called the infinitive. *To carry* and *porter* are thus infinitives.

When verbs make plain statements they are said to be in the indicative mood, and if the action is now going on we have what is called the

PRESENT INDICATIVE.

I carry	je porte
thou carriest	tu portes
he (she, it) carries	il (elle) porte
we carry	nous portons
you carry	vous portez
they carry	ils (elles) portent

In English the pronoun *I* is always written with a capital. In French *je* is always written with a small *j*, except when it begins a sentence.

If we call the part of the word that does not change, the *stem*, and the part that does, the *termination*, then *carr-* and *port-* are the stems. In English we have three terminations : *-y, -iest* and *-ies ;* in French we have five : *-e, -es, -ons, -ez, -ent.*

Not only has the French verb more terminations, but they *tell us more.* If I say in English " carr*iest* " you know that it must be used with *thou,* and " carr*ies* " can only be used with *he* (*she* or *it*). These terminations, therefore, give us definite information. But try " carr*y* " : this may go with *I* or *we,* or *you* or *they.* In French only the termination *e* leaves us in any doubt : *es* always goes with *tu, ons* always with *nous, ez* always with *vous, ent* always with *ils* (or *elles*). Thus the French *portez* means *you carry* and nothing else. In other words, you *must* use two words in English for what *may* be expressed by one in French.

This is what is meant by saying that English is in some ways at least a more analytic language than French. It breaks up into two or more words what can be expressed in French by one. This is seen better still in the

FUTURE INDICATIVE.

I shall carry	je porterai
thou wilt carry	tu porteras
he (she, it) will carry	il (elle) portera
we shall carry	nous porterons
you will carry	vous porterez
they will carry	ils (elles) porteront

If I wish to telegraph to a Frenchman something in which the words *I shall carry* occur, I need spend only one penny on them; for the one word *porterai* can mean nothing else but the whole three words *I shall carry*. In English, I cannot escape even with twopence, for *shall carry* might mean *we* shall carry. We must spend the whole threepence on *I shall carry*.

This difference caused by the different pronouns is known in grammar as *person*. The person speaking is always *first* person; so *je* and *nous* which mean *I* and *we* are first person. The person spoken to is always second person; so *tu* and *vous* which mean *thou* and *you* are second person. The person or thing spoken about is always third person; so *il* and *ils* which mean *he* and *they* are third person. *Elle* and *elles* which mean *she* and *they* (if all that are meant by *they* are feminine) are also third person.

If you look now at the terminations of the verb in the future indicative, you will note that they are all different; no two are alike. If the present, two out of the six end in *e*. This time no two have the same termination. Yet there is a general resemblance to the endings of the present. In fact in all tenses of French verbs the second person singular *almost always* ends in *s*, the first person plural in *ons*, the second person plural in *ez*, and the third person plural in *nt*.

Exercise I

(*a*) Put the proper pronouns before the following verbs : (1) lavions; (2) tais; (3) marchent; (4) travaillez; (5) tenaient; (6) aimons; (7) étais; (8) cours; (9) mettez; (10) mettiez.

(*b*) Put the proper terminations to the following verbs: (1) tu aime-; (2) ils étaie-; (3) nous cour-; (4) vous march-; (5) tu marche-; (6) nous ten-; (7) tu parle-; (8) ils craignaie-; (9) nous aimi-; (10) vous tranchi-.

(*c*) Write out the following in French : (1) you carry; (2) you will carry; (3) I shall carry; (4) I carry; (5) they carry; (6) we shall carry; (7) thou carriest; (8) you shall carry; (9) he carries; (10) he shall carry.

(*d*) Write out in French the following parts of the verb *porter* : (1) first pers. sing. pres. ind.; (2) first pers. pl. fut. ind. ; (3) second pers. pl. fut. ind. ; (4) first pers. pl. pres. ind.; (5) third pers. sing. pres. ind.; (6) second pers. sing. pres. ind.; (7) third pers. pl. pres. ind.; (8) second pers. sing. fut. ind.; (9) first pers. sing. fut. ind.; (10) third pers. pl. fut. ind.

LESSON II

GENDER

There is another way in which French words change their terminations to the great inconvenience of English students. There is in grammar a thing called gender, of which we English people can talk with indifference—it gives us so little trouble. With us, in fact, gender corresponds to sex; the name of a male creature is *masculine*, of a female *feminine*, of an inanimate object, neither masculine nor feminine, but what our grammars call *neuter*. A horse is masculine, a cow is feminine, a table is neuter, and there is no more about it. But in French a table (*table*) is feminine; a camel (*chameau*) and a squirrel (*écureuil*) are always masculine, while a mouse (*souris*) and a lark (*alouette*) are always feminine; and there is no neuter at all. As a matter of fact gender in French is determined not so much by the sex of the thing signified as by the form of the word, particularly its termination : it is a matter of words not things.

As there are only two genders in French, if we had any rule for finding out which nouns are feminine, we could take it for granted that all the rest are masculine. Unfortunately no satisfactory rule can be given, but the following, from La Bruyère's *L'Emploi du Genre Facilité* (Hachette, now out-of-print), is the most useful. According to this rule all nouns ending with the following termination are feminine :—

> ale, ole, ule ; ure, ère, eur ;
> rre, lle, ie, ié ; ée, ue, ion ;
> be, ce, de ; fe, ne, pe ;
> se, te, té ; ve, he, aison.

fière ?

Speaking generally *e* is a feminine termination. Observe that nearly the whole of the endings in the list above finish with *e*. Many nouns change from masculine to feminine by just adding an *e*. Thus, *cousin* is a male cousin, *cousine* a female one. *Ami* = a male friend ; *amie* = a female friend.

In French a noun obviously meaning a male person is usually masculine, *e.g.*, *porteur* (bearer, or one who carries) is masculine in spite of the above rule. But sometimes the rule over-rides all common sense ; and we have a sentinel (*sentinelle*) always feminine, because of the ending *lle*, and *Majesté* is always feminine, even when applied to a king, because it ends in *té*.

Corresponding to this difference in gender of nouns there is a difference in the form of the adjectives or qualifying words. *Homme* = man, and *femme* = woman. *Petit homme* = little man. But if we wish to say *little woman* we must add an *e* to the adjective to make it " agree with " the noun, thus *petite femme*.

This is easily understood, but when the words *his* and *her* are used, great trouble arises. The French for *his* is *son* and the feminine of *son* is *sa*. But in using them it has to be continually kept in mind that the gender is determined not by the sex of the one possessing, but by the gender of the thing possessed. *Table* is feminine, so we must say *sa table* whether the table belongs to a man or a woman. *Cœur* (heart) is masculine, so we must say *son cœur* even if we speak about a lady's heart. In short, *son* can be either *his* or *her*, and so can *sa*. *Sa maison* may be *his house* or *her house*; and *son frère* may be *his brother* or *her brother*.

Like *son* and *sa* are *mon* and *ma* meaning *my*, and *ton* and *ta* meaning *thy*. The article *the* has also two forms in French, *le* (m.), *la* (f.).

Exercise 2

[Revise the whole lesson, getting up the table of genders by rote.]

Put in the French word for each of the words in italics.[1]
1. *His* maison. 2. *The* cathédrale. 3. *My* terre. 4. *Her* clémence. 5. *Thy* beauté. 6. *His* femme. 7. *The* charrette. 8. *My* mélancolie. 9. *Thy* terrain. 10. *The* misère. 11. *Thy* courage. 12. *His* pitié. 13. *Her* rumeur. 14. *Thy* capote. 15. *The* boue. 16. *His* médecin. 17. *His* marche. 18. *Thy* preuve. 19. *The* fève. 20. *The* molécule.

[1] You do not need to know the meaning of the French words in this exercise. All you have to do is to look at the endings. Compare them with your table, and thus discover whether they are masculine or feminine.

LESSON III

NUMBER

In French as in English the singular of a noun is made into the plural by adding *s*; *soldat* = a soldier, *soldats* = soldiers. If the singular already ends in an *s*, or something equal to an *s*, there is no change made at all. *Bois* = either wood or woods : *nez* = nose or noses : *voix* (f.) = voice or voices.

Adjectives form their plurals just like nouns.

The following table gives some very important plurals : note that the plurals are both masculine and feminine. *These words can be used only before nouns.*

	Masc.	*Fem.*	*Plural.*
my	mon	ma	mes
thy	ton	ta	tes
his or her or its	son	sa	ses
our	notre	notre	nos
your	votre	votre	vos
their	leur	leur	leurs
the	le	la	les

Adjectives agree with their nouns not only in gender, but also in number. Thus *le bon enfant* = the good child; *les bons enfants* = the good children. This rule holds even if there is a verb between the noun and its adjective; *e.g.*, *les enfants sont petits* = the children are little.

I am—*je suis*.	we are—*nous sommes*.
thou art—*tu es*.	you are—*vous êtes*.
he (or she) is—*il* (or *elle*) *est*.	they are—*ils* (or *elles*) *sont*.

la maison, the house.	*sûr*, sure.
le château, the castle.	*grand*, tall, great, big.
le touriste, the tourist.	*intéressant*, interesting.
la ville, the town.	*petit*, small, little.

B

la voiture, the car (also railway coach)

la rue, the street.

visiter, to visit.

monter to mount, to get (into).

large, wide (*not* large).

dans (prep.), in, into.

que (conj.), that.

le garçon, the boy.

jeune, young.

Remember that you make an adjective feminine by adding an *e*, *if there is not an e at the end already*. Adjectives ending in *e* like *habile* = clever, are either masculine or feminine. This applies to *e mute* only: the feminine of *aîné* is *aînée* (elder).

Exercise 3(a)

1. Les rues sont larges. 2. La grande ville est intéressante. 3. La maison est petite. 4. Nous sommes jeunes. 5. Les petites maisons sont intéressantes. 6. Je suis sûr que les touristes visiteront le château. 7. Nous sommes sûrs que nos amis visiteront la ville. 8. Notre ami est dans la petite maison. 9. Leurs amis sont jeunes. 10. Le jeune touriste monte dans sa voiture. 11. Le petit garçon portera la table. 12. Nos jeunes amis monteront dans notre voiture. 13. Elle est sûre que son frère visitera la maison. 14. Les maisons dans notre ville sont intéressantes. 15. Sa Majesté visitera le château. 16. Ils sont sûrs que mon ami et son cousin sont petits. 17. Les rues dans notre ville sont larges. 18. Les touristes monteront dans leur grande voiture.

Exercise 3(b)

1. The sentry is tall. 2. His house is interesting. 3. They are small. 4. My brother visits the house. 5. The little boys carry their table. 6. I am sure that his brother will visit the town. 7. The tourists get into their car. 8. She is sure that I shall visit the castle. 9. His young

friends will get into his big car. 10. They are sure that we shall visit the big house. 11. The streets in our town are wide. 12. His Majesty will visit the little town. 13. Our car is small. 14. The little boys are in the big house. 15. We are sure that the town is interesting. 16. The tourists are in their little car. 17. They will carry their brother into the house. 18. The tourists will visit the big castle.

LESSON IV

CONTRACTIONS OF WORDS

Everything must give way to the necessity for a pleasant sound in reading or speaking French. To say *le enfant* would be difficult, and would not sound well. Accordingly the *e* is omitted altogether before a vowel, and an apostrophe is put in its place. The word now reads and sounds *l'enfant*. The same thing happens with *la* before a vowel. *Eau* (water) is feminine, yet we do not write *la eau* but *l'eau*. The plural *les*, however, does not get cut short: we write *les enfants*.

Two important words are *à* = *to* or *at*, and *de* = *of* or *from*. When these come along with the article they do not sound well in a Frenchman's ear. *To the boy* would naturally be *à le garçon*, and *of the boy*, *de le garçon*. But the rule about easy and pleasant sounds comes in again, and the words *à le* and *de le* are shortened into *au* and *du* respectively—*au garçon*, to the boy, *du garçon*, of the boy. The plural *à les garçons*, *de les garçons* is equally unpleasant to French ears, so we have again a contraction *aux garçons* and *des garçons*. So we have :—

à le = au   à les = aux
de le = du   de les = des

Note that *à la* and *de la* are never contracted into *au* and *du*.

If a noun begins with a vowel or *h* unsounded the *à le*
and *de le* are never combined. To the emperor = *à
l'empereur*, of the man = *de l'homme*.

I have = *j'ai*	we have = *nous avons*
thou hast = *tu as*	you have = *vous avez*
he has = *il a*	they have = *ils ont*

Note (1) the elision of *e* in *je ai* making it *j'ai*. (2) The
third plural differs from *they are* by having no *s* before *ont*.
Ils sont (they are) sounds *ilsson*; *ils ont* (they have) sounds
ilzon.

et, and.	*fruit*, fruit.
mais, but.	*arriver*, to arrive.
année, year.	*parler*, to speak.
ouvrier, workman.	*écouter*, to listen, to
honneur, honour (m., *h* not	listen to.
sounded).	*travailler*, to work.
vers, towards.	*marcher*, to walk, march.
fils, son.	*manger*, to eat.
argent, money, silver.	*chanter*, to sing.

**Note.—In all the lists of words that follow, the gender is
not indicated unless the word is an exception to the rule of
terminations on p. 31.**

Thus *année* above, should be feminine because it ends
in *ée*. It *is* feminine, so no mark is made. *Honneur* on
the other hand should be feminine because it ends in *eur*;
but since the word is an exception and is masculine the
letter *m.* is added. By continually referring to the list of
feminine terminations you will rapidly acquire the power
of readily separating masculines from feminines at sight.

Exercise 4(a)

1. Les soldats de l'empereur arrivent au château. 2.
Les hommes de l'armée de l'empereur sont jeunes, mais

grands. 3. L'ouvrier travaille dans la grande rue. 4. Les soldats marcheront vers la ville. 5. L'empereur parlera aux soldats. 6. Nous écoutons l'alouette : elle chante dans les bois. 7. Les ouvriers sont dans la petite maison. 8. L'honneur et l'argent sont aux habiles ouvriers. 9. Les cinq enfants de l'ouvrier marchent vers le château du grand empereur. 10. Nous mangerons les fruits. 11. Vous avez l'argent, mais vous parlez et nous travaillons. 12. Je suis sûr que l'empereur arrivera au château. 13. Les soldats de l'empereur chantent et nous écoutons leurs voix. 14. Les touristes parlent au petit enfant de l'ouvrier. 15. Vingt soldats marchent vers le château du grand empereur. 16. Nous sommes sûrs que les alouettes chantent dans les bois. 17. Cinq touristes arrivent au château dans leur grande voiture. 18. Les enfants marchent vers le château de sa Majesté et parlent aux sentinelles.

Exercise 4(b)

1. We are listening to the larks : they sing in the woods. 2. I have the workmen's money : they are at the castle. 3. The fruits of the year are good. 4. The bearer of the money will speak to the workmen. 5. I will speak of the sentry to the emperor. 6. The men listen to the squirrels in the woods. 7. The little children of the emperor will visit the castle. 8. The tourist will eat in my house, but the workmen will eat in the street. 9. The soldiers of the emperor will march towards the castle. 10. The children of the emperor speak to the sentry. 11. They have a young lark and a squirrel. 12. The young children of the workmen are at the house. 13. I am sure that you have the money of the workman. 14. The brother of His Majesty will arrive with the soldiers. 15. She is young but tall. 16. We will carry the money to the emperor. 17. I listen to the voice of the young man in the street. 18. She is at the house of her friend. 19. The wide streets of the town are interesting to the tourists.

LESSON V

THE SAXON GENITIVE

In one particular the French have broken through their rule, and are more analytic than the English. We say, *the man's books ;* the French must say, *les livres de l'homme.* So *the queen's money* must appear as *l'argent de la reine. John's hat = le chapeau de Jean.* This English possessive is called the Saxon genitive, or possessive, and is much more convenient than the French form. You must be continually on your guard in translating it.

There is another example of the effect of the French dislike of troublesome sounds, which sometimes leads to confusion. *Ame* is feminine, so we ought to write *ma âme* for *my soul.* French ears dislike this, yet French people do not treat *a* so unceremoniously as they treat *e.* Since *a* cannot be elided (except in the one case of the word *la,* NOT *là*), the sound is made pleasant by simply using the masculine form before every feminine noun beginning with a vowel : *mon âme, son innocence, ton année,* though all three are feminine.

In fact *e* is the only letter that the French generally cut out. In one case only is *i* elided. *Si* means *if,*[1] and when it comes before *il* or *ils,* the *i* is omitted, and we have *s'il* or *s'ils. Qui* means *who,* and never loses its *i ; que* means *whom,* and always loses its *e* when the next word begins with a vowel. *Le roi qui aime les soldats =* the king who loves the soldiers. *Le roi qu'aiment les soldats =* the king whom the soldiers love.

The endings of the past tense in French (called the *imperfect,* because it gives no indication of the exact time referred to) are always the same : *ais, ais, ait ; ions, iez, aient.*

---

[1] *Si* also means *whether.*

Was	*Had*	*Loved*
j'étais	j'avais	j'aimais
tu étais	tu avais	tu aimais
il était	il avait	il aimait
nous étions	nous avions	nous aimions
vous étiez	vous aviez	vous aimiez
ils étaient	ils avaient	ils aimaient

Nouns ending in *al* make their plural in *aux*, as in *général*, *généraux*. Nouns ending in *eau*, *au*, *eu*, *œu*, also form their plural by simply adding *x* : *chapeau* = a hat, plural *chapeaux* ; *eau* = water, plural *eaux*.

VOCABULARY.

là, there	*affaire* (f.), affair.
ici, here	*couper*, to cut.
mari, husband.	*traverser*, to cross.
général, general.	*fleuve* (m.), river.
cheval, horse.	*bateau*, boat.
très, very.	*fardeau*, burden.
un (m.), *une* (f.), a or an.	*pour*, for, in order to.
nombreux, numerous.	

Exercise 5(a)

1. L'enfant du général traversait le fleuve. 2. Son mari était très pauvre. 3. Le mari de mon amie portait l'argent à son cousin. 4. Les soldats qui arrivaient à la grande ville étaient très jeunes. 5. S'il traverse la rue, il arrivera au château de l'empereur. 6. Les touristes qui visitent la ville sont très nombreux. 7. Le bois que coupaient les soldats est bon. 8. Ses affaires sont très mauvaises. 9. Les fruits qu'aiment les petits garçons sont là. 10. Si vons parlez à mon alouette elle chantera. 11. Les pauvres animaux portaient les fardeaux. 12. Les châteaux que visitent les touristes sont très intéressants. 13. Si vous

arrivez ici pour visiter le château de l'empereur, vous parlerez à la sentinelle. 14. Les garçons qui aimaient les fruits étaient au bois. 15. Les fardeaux qu'il porte au château sont grands. 16. Les bateaux qui traversaient le fleuve sont ici. 17. Si elle monte dans ma voiture elle arrivera à la maison. 18. Les chevaux du général traversaient les rues de la ville. 19. Je parlerai aux sentinelles si elles sont là. 20. L'enfant qu'elle portait était le petit garçon de l'ouvrier.

Exercise 5(b)

1. Her husband's affairs were bad. 2. The tourist's hat was in the waters of the river. 3. The tourists who visited the castle were very numerous. 4. The soldiers' horses carried their burden to the town. 5. The children whom she loved were here. 6. If she crosses the street she will arrive at a workman's house. 7. The boys who were cutting the wood are the children of the young soldier. 8. If he arrives he will cross the river in order to visit the castle. 9. I shall eat the fruit if it is here. 10. The man who was there cut the wood. 11. The workman who was cutting wood is Jean's cousin. 12. Our boats crossed the river. 13. The soldiers who had the horses marched towards the river. 14. If you sing, he will listen. 15. The house was her affair. 16. Her Majesty the Queen will visit the town. 17. If you speak of the affair to John he will listen. 18. If we get into their car we shall arrive at the town. 19. They crossed the river in order to speak to the small boys in the wood. 20. The workmen who were here are very clever.

LESSON VI

REGULAR VERBS—CONJUGATIONS—PARTICIPLES

There are two main kinds of French verbs, the regular and the irregular. About the regular verbs certain general rules can be laid down regarding their forms, while the irregular verbs get their name from the fact that their forms are all more or less exceptional. Two of the verbs we have been dealing with (*être* = to be; and *avoir* = to have) are irregular; all the rest that we have had are regular.

The infinitive of a verb is the part that is always used to give the meaning of a verb. If we wish to convey the idea of *marching* in French we speak of the verb *marcher* = to march. Of this word, *march* may be called the stem, *er* the termination. Every part of the verb must have *march* as a part of it; while *er* is the sign of the infinitive. You must have noticed that all the regular verbs we have yet come across end in *er*. But there are other verbs that have the infinitive ending in *ir*, others in *oir*, others in *re*, thus fin*ir* = to finish, recev*oir* = to receive, perd*re* = to lose. There are thus four great classes of regular verbs in French called the four Conjugations. The infinitive in the First Conjugation ends in *er*, in the Second in *ir*, in the Third in *oir*, and in the Fourth in *re*. Most French verbs belong to the First Conjugation, while the Third is so small that we shall not speak of it just yet.

In English when we use the words *speaking, finishing, losing*, we are said to use the present participle. Obviously *ing* is the termination which marks the present participle. In French the corresponding termination is *ant*. Parl*ant* = speaking; perd*ant* = losing. We would expect fin*ant* to mean finishing; but in this Second Conjugation some of the forms require the assistance of an extra syllable *iss*, which means nothing,[1] but makes the sound pleasanter to Frenchmen. *Finishing* is thus fin*issant*.

The part of the English verb that we use with *have* or *had* or *is* or *was* is called the *past participle*, thus: have *spoken*, had *finished*, is *lost*. In French we have the past

[1] Now, at any rate: the *iss* represents the *esc* of the Latin verb from which the French ones are derived.

participles *parlé, fini, perdu* where *é, i* and *u* are the terminations that indicate the past participle.

The name *participle* indicates that the word to which it is applied has *part* of the nature of a verb, and *part* of the nature of an adjective. Sometimes the verbal part gets the upper hand, and sometimes the adjective part. *Remarquant* is the present participle of the verb *remarquer*, to notice. In this word the verbal part has usually the upper hand. In *tremblant* (from *trembler* to tremble) we may use the word as an adjective. *La fille tremblante* means the trembling girl. Here we are thinking more about describing the person than about what she is doing. When a participle is used as an adjective it *agrees with* its noun in number and gender. The rule is that when the verbal part gets the upper hand, the participle does not agree, but when the adjective part gets the upper hand, the participle does agree. The same is true about the past participle. She has killed = *elle a tué*. Here *tué* does not agree with *elle*, because the action is the important thing. She has been killed = *elle a été tuée*. Here *tuée* does agree with *elle*, because the important thing here is the state in which *she* is. In other words, *tuée* is really an adjective. We think less of the action than of the result of the action. Hence we get the rule that a past participle used with *être* agrees with its subject; but the past participle does not agree with the subject when used with *avoir*.

The past participle of the verb *être* is *été*. Now, *été* is often used along with other past participles, and when thus used those other past participles always agree with their subjects. The hand has been squeezed = *la main a été serrée*. The soldiers have been killed = *les soldats ont été tués*. But when we say the soldiers have killed, we have only *les soldats ont tué*. We have *ont* in both sentences about the soldiers; it is because we have *été* that the participle agrees in one of them. It is comforting to know that *été* itself never changes either for number or gender; it is always plain *été*.

Notice the two ways of translating the following. The second form is the more usual one.

Elle a chanté	She has sung, or simply she sang.
Elle a été polie	It (f.) has been polished, or simply it was polished.
Ils ont remarqué	They have noticed, or simply they noticed.
Elles ont rougi	They have blushed, or simply they blushed.
Les tables ont été polies	The tables have been polished, or simply the tables were polished.

The following table should now be thoroughly mastered :—

	1st Conj.	2nd Conj.	4th Conj.
Infin.	parler	finir	perdre
pres. part.	parlant	finissant	perdant
past part.	parlé	fini	perdu

PRESENT INDICATIVE.

je parle	je finis	je perds
tu parles	tu finis	tu perds
il parle	il finit	il perd
nous parlons	nous finissons	nous perdons
vous parlez	vous finissez	vous perdez
ils parlent	ils finissent	ils perdent

par, by	*avec*, with.
remarquer, to notice.	*donner*, to give.
polir, to polish.	*vendre*, to sell.
tuer, to kill.	*livre*, a book.
punir, to punish.	*mère*, mother.
rendre, to give up, render.	*marchand*, merchant.
train, train.	*voie*, railway line, track.

Exercise 6(a)

1. Le touriste donne l'argent à l'habile ouvrier. 2. Les garçons qui ont été punis sont les enfants du marchand. 3. Les hommes qui ont tué votre cheval sont au bois avec mon ami. 4. Le livre que vous avez vendu au marchand était très intéressant. 5. Nous sommes sûrs que les soldats ont été punis. 6. Si le général rend la ville ses soldats traverseront le fleuve avec leurs chevaux. 7. Nous avons été au château avec les ouvriers qui ont coupé le bois. 8. Je suis sûr que son mari a été tué par les soldats. 9. La femme qui a chanté est à la maison. 10. Les petits garçons qui ont perdu leurs livres ont été punis. 11. J'ai écouté les filles qui chantaient. 12. Les touristes ont vendu leur automobile au marchand. 13. J'ai fini le livre que vous avez donné à mon cousin. 14. Les tables ont été polies. 15. Les chevaux qui traversaient la voie ont été tués par un train. 16. Le train a tué deux hommes. 17. Le livre qu'il a perdu est ici. 18. Si nous traversons la voie nous arriverons au château. 19. Le général visitera le château que la reine a rendu. 20. J'ai remarqué un grand jeune homme qui parlait à votre mari.

Exercise 6(b)

1. His daughter is lost. 2. His books were given to the poor. 3. The merchant's big house has been sold. 4. We noticed the sentry who spoke to the workmen. 5. I am sure that the horses are lost. 6. We have lost the money which he gave to the woman. 7. If you walk towards the town you will cross the line. 8. The tourist who got (imperfect) into the train has lost his hat. 9. The children who were killed were the merchant's little girls. 10. I noticed the boy who cut the wood. 11. They gave up the town to the emperor's soldiers. 12. His mother walked towards the house with her husband. 13. He lost the

money, but his brothers have been punished. 14. The table was polished by the workmen. 15. The train killed the horses which crossed the railway line. 16. They sold their boats to the soldier's young brother. 17. The poor woman who was in the wood with her children has been killed. 18. We are sure that the books are lost. 19. We noticed the girl who sang in the street. 20. The horse which I noticed has been sold.

LESSON VII

PAST TENSES AND PROGRESSIVE FORM

The *imperfect* we have already learned. It is exactly the same for the Second and Fourth Conjugations, except that the Second requires its assistant syllable, *iss* :—

1st Conj.	2nd Conj.	4th Conj.
tuais	punissais	rendais
tuais	punissais	rendais
tuait	punissait	rendait
tuions	punissions	rendions
tuiez	punissiez	rendiez
tuaient	punissaient	rendaient

Since the imperfect gives no clear indication of the exact time at which an event took place it may be translated in different ways : (1) I killed; (2) I was killing; (3) I used to kill. The first is purely general; the second is called the progressive form; the third is specially characteristic of the imperfect tense.

The progressive form is not confined to the imperfect, for we can say *is killing*. There is here a source of much trouble to beginners. The progressive form must never be translated into French by the present participle. *Il parle* = he is speaking (as well as *he speaks*); *il parlait* = he was speaking (as well as *he spoke*). It is because English is so analytic that the present participle has this work thrown upon it among us. NEVER use the verb *être* along with any present participle which implies that anything is going on.

There are two other important past tenses in French named the *past definite* and the *past indefinite*. The former is sometimes called the *preterite*, but more often the *past historic*. It means that the event in question took place once for all at a certain time.

PAST HISTORIC.

1st Conj.	*2nd Conj*.	*4th Conj*.
portai	finis	rendis
portas	finis	rendis
porta	finit	rendit
portâmes	finîmes	rendîmes
portâtes	finîtes	rendîtes
portèrent	finirent	rendirent

The past indefinite [1] is the most commonly used of all the past tenses in French, and yet it is very rarely used by English students. Make up your mind to use this tense as often as you can, especially in conversational style. It is what is called a compound tense, being made up of the verb *avoir* and the past participle of the verb we wish to use. We have already used it in the exercises without knowing its name.

PAST INDEFINITE.

	1st	*2nd*	*4th*
j'ai	parlé	fini	perdu
tu as	,,	,,	,,
il a	,,	,,	,,
nous avons	,,	,,	,,
vous avez	,,	,,	,,
ils ont	,,	,,	,,

[1] Sometimes also called the *perfect*.

Il a parlé seems a roundabout way of saying *he spoke,* but it is the common French way, and should be imitated. The use of this tense began comparatively late in the history of the French language, but its use is now so common as to warrant all this repetition of ours about it. Be careful, too, in translating from French into English not to write *he has lost* but *he lost*—unless indeed the context demands the longer form.

porte, door, gate.	*chambre* (f.), room.
soir, evening (in general)	*remplir*, to fill.
soirée, a whole evening.	*sur*, on.
fermer, to shut.	*poche*, pocket.
doucement, gently.	*fenêtre*, window.
triste, sad.	*entendre*, to hear.
vite, quickly, fast	*casser*, to break.
	travail, work.

Exercise 7(a)

1. Il a rempli sa poche d'argent.[1] 2. Elle a fermé doucement la porte de sa chambre. 3. Elle finissait son travail. 4. Les soirées sont très tristes dans sa maison. 5. Nous avons entendu parler le général. 6. J'ai remarqué un petit garçon qui remplissait ses poches de fruits. 7. La rue est remplie de chevaux. 8. Les touristes marchaient vite vers la ville pour visiter le château que j'ai remarqué. 9. Ils ont cassé les fenêtres de la maison de l'ouvrier. 10. Il avait l'argent dans sa poche. 11. Nous avons vite fini notre travail. 12. Nous avons donné l'argent au jeune homme qui visitait mon cousin. 13. Nous entendons la voix du marchand qui vend les livres. 14. Nous écoutions les alouettes au bois. 15. Ils ont rempli la chambre d'hommes. 16. Si vous montez dans ma chambre vous remarquerez un livre sur la table. 17. Si vous avez fini

[1] After the verb remplir *de* means *with*.

votre travail, je donnerai vos livres au fils du marchand.
18 Nous avons remarqué le touriste qui montait dans le
train. 19. La fenêtre qu'il fermait à été cassée par un
petit garçon. 20. Ses poches sont remplies de fruits.

Exercise 7(b)

1. She is finishing her work. 2. We have finished our
work. 3. He was filling his pockets. 4. They broke the
windows of the merchant's house. 5. The evenings with
my father were sad. 6. He heard the boy speaking
(infinitive). 7. We heard a man singing in your room.
8. We used to cross the railway line in order to arrive
quickly at the town. 9. They used to fill their pockets
with money. 10. Five rooms in the house are for the boys.
11. I heard the man who was gently shutting the door of
his room. 12. We have lost the book which you gave to
my cousin. 13. You will notice that the window of my
room is broken. 14. The tourist is selling his car to the
merchant's son. 15. The streets are filled with soldiers:
they are marching towards the castle. 16. If you listen
you will hear the train which is crossing the river. 17. We
will give the money to the boy whom you noticed in the
street. 18. We spoke to the sentry at the gate of the
castle. 19. The boys who broke the window have been
punished. 20. He had in his pocket the money which you
lost.

LESSON VIII

REVISION OF VERBS—NEGATION

To revise all that has gone before about the tenses, we
give a table of the terminations of the Regular verbs. In
the meantime you have to deal only with the first half
of the table. The conditional and the subjunctive and

TABLE OF TERMINATIONS OF REGULAR VERBS.

CONJUGATION	I.	II.	III.	IV.
Infinitive	er	ir	evoir	re
Present Participle	ant	issant	evant	ant
Past Participle	é	i	u	u
Present	e es e ons ez ent	is is it issons issez issent	ois ois oit evons evez oivent	s s — ons ez ent
Imperfect	ais ais ait ions iez aient	issais issais issait issions issiez issaient	evais evais evait evions eviez evaient	ais ais ait ions iez aient
Future	erai eras era erons erez eront	irai iras ira irons irez iront	evrai evras evra evrons evrez evront	rai ras ra rons rez ront
Conditional	erais erais erait erions eriez eraient	irais irais irait irions iriez iraient	evrais evrais evrait evrions evriez evraient	rais rais rait rions riez raient
Subjunctive Present	e es e ions iez ent	isse isses isse issions issiez issent	oive oives oive evions eviez oivent	e es e ions iez ent
Subjunctive Imperfect	asse asses ât assions assiez assent	isse isses ît issions issiez issent	usse usses ût ussions ussiez ussent	isse isses ît issions issiez issent
Imperative	e ons ez	is issons issez	ois evons evez	s ons ez

the imperative will be taken up by-and-by. What you should do just now is to take the stem of several verbs, one after the other, and run down the table putting in the terminations after the stem. The oftener you do this the better. The following are stems to practise on in each of the Conjugations. First Conjugation: *march-, tu-, parl-, aim-, dans-, chant-*; Second Conjugation: *fin-, roug-, pun-, bât-, enrich-, rempl-*; Fourth Conjugation: *rend-, vend-, entend-, perd-, répond-, défend-*.

The Third Conjugation we have not yet touched. But you will do well to practise it here along with the others, for the sake of comparison. It contains only seven verbs in all. The following is the complete list :—

apercevoir = to perceive
concevoir = to conceive.
décevoir = to deceive.
devoir = to owe.

recevoir = to receive.
redevoir = to owe still.
percevoir = to collect (such things as taxes or rents).

Of these *devoir* is very important. It is interesting to note that in it the stem is reduced to one letter *d*. We give the first of each of the tenses of *devoir to* show how to do the others. Going down the table under III. we have : *devoir, devant, dû* (a circumflex is added in this case to distinguish it from *du* = of the), *dois, devais, devrai, devrais, doive, dusse, dois.*

French requires two words to express a negative, one going before the verb, the other after. These two words are *ne* and *pas*. Of these only *ne* is really negative; *pas* means merely a step. We say in English I will not go *a step*, which is exactly the same as the French form, only the French use it with all verbs as well as with *go*. We also say : I do not believe it *a bit*; and the French say : I do not believe it *a point*. In this case they use *ne . . . point* instead of *ne . . . pas*. *Ne . . . point* is the stronger way of stating a negative, but *ne . . . pas* is

what is almost always used. In older French we sometimes come across *ne . . . goutte*, which means *not . . .
a drop*. It is clear, then, that the second negative is merely
added to strengthen the first; in French it *must* be added,
in English it is usually dropped.

Examples of negative forms of verbs: *il ne parle pas,
nous ne tuons pas les lapins* (lapin = rabbit), *elle ne finissait
pas*. If the verb begins with a vowel the *e* of *ne* is elided:
il n'aime pas, elle n'était pas, nous n'avons pas. In compound tenses the *ne* and *pas* are put before and after the
little verb, and not after the past participle: *il n'a pas
parlé, vous n'avez pas entendu, elle n'est pas perdue, elles
n'avaient pas pleuré*.

vie, life.	*regarder*, to look at, watch.
beaucoup, much, many.	*mener*, to lead.
mot, word, saying.	*montre*, watch.
demain, to-morrow.	*champ*, field.
marque, mark, make	*chercher*, to look for.
(of car, etc.).	*laisser*, to leave.
mort (f.), death.	

Exercise 8(a)

1. La vie n'est pas triste. 2. Vous ne parlez pas doucement. 3. Les garçons ne couperont pas demain le bois.
4. Le général n'a pas rendu la ville. 5. Les chevaux n'ont
pas été tués. 6. Les animaux n'étaient pas menés ici.
7. J'ai tué le lapin mais je n'ai point tué l'alouette. 8.
Nous ne regardions pas vos livres, nous cherchions mon
chapeau que j'ai laissé dans votre chambre. 9. Si vous
n'écoutez pas, vous n'entendrez pas ses mots. 10. Je
n'aimais point la vie qu'il menait. 11. Je suis sûr qu'elle
n'est pas ici. 12. Je ne chercherai pas l'argent que vous
avez perdu. 13. Si vous ne montez pas vite dans le train,
nous n'arriverons pas. 14. Sa montre n'est pas d'une

très bonne marque. 15. Je n'ai pas remarqué les animaux que vous cherchez. 16. Ils parlaient vite et je n'ai pas entendu un mot. 17. Je suis sûr que nous devons beaucoup au marchand. 18. Nous ne recevrons pas l'argent qu'il doit. 19. Les soldats n'ont pas mené leurs chevaux à l'eau. 20. Les ouvriers n'ont pas coupé le bois : ils travaillent dans les champs.

Exercise 8(b)

1. The train will not arrive. 2. Your books are not here. 3. I am not sure whether she will visit the castle. 4. He will not listen[1] to a word. 5. The windows have not been broken. 6. You will not hear his voice if you do not listen. 7. The tourists will not arrive to-morrow. 8. The animals have not been led to the water. 9. I was not looking for my money, I was looking for his watch. 10. If she does not get into the train quickly, she will not arrive at the town. 11. The child's rabbit has not been killed. 12. The tourists who owe the money to my father are getting into their car. 13. If you shut the door he will not hear a word. 14. Her husband's affairs are not very good. 15. The life which he was leading was not interesting. 16. I did not notice the boats which were crossing the river. 17. The castle has not been given up. 18. We will look to-morrow for the money which you have lost. 19. We are sure that he was not filling his pockets with money. 20. I will not give to the workman the money which you owe to the merchant.

[1] Remember that *écouter*, *regarder*, *chercher* mean respectively to listen *to*, to look *at*, to look *for*. The preposition is omitted when translating into French. So also *payer*, to pay, or to pay *for*.

LESSON IX

FEMININE OF ADJECTIVES

The verbs *être* and *avoir* have the same three past tenses as ordinary verbs, and the same compound tenses. The following tables have to be carefully studied :—

Infinitive, *être*	*avoir*
Pres. part., *étant*	*ayant*
Past part., *été*	*eu*
Imperfect. (*See* p. 39).	

PAST HISTORIC (PRETERITE).

fus	eus
fus	eus
fut	eut
fûmes	eûmes
fûtes	eûtes
furent	eurent

PAST INDEFINITE

j'ai été	j'ai eu
tu as été	tu as eu
il a été	il a eu
nous avons été	nous avons eu
vous avez été	vous avez eu
ils ont été	ils ont eu

Observe the *y* in *ayant*. You would expect *v*, but *avant* is already a French word meaning *before*, so *having* is always *ayant*. In the expression *I have had*, *have* and *had* are parts of the same verb, but *have* is called the auxiliary, and *had* the principal verb. So in French *ai* and *eu* are parts of the same verb *avoir*, but *ai* is the auxiliary and *eu* is the principal. Of course, when *ai* stands by itself without another verb it is itself a principal verb, *e.g.*, *J'ai un livre* = I have a book. Here *ai* is a principal verb.

The general way to make an adjective feminine is to add an *e* to the masculine unless there is an *e* there already. But if the word end in *é* another *e* must be added, as *porté* (m.), *portée* (f.) = carried.

But there are some exceptions to this rule that are so common that we must notice them at once.

If the adjective ends in *x*, the *x* is changed into *se*, as :—

joyeux	*joyeuse*	joyful or joyous
nombreux	*nombreuse*	numerous
heureux	*heureuse*	happy
except		
vieux	*vieille*	old

If the adjective ends in *f*, the *f* is changed into *ve*, like our English half, halves.

actif	*active*	active
bref	*brève*	short
neuf	*neuve*	new (*i.e.* brand new)
vif	*vive*	lively

Adjectives which end in *el*, *eil*, *ien*, *on* and *et*, double the last consonant before adding the *e*.

immortel	*immortelle*	immortal
pareil	*pareille*	equal to, or similar
ancien	*ancienne*	ancient (or former)
bon	*bonne*	good
muet	*muette*	dumb, silent

Some adjectives ending in *er* and *et* besides adding an
e put in a grave accent on the *e* they have already.

cher	*chère*	dear
complet	*complète*	complete, full (of vehicles, etc.)

The following adjectives are quite irregular, but they
occur so often that it will pay you to get them up now.

bas	*basse*	low
beau	*belle*	fine, pretty
bénin	*bénigne*	benign
blanc	*blanche*	white
épais	*épaisse*	thick
exprès	*expresse*	express
favori	*favorite*	favourite
fou	*folle*	foolish, mad
frais	*fraîche*	fresh
franc	*franche*	frank, open
gentil	*gentille*	pretty, nice, kind
gras	*grasse*	fat
gros	*grosse*	big, stout
las	*lasse*	weary, tired
long	*longue*	long
malin	*maligne*	cunning, malignant
mou	*molle*	soft
nouveau	*nouvelle*	new
public	*publique*	public
sec	*sèche*	dry

It is worth noting that the above rules apply to nouns
ending in *x* and *f* and *et*, etc., thus : *époux* = a husband,
épouse = a wife ; *veuf* = a widower, *veuve* = a widow ; *sujet*
= a subject, *sujette* = a female subject ; *lion* = a lion,
lionne = a lioness ; *sot* = a he fool, *sotte* = a she fool ;
païen = a pagan, *païenne* = a female pagan.

Exercise 9(a)

1. Elle a été heureuse. 2. Il a eu une vie brève[1] et joyeuse. 3. Nous n'avons pas eu beaucoup[2] de fruit. 4. Les rues de notre petite ville ne sont pas très longues. 5. Ayant beaucoup marché elle est lasse. 6. Nous avons remarqué une belle petite fille qui marchait avec la veuve. 7. Il portait un habit neuf et un chapeau blanc. 8. Je suis sûr que son épouse est folle. 9. L'animal que vous regardez est le cheval favori de l'empereur. 10. J'écoute la fille qui chante dans la rue : elle a une belle voix. 11. Le général a fini sa vie publique. 12. J'ai vendu ma voiture : elle n'est pas neuve, mais elle est bonne. 13. Les portes du château sont très épaisses. 14. Ayant perdu sa fille favorite, il est très triste. 15. Avant la mort de sa chère épouse il menait une vie active. 16. Les chambres des vieilles maisons sont très basses. 17. La vieille femme qui traverse la voie est la veuve de l'ancien marchand Dubois. 18. Je vendrai ma maison : elle n'est pas sèche. 19. Nous arriverons avant demain dans une voiture neuve. 20. La vie est très chère et je dois beaucoup d'argent.

Exercise 9(b)

1. He was (past historic) there before the evening. 2. Having a brand new house his wife is happy. 3. The white house is low but pretty. 4. The stout man's daughter got into the train. 5. His long life was lively and happy.

[1] The rules for the position of adjectives in French have not yet been explained. For the present they may be summarised as follows : Brief and common adjectives come *before* the noun. Long or unusual adjectives, together with adjectives of colour, come *after* the noun. If two adjectives qualify the same noun they both follow the noun in French.

[2] Words of quantity in French when followed by a noun require the insertion of *de* or *d'* before the noun. This applies to adverbs and nouns of quantity, but not to numerals, *e.g.* Beaucoup d'argent. Une livre de beurre (*m.*), a pound of butter : *but* cinq chevaux.

6. The old woman has been killed by a train. 7. The years of a man's life are not long but short. 8. The horse was carrying a big burden. 9. You will not hear the old woman speak : she is dumb. 10. The ex-general will visit His Majesty before to-morrow. 11. She is tired, but she will look to-morrow for the new hat which she has lost. 12. The two old castles have been sold to the merchant's widow. 13. I noticed ten soldiers who were crossing the river. 14. Having left his hat at the castle the tourist spoke to the sentry at the door. 15. She used to be lively and happy before the death of her husband. 16. She is very old, but she is not immortal! 17. The thick doors of the castle were shut to the tourists. 18. His new car was of a fine make. 19. His life has not been happy, but he will receive much honour at his death. 20. We gave a pound of fresh butter to the poor widow.

LESSON X

CONJUNCTIVE PRONOUNS

There are two kinds of personal pronouns in French, called respectively conjunctive and disjunctive. The conjunctive pronouns are always used in close and necessary connection with verbs. Thus all the personal pronouns that we have used up to this point have been conjunctive. Further, they have always been the *subjects* of sentences; but conjunctive pronouns can be *objects* as well.

Subject.	*Object.*
je	me
tu	te
il	le
elle	la
	lui (both *m.* and *f.*)

Subject.	*Object.*
nous	nous
vous	vous
ils	les
elles	les
	leur (both *m.* and *f.*)

One very marked difference between French and English here comes out. In French, conjunctive pronouns, when objects, come *before* the verb instead of after as in English. The king killed him = *le roi le tua.* He carries me = *il me porte.* They will listen to you = *ils vous écouteront.* She will love thee = *elle t'aimera.* Thou lovest them = *tu les aimes.* Our mother washes us = *notre mère nous lave.* The king gave her up = *le roi la rendit.*

In a compound tense the object-pronoun comes before the auxiliary verb. She has loved him = *elle l'a aimé.* But here a very queer rule comes up. When the *direct object* comes *before* the verb in French the past participle agrees with the *object.* This seems at first senseless, but suppose you try to translate into French : She has loved *her*, you set about it and produce *elle l'a aimé*, which is exactly what we have already used for : She has loved him. If now we add an *e* we get *elle l'a aimée*, which by our rule can mean nothing but : She has loved *her*. Note that *aimée* does not agree with *elle* but with *l'*, which stands for *la*. The following examples will help you to understand the rule. She has loved them = *elle les a aimés* (if *them* refers to masculines), or *elles les a aimées* (if *them* refers to feminines). They have killed her = *ils l'ont tuée.*

It has to be noted that *il* and *elle* may stand for *it.* If the English word to which *it* refers is masc. we use *il*, if fem. we use *elle.* Speaking of our arm we say, *il est fort*, but of our hand, *elle est forte.* Speaking of the table we say, *il l'a polie*, he has polished it; of a book we say, *ils l'ont perdu*, they have lost it; of pockets, *ils les ont remplies*, they have filled them.

frapper, to strike, hit, knock	*chaise*, a chair.
	magasin, shop.
trouver, to find.	*dame*, lady.
vu, seen.	*oncle*, uncle.
boîte, a box.	*tante*, aunt.
or, gold.	*officier*, officer.
acheter, to buy.	*parce que*, because.
penser, to think.	*pendant que*, while.

Exercise 10(a)

1. La dame est ici : vous l'avez vue. 2. Nous les avons vus. 3. Ma tante est une dame triste mais bénigne. 4. La boîte fut perdue mais mon oncle l'a trouvée. 5. La boîte était remplie de livres. 6. J'ai perdu mes livres, mais elle les a trouvés. 7. Pendant que la vieille femme traversait la voie le train l'a tuée. 8. Je suis sûr qu'elle était là, parce que je l'ai vue. 9. Le marchand n'a pas acheté la voiture : il l'a vendue. 10. Je pense que les magasins dans la ville sont très bons. 11. Nous avons parlé à la sentinelle : elle nous a écoutés. 12. Vous cherchez les fruits : je suis sûr que le petit garçon les a mangés. 13. J'ai frappé à la porte de la maison, parce qu'elle était fermée. 14. Vous cherchez vos livres ? Votre oncle les a vendus. 15. Les chapeaux furent perdus, mais je les ai trouvés et je les ai laissés sur la table dans votre chambre. 16. Nous avions une belle chaise mais nous l'avons vendue. 17. La dame parlait à l'officier : je l'ai remarquée. 18. Il a trouvé sa maison remplie de soldats. 19. Il a traversé la rue pendant que je polissais la table. 20. Je pensais que nous visiterions les châteaux : mais ils sont fermés.

Exercise 10(b)

1. He has struck me. 2. I have struck her. 3. We have seen them. 4. She has seen us. 5. I was looking at the window : you have broken it. 6. I had 7 books but I have lost them. 7. Their chair is here : they have polished it. 8. She sang and we listened to her. 9. The soldiers marched towards the castle and we watched them. 10. I noticed her while I was speaking to the tourist. 11. I knocked at the door : it was shut. 12. I had a watch, but I have sold it to one of my friends. 13. His father will strike him, because he has filled his pockets with fruit. 14. We found a watch and I have given it to his aunt. 15. We shall not cross the river : the boats are filled with water. 16. I think that we have seen her with my uncle. 17. They were getting into their car : I heard them. 18. He gave his watch to the boy and he will strike him if he has lost it. 19. The merchant has not bought the chair : he has sold it. 20. If the shop is shut we will knock at the door.

LESSON XI

DISJUNCTIVE PRONOUNS

Disjunctive pronouns are those which do not directly depend upon a verb.

Conjunctive.	*Disjunctive.*
je	moi
tu	toi
il	lui
elle	elle
nous	nous
vous	vous
ils	eux
elles	elles

Since some of the words are found in both lists, you may wonder how you are to distinguish conjunctive from disjunctive pronouns. This distinction is always to be found in the work done by the pronoun in the particular case in which we happen to be interested. In other words, the distinction depends upon the function of the word—not upon its form. The following are the main functions of the disjunctives. 1. They are used when a reference is made to a previous statement without repeating the verb. Somebody says for example: *Je l'ai vue* = I saw her. If I wish to say *I also* I must put it *moi aussi*. This is particularly noticeable about answers to questions. *Qui a tué Cock Robin?* The sparrow's reply ought to be *moi*. If, however, the sparrow repeats the verb of the original sentence he must use *je*: *Je l'ai tué*. 2. This leads us to the second use, for if the sparrow was proud of his deed—as the story seems to imply—he might have used *both* forms for the sake of *emphasis*, and said *Moi, je l'ai tué*. 3. Disjunctives are used in exclamations: *I, kill him!* the sparrow might have said had he put in a plea of "not guilty"—*Moi, le tuer!* Notice that *moi* is not here directly dependent on the verb, which is in the infinitive. Similarly we have—*Lui, parler français!* = *he*, speak French! 4. In enumerations we use disjunctives. You, he and I is *vous, lui et moi*. If these have to be followed by a verb they must be all gathered up into one conjunctive pronoun which must be responsible to the verb. In this case it would be: *Vous, lui et moi, nous l'avons vu.* The rule is that if *any* pronoun of the number is first person the verb must be first person; if there be no first person but there is a second then the verb must be second; only if all the pronouns are third can this verb be third. *Vous et lui, vous l'avez vu. Son mari, elle et lui l'ont vu.* When all the nominatives are of the third person it is not necessary to gather them up in the conjunctive pronoun. *Ils* can be put in or not just as you please. It is usually left out.

5. The remaining important use of the disjunctives is after prepositions. *A moi*, to me, *pour elle*, for her, *devant elles*, before them (if fem.), *devant eux* (if masc.).

avant, before (in time or order).	*pain*, bread.
devant, before (in place).	*palais*, palace.
quant à, as for.	*gauche*, left.
malgré, in spite of.	*droit*, right.
au-dessus, above.	*sous*, under.
au-dessous, below.	*c'était*, it was.
c'est, it is.	*gare*, station.

Exercise 11(a)

1. C'est lui qui m'a frappé. 2. Quant à moi, je la trouverai malgré vous. 3. Eux dans le palais et moi dans le magasin. 4. Vous et elle, vous trouverez la rue à (votre main) [1] gauche. 5. C'est moi qui ai l'argent, parce que je suis habile. 6. Eux, elles et nous, nous avons cassé la boîte. 7. Vous les avez vus? Moi aussi. 8. Lui et elles sont pauvres. 9. C'est vous qui l'avez vendu. 10. Moi, j'ai vu la sentinelle : elle était devant la porte du château. 11. J'ai regardé à droite et à gauche, mais je ne l'ai pas vue. 12. Votre chapeau ! C'était elle qui l'a perdu et moi qui l'ai trouvé. 13. Malgré vous, j'arriverai avant elle à la ville. 14. Moi, le frapper ! C'est ridicule ! 15. Si nous marchons vite, vous et moi, nous arriverons au château avant eux. 16. Quant à la vieille dame, elle a été tuée. 17. Ce n'est pas lui, c'est elle qui a vendu sa montre. 18. Nous aussi, nous l'avons vue : elle traversait la rue avec son oncle. 19. C'était la main gauche qui était coupée. 20. Lui, il marche vite : il arrivera avant nous à la gare.

[1] The word *main* (hand) is usually omitted : *à gauche* and *à droite* are all that are required.

Exercise 11(b)

1. As for her, he killed her. 2. In spite of him, I shall sell my car. 3. It was she who was above. 4. They and I are not happy because we are poor. 5. It was he who left his hat in the train. 6. I, fill my pockets with money ! It is ridiculous ! 7. The boy and I have seen them. 8. You will notice the house on the right. 9. He and they are not with my uncle. 10. As for them, they are very happy. 11. In spite of me he struck her. 12. Your window ! It was he who broke it. 13. Who has seen them? I. 14. He, she and I are tired. 15. Their car was before the station : I noticed it. 16. As for the money, I have lost it. 17. They ! I shall not speak of them. 18. It was she who was walking towards the river. 19. I was there with him : she also. 20. You and she have plenty of (much) money.

LESSON XII

THE INTERROGATIVE FORM

Questions are asked in French as in English by putting the subject after the verb. *Avez-vous ?* = have you? *Sommes-nous ?* = are we? *Est-il ?* = is he? *Etaient-elles ?* = were they (*f.*) ? Sometimes the French ear demands the insertion of a *t* to separate two vowels. *A-il ?* should equal has he? but the insertion of a *t* certainly makes this more easily sounded as *a-t-il ?* This occurs in other forms as in *va-t-il ?* = does he go? and *appelle-t-elle ?* = does she call; but *a-t-il* is the commonest example.[1]

With nouns the question form is a little different from ours. We ask : *Do* the soldiers march? Now this

[1] This *t* really represents the final *t* of the third person which has been worn away. Its only value now is to help the sound.

auxiliary *do* is never translated into French, whether in a question or in a direct statement. In : The soldiers do march, the *do* is simply omitted and the present tense used : *Les soldats marchent.* We might put this in question form by merely transposing subject and verb : *Marchent les soldats ?* But the French do not use this form. They prefer to make a round-about question : Is it that the soldiers march? = *est-ce que les soldats marchent ?* Here the whole burden of the question is thrown upon the three little words *est-ce que*, the rest of the question being put in the form of an ordinary statement. We can thus make any statement into a question by merely putting *est-ce que* before it. *La princesse est morte* gives : *Est-ce que la princesse est morte ?* = is the princess dead ? Will the traveller sell the vacuum cleaner ? = *est-ce que le voyageur vendra l'aspirateur électrique ?*

Another way of making questions is to place the noun first, and then form the question by placing a pronoun after the verb. *Was the emperor in the palace ?* becomes : The emperor, was he in the palace ? = *l'empereur était-il dans le palais ?* Has John seen him = *Jean l'a-t-il vu ?* Did your aunt weep = *votre tante a-t-elle pleuré ?* In such cases there is a little emphasis laid upon the noun by its being placed first, but it is quite a good way of asking questions all the same. The *est-ce que* way is on the whole preferable, however.

A sentence like *Where was your uncle ?* = *votre oncle où était-il ?* suggests two points of interest : (1) In sentences referring to persons it is customary to show politeness by putting in M. (short for Monsieur), Mme. (Madame), Mlle. (Mademoiselle) before the noun. Thus : *Où est monsieur votre père ? J'ai vu madame votre tante.* (2) With interrogative words like *où* = where ? *quand* = when ? *comment* = how ? it is not necessary to use pronouns. *Où est monsieur votre oncle ?* How do your affairs go ? = *comment vont vos affaires ?* The pronouns, however, can be used if you wish, as : *Vos affaires, comment vont-elles ?* or better, *Comment vos affaires vont-elles ?*

When negation is combined with interrogation the *ne . . . pas* are placed before the verb and after the pronoun respectively in the emphatic form. Is the house not dry? = *la maison n'est-elle pas sèche ?* But in the *est-ce que* form the *ne . . . pas* go with the original verb : *est-ce que la maison n'est pas sèche ?* Did you not see her? = *ne l'avez-vous pas vue ?* or *est-ce que vous ne l'avez pas vue ?* Have we not struck them (*m.*)? = *ne les avons-nous pas frappés ?* or *est-ce que nous ne les avons pas frappés ?* Are they (*f.*) not tired? = *ne sont-elles pas lasses ?* or *est-ce qu'elles ne sont pas lasses ?*

heure, hour.	*temps*, time.
plaisir, pleasure.	*raconter*, to relate.
rester, to remain.	*durer*, to last.
gens, people.	*dépenser*, to spend (of money).
encore, again or yet.	*tomber*, to fall.
histoire (f.), story.	*manquer*, to miss.
ramasser, to gather.	*passer*, to pass, to spend (of time).

Exercise 12(a)

1. L'empereur n'a-t-il pas perdu ses chevaux? 2. Quand sera-t-elle à la maison. 3. Comment la trouvera-t-elle? 4. Quand l'officier vous a-t-il donné l'argent? 5. N'a-t-il pas encore dépensé l'argent que je lui ai donné? 6. Le touriste n'a-t-il pas manqué le train? 7. Où sont les pauvres gens? Ils ramassent l'argent que le marchand a laissé tomber. 8. Les histoires qu'il raconte sont longues. 9. Est-ce que les soldats marcheront encore au château? 10. Quand votre cousin arrivera-t-il? 11. Le château est là. Ne l'avez-vous pas encore visité? 12. Comment

c

vont ses affaires ? A-t-il perdu beaucoup d'argent ? 13.
Je vous laisserai ici : mais ne perdons-nous pas notre
temps ? 14. L'officier, ne parlait-il pas à la sentinelle
quand vous l'avez vu ? 15. Resterez-vous ici beaucoup de
temps ? Une heure. 16. Ne manquera-t-il pas le train,
s'il ne marche pas vite ? 17. Les plaisirs de la vie ne sont-
ils pas grands ? 18. Ne vous a-t-elle pas encore raconté
l'histoire de la mort de son mari ? 19. Est-ce que le
touriste a beaucoup dépensé ? 20. Les ouvriers, n'ont-ils
pas perdu leur temps ?

Exercise 12(b)

1. Do the soldiers spend much ? 2. Doesn't she walk
quickly ? 3. How does the money last ? 4. Has he missed
the train again ? 5. Were you not gathering the wood ?
6. Shall we not remain here an hour ? 7. How do the boys
spend their time ? 8. Will not the officer be here ? 9. Did
you not hear the story which he was relating ? 10. Did
not the people of the town look at the soldiers who were
passing ? 11. Will not your aunt give you the money ?
12. Hasn't your cousin yet found his money ? 13. Were
they not speaking to the officer when I saw them ? 14.
How did you find her ? 15. Shall we not walk towards
the station ? 16. Was not the old woman killed ? 17. Do
the tourists spend much money in this town ? 18. Haven't
you seen them ? 19. Isn't the lady your aunt ? 20. Will
you not tell me the story ?

LESSON XIII

REFLEXIVE VERBS

There is a troublesome pronoun which we have up till
now omitted to mention. Its conjunctive form is *se*, its
disjunctive *soi*. *Se* is used only with certain verbs called

reflexive verbs, *i.e.* verbs which have the same person or thing for subject and object, verbs in which the action is reflected from the subject back upon itself. *He washes himself.* Here *he* and *himself* mean the same person. The action passes from *he* back to *himself.* We are therefore dealing with a reflexive verb. Its French form is *il se lave.* The plural is *ils se lavent* or *elles se lavent.*

You note that *se* does for both singular and plural, both masculine and feminine. It is, however, of the third person, and cannot be used in a sentence like *I wash myself*, which must be rendered *je me lave.* The object pronoun must be of the same number and person as the subject pronoun. The following table makes this clear.

je me lave	nous nous lavons
tu te laves	vous vous lavez
il (or elle) se lave	ils (or elles) se lavent

Observe that in each case the first pronoun is the subject and the second the object, even when (as in *nous nous lavons*) both pronouns are identical. Obviously, then, there is no great difficulty about reflexive verbs. They are merely ordinary verbs having as objects pronouns which mean the subjects.[1]

The object-pronouns of reflexive verbs are often called

---

[1] Sometimes the reflexive force of the verb is not so clear as in *se laver* or *se couper.* We say in English *to repent*, the French make *se repentir* = to repent oneself. Similarly *to run away* or *make off* is rendered by *s'enfuir* or *se sauver.* In these cases we can always supply the object in English though it makes a very clumsy phrase : *To make oneself off*, or *to save oneself*, for example. The verb *se trouver* is very common. It can be used in its ordinary meaning : *Je me trouvais là*, I found myself there. But in its more common use it is applied to inanimate objects instead of the verb *to be.* In the house there was a table = *dans la maison se trouvait une table.* He had a pipe in his pocket, may be rendered *Une pipe se trouvait dans sa poche.* The slight difference between *se trouver* and *être* may be represented by a feeling of " there happened to be " in the case of *se trouver.*

reflexive pronouns, and are usually known by the termination *self*—myself, thyself, himself, etc. But here arises confusion in English, for we can use those pronouns in two quite distinct ways. *I cut myself:* here *myself* is an ordinary reflexive pronoun, and is put into French by *je me coupe.* *I myself cut the bread*: here *myself* is something quite different. It is not the object of *cut*; it is not even the subject. The sentence could get along quite well without it; its only use is to give emphasis. *I* and *myself* are obviously the same person. Now the French word for *same* is *même.* Accordingly this form of *myself* is written *moi-même.* *Moi-même je coupe le pain.* The two forms of *myself* may occur in one sentence. I might want to say *I myself cut myself* (*i.e.* no other body cuts me). In French this would read: *Moi-même je me coupe.* The *même* or emphatic form is made by adding *même* to the disjunctive pronouns: thus *moi-même, toi-même, lui-même, elle-même, soi-même.* Since *même* is an adjective it must agree with the plural pronouns, so we have *nous-mêmes, vous-mêmes, eux-mêmes,* and *elles-mêmes.*

The difference between *lui-même* and *soi-même* is that the latter is more vague and general. *Lui-même* = himself; *soi-même* is nearer to *oneself.*

This and *that* (as adjectives) are represented in French by the little word *ce.* The feminine form is *cette,* and the plural for both masculine and feminine is *ces.* *Ce loup* = this (or that) wolf; *cette boucherie* = this (or that) butcher's shop; plural, *ces loups* and *ces boucheries.*

If a masculine noun begins with a vowel, *ce* is felt to be unsatisfactory. *Ce officier* does not sound well, so we write *cet officier.*

ce or *cet* (m.)   *cette* (f.)   *ces* (m. or f.)

se coucher, to lie down, go to bed   *s'amuser,* to amuse oneself.
se hâter (*de*), to hasten (to).   *s'éveiller,* to awaken.

se glisser, to slip oneself.
se trouver, to find oneself.
se lever, to raise oneself, get up.
se cacher, to hide oneself.
s'habiller, to dress oneself.

se fourrer, to thrust oneself.
se tromper, to deceive oneself, to be mistaken.
s'enrichir, to enrich oneself.

Exercise 13(a)

1. Maintenant je me couche. 2. Il se sauve. 3. Je le sauverai. 4. Je couperai le pain moi-même. 5. Il se hâte de s'enrichir. 6. Ne se couche-t-il pas? 7. Nous ne nous habillons pas. 8. Il nous amuse beaucoup. 9. Nous nous amuserons. 10. Malgré moi elles s'amusaient. 11. Est-ce que le garçon ne s'éveille pas? 12. Où cet homme se cache-t-il? 13. Est-ce que cette table se trouve dans votre maison? 14. Quand vous coucherez-vous? 15. Je suis sûr que vous vous trompez. 16. Je l'éveillerai moi-même. 17. Nous nous habillerons vite. 18. N'avez-vous pas remarqué ce beau magasin, ces vieilles maisons et cet hôtel? 19. Je me hâterai de me lever. 20. Nous nous cacherons sous la table. 21. Nous le trouverons nous-mêmes. 22. Elle est lasse : elle ne s'éveillera pas avant demain.

Exercise 13(b)

1. This evening she will awaken. 2. Are you washing? 3. He does not deceive himself. 4. When do you get up? 5. Will the children not hasten? 6. Where are you hiding yourself? 7. Will you not go to bed? 8. I will dress myself. 9. I myself will dress him. 10. This merchant will not enrich himself. 11. He slipped into the house in order to escape. 12. Do these books amuse you? 13. Your money? He was slipping it into his pocket. 14. They were slipping into the house. I saw them. 15. I

will speak to him myself. 16. His father struck him but he got up. 17. They have hidden it themselves. 18. You are mistaken if you think that I spoke to that man. 19. That merchant will not deceive you. 20. When will this officer wake up?

LESSON XIV

VERBS USED WITH ÊTRE INSTEAD OF AVOIR

One striking peculiarity about reflexive verbs is that all their compound tenses are made with *être,* and not with *avoir* like ordinary verbs. *Il l'a coupé* = he has cut it. But: he has cut himself = *il s'est coupé.* So: I had washed myself = *je m'étais lavé;* thou hast hidden thyself = *tu t'es caché;* I have been mistaken = *je me suis trompé.*

PAST INDEFINITE.	PLUPERFECT.
je me suis couché	je m'étais couché
tu t'es couché	tu t'étais couché
il s'est couché	il s'était couché
elle s'est couchée	elle s'était couchée
nous nous sommes couchés	nous nous étions couchés
vous vous êtes couchés	vous vous étiez couchés
ils se sont couchés	ils s'étaient couchés
elles se sont couchées	elles s'étaient couchées

This use of the verb *être* instead of the verb *avoir* is not confined to the reflexive verbs. Many other verbs require *être,* and the distinction between verbs with *avoir* and verbs with *être* often gives rise to unnecessary confusion. The distinction may be clearly made as follows: All verbs are used with *avoir* except those *which indicate an action followed by a corresponding state.*

This is somewhat abstractly put, but concrete examples will make the rule plain. Always put the case to yourself in the form of a question. Take the verb *arriver* = *to arrive*. This is the question to put to yourself. If you have arrived, *are* you arrived? The answer is obviously, Yes. Then use the verb *être*. If I *kill*, am I killed? Answer, No. Therefore you use *avoir*. Thus *je suis arrivé*, but *je l'ai tué*. If you *have* come, gone, fallen, descended, then you *are* come, gone, fallen, descended, therefore we use *être* with these verbs. On the other hand, if I *have* eaten it does not follow that I *am* eaten, or if I *have* drunk that I *am* drunk. So with these verbs we use *avoir*.

Students sometimes object that if they *have* fallen it does not follow that they *are* fallen, because they may have got up again. But so far as the verb is concerned— and that is all that we have here to do with—they are fallen.

If this test is applied to reflexive verbs it will give the verb *être* every time. If I have washed myself, I am washed; if I have cut myself, I am cut; if I have hidden myself, I am hidden, and so on. Therefore all reflexive verbs take the verb *être*.

There are two little words that are really pronouns, but are different from all the pronouns we have had : they are *en* and *y*.

En means *of it*, as in *j'en ai entendu* = I have heard of it. When used with verbs it comes before them just like any other object pronoun. Its most usual use is when we have been talking of a number of things, and then refer to a certain number of them. Then it is really equal to *of them*. In English it is nearly always untranslated ; in French it must *on no account* be omitted. Talking of books, for example, you say in English " I have five." You do not think of putting in " of them," though you can put it in if you like. In French it *must* be *j'en ai cinq* = I of them have five. " Have you seen the soldiers ? No, but he saw one " = " *Avez-vous vu les soldats ? Non, mais il en a vu un, lui."* Besides *of it* and *of them, en* can mean *of him, of her, from it, some of them, any* and other things; but these meanings you will learn from practice in reading.

Y also has a great many meanings, but as *en* has always underlying it the idea of *de = of* or *from*, so *y* has always underlying it the idea of *à = to* or *in*. Thus some of the main meanings of *y* are : *to it, to him, to her, in it, in them, to them, therein.* The *it*, or *him*, or *her*, or *them*, must always refer to a word previously used.

Souvent femme varie, bien fol qui s'y fie.	Woman varies often, (he is) indeed foolish who trust himself *to her*.

Talking of a question you may say *j'y ai répondu =* I have answered (to) it.

Y occurs in a peculiar but very useful phrase, *il y a*, which means *there is* or *there are; il y avait =* there was or *there were. Il y a* put before a period of time is usually translated *ago. Il y a deux années =* two years ago.

As a matter of practice it may be said that *y* is now used only in connection with things, not persons.

bien, very, indeed.	*lu*, read.
mois, month.	*un (une) autre*, another.
semaine, week.	*Guillaume*, William.
combien, how much, how many ?	*Pierre*, Peter.
couteau, a knife	*demeurer*, to live.
aise, glad (*aisé =* easy).	*chose* (f.) thing.

Exercise 14(a)

1. Elle est tombée dans la rue. 2. Il a perdu son argent il y a trois mois. 3. Il sera ici demain : j'en suis bien aise. 4. Nous ne nous sommes pas couchés. 5. N'avez-vous pas lu ce livre ? Non. Mais j'en ai entendu parler. 6.

Je n'ai pas beaucoup de livres, mais j'en vendrai cinq.
7. Ils demeuraient dans cette rue il y a six mois. 8. Il y a
sept jours dans la semaine et le lundi (Monday) en est un.
9. Mes cousins étaient arrivés à la maison avant la mort de
leur père. 10. Nous sommes restés ici une heure, parce
que notre voiture ne marche pas. 11. Avez-vous vu
cette maison? Nous y demeurons. 12. Il m'a raconté
une chose bien intéressante : je vous en parlerai. 13. Nous
nous sommes trompés : je suis sûr que sa maison ne se
trouve pas dans cette rue. 14. Si vous n'aimez pas ce
livre, je vous en donnerai un autre. 15. Cet officier est
très riche ; il a deux voitures et maintenant il va en
acheter une autre. 16. Combien de temps resterez-vous
ici? Une heure ou deux, je n'en suis pas sûr. 17. Je ne
me fie pas à cet homme. 18. Il y avait deux sentinelles à
la porte du château : maintenant il y en a trois. 19. Si
elle n'avait pas marché vite, elle ne serait pas tombée.
20. Elles ne se sont pas encore levées.

Exercise 14(b)

1. My cousins Peter and William have arrived. 2.
Where are the knives? There were two on the table.
3. We are very tired. We haven't been to bed this week.
4. I do not like that woman because I do not trust her.
5. Have the boys not hidden themselves in the street?
6. I had five books but I have given him one. 7. Four
years ago we used to live in a big house. 8. Hasn't your
husband yet got up? 9. She fell into the water while
she was crossing the river. 10. Did you notice that
house on the left? My uncle lives in it. 11. I myself
have seen the man who killed himself. 12. If you do not
work you will not grow rich. 13. She has arrived and I am
very glad of it. 14. If you have read this book we will give
you another. 15. I was sure that she had made a mistake.
16. He was getting up but he had not dressed himself. 17.

Would she have fallen if she had not walked quickly?
18. I will give you my book if you haven't one.   19. We
visited the castle and we stayed there an hour.   20. She
has worked hard (much) but she has not grown rich.

LESSON XV

FIRST READING LESSON

The time has now come for facing a bit of real French.
Up till now we have been dealing with bits specially prepared for you, and made to suit your limited vocabulary.

Since this is your first attempt at translation you must
be prepared for the trouble of turning up a fair number of
words in the vocabulary at the end of the book, but every
translation you make will leave you with a bigger vocabulary
of your own.   But you will find that a good many of the
words are already old friends.   At first sight it appears that
by the help of a French dictionary you could translate
any passage in French without knowing any grammar at all;
all you would require would be patience enough to turn up
each word.   But this is not so.   The dictionary does *not*
give every word that you meet with when you read a French
book.   Take the simple word *était* for instance, which is not
in the dictionary.   It is true that you know that this word
is *formed from* another word; that it is in fact the imperfect
of *être*, and *être* is in the dictionary.   There is here a
little resemblance between *être* and *était* which helps you
to see that the latter comes from the former.   In the
same way when you get a little farther down and come
to *pouvait* and look up the dictionary and find no trace of
pouvait but find a verb *pouvoir* which means *to be able*,
you have no difficulty in guessing that *pouvait* is the imperfect of *pouvoir*.

Again, suppose you come upon the word *disait* and
turn up your dictionary, quite expecting to find a verb

diser or *disoir* or *disir* or *disre*. But you find none of these. You feel that *disait* is the 3rd sing. imperfect of a certain verb, but what that verb is you have no idea. What is to be done? In all such cases turn to your Table of Irregular Verbs (p. 209) under the proper letter, and run your eye along the verbs. You are certain to pick up some bit exactly like the bit you are troubled about. In the present case, for example, we find *dire* = to say; and running our eye along, we find *disant, dit, je dis, je dis*. The *r* of *dire* seems to throw us out, but *disant* puts us straight again. Sometimes the first letter is the only thing the two parts have got in common. Thus if we come across *mû* in reading, we look up *m* in our Irregular Verbs and find that it comes from *mouvoir* = to move.

Translation may be done in two different ways—*literal* and *free*. In the literal translation the meaning is given from the French word by word, and the English rendering reads very stiffly, and is sometimes hardly intelligible. The free translation on the other hand takes the meaning of the passage as a whole, and turns it into good English. The literal translation pays more attention to the French form, the free translation to the English. You will understand this better when you read in Part II (p. 163) the two translations of the first extract.

Your first translations are better to be pretty literal. By-and-by you will be able to think more about the English. In any case use your wits to try and discover the meaning of a word for yourself, before checking your interpretation by referring to the vocabulary at the end of the book or a dictionary.

Translation I

Mon frère aîné n'avait que dix-huit ans quand il a visité Paris pour la première fois, et ce qui l'a beaucoup impressionné c'est l'animation et la largeur des rues. A Londres, les rues même les plus grandes n'avaient que soixante pieds

de large et les petites n'en avaient que vingt. A Paris,
surtout dans les beaux quartiers de la ville, c'était tout
à fait différent. Les rues étaient larges et bien éclairées et
ce n'est pas sans justice qu'on a appelé Paris " la ville
Lumière." A cette époque les automobiles étaient encore
peu nombreuses : en effet on n'en voyait guère et les
piétons n'avaient aucune difficulté à traverser les rues.
On pouvait flâner sans méfiance : ce qui n'est plus possible.

After you have translated the above and carefully compared your version with that given in Part II you should
be able to do the following exercise without much difficulty.

Exercise 15

1. This boy is young : he is only 8 years old. 2. One
of the tourists was able to get into the train. 3. They say
that he has bought a motor-car which goes very fast. 4.
What annoys me is that I have lost my money. 5. They
say that the lady who lived in this old house has killed
herself. 6. Have you seen any of them? 7. He sold his
horse which was 10 years old. 8. He fell into the river,
which was very amusing. 9. This window is three feet
broad, but the other is only two. 10. The liveliness of
the city has impressed them (very) much. 11. I used
to have many books, but now I have only seven. 12. The
horse fell and was not able to get up. 13. Aren't the
streets here well lighted? 14. To look at the shops is
amusing. 15. I was looking at the numerous cars which
were passing. 16. I have read a book which I don't like.
17. To listen to his stories is scarcely amusing. 18. They
say that she has hidden herself in my shop : which is not
possible. 19. I saw them this evening for the first time.
20. I have only bought two pounds of butter.

LESSON XVI

COMPARISON OF ADJECTIVES AND ADVERBS

When an adjective is used about one thing without reference to anything else, the adjective is said to be in the *positive* degree. When we compare the qualities of two things by means of adjectives, we use the words *plus* = more, and *moins* = less; *plus habile* = more clever, *moins triste* = less sad. This is called the comparative degree of the adjectives, and naturally implies that there are two things compared.

The result of the comparison may be that one of the things has more of the quality in question than the other, or less; or it may happen that the objects are equal in respect of this quality. Thus we have three forms of comparison.

Il est *plus* habile *que* moi = He is more clever than I.
Il est *moins* habile *que* moi = He is less clever than I.
Il est *aussi* habile *que* moi = He is as clever as I.

When more than two objects are compared we have the *superlative* degree, of which the English form ends in *est*, or is made with *most :* clever*est* or *most* clever. The superlative is indicated in French by the article *le* or *la* before *plus* or *moins*. *Il est le plus habile garçon de sa classe. Elle est la plus belle fille de la ville.* Notice the *de* after the superlative for *in* his class, and *in* the town—not *dans*.

This method of comparison is very easy; but there are a few—and these the most commonly used—adjectives that are irregularly compared. They had better be learnt now, and as each has a corresponding adverb, we give them in pairs.

Positive.	Comparative.	Superlative.
adj. (good) bon	(better) meilleur	(best) le meilleur
adv. (well) bien	(better) mieux	(best) le mieux
adj. (bad) mauvais	(worse) pire	(worst) le pire
adv. (badly) mal	(worse) pis	(worst) le pis
adj. (little) petit	(less) moindre	(least) le moindre
adv. (little) peu	(less) moins.	(least) le moins

You must be very careful in distinguishing between these pairs. The adjectives always go with *nouns or pronouns;* the adverbs with *verbs, adjectives or other adverbs. Elle est la meilleure* = she is the best. *Elle danse le mieux* = she dances best. You observe that the *le* of the adverb never changes. *La princesse était la pire* = the princess was the worst. *La princesse a parlé le pis* = the princess has spoken worst. *Mon cousin (était) le moindre* (or *le plus petit*) [1] *de sa famille* = My cousin was the smallest of his family. *Le plus petit enfant pleura le moins* = The smallest child wept least.

mouchoir, a handkerchief.	*aller,* to go
faire, to do, make.	*campagne,* country.
voleur, the thief.	*minute,* minute.
pris, taken	*minuit* (m.), midnight.
l'agent de police, the police-man	*chemin,* way.
	route, road.

Translation II

Tout le monde sait très bien que Londres est la plus grande ville de l'Europe. Paris est loin d'être aussi grand que la capitale de l'Angleterre. Mais, s'il est moins vaste, il est en revanche, du moins à l'avis des Français, de beaucoup plus agréable. Et à en juger par le grand nombre de touristes qui visitent la ville, il est évident que les étrangers

[1] *le plus petit* is preferred when actual size is meant; *le moindre* when the meaning is metaphorical.

se rendent compte de la beauté de Paris. L'Exposition, une des plus grandes et des plus variées qu'on a vues depuis la fin de la guerre, a attiré des foules de visiteurs. Pour les touristes qui redoutent le trajet de la Manche le meilleur moyen d'aller à Paris, c'est de faire le voyage par avion : mais ce n'est pas le moins cher. Les gens qui ont plus de loisir ne sauraient mieux faire que d'y aller en automobile. Les routes sont bonnes : on voit bien la campagne : en suivant la route nationale il est presque impossible de perdre son chemin. Et l'on peut faire facilement le voyage en deux jours, vu que Paris n'est qu'à trois cents kilomètres de Calais. En France, comme dans la plupart des pays du monde, les véhicules tiennent la droite, mais le touriste intelligent s'accoutumera sans la moindre difficulté à ce règlement. Il n'a qu'à se dire: " je suis résolu de ne pas l'oublier," et en quelques minutes il se moquera de l'anxiété qui l'a torturé dès le moment où, du pont du paquebot, il a aperçu la côte française.

Exercise 16

1. She is old but she sings better than her daughter. 2. You work badly, but I am sure that you will work better before the end of the year. 3. He is the greatest man in the country. 4. Peter is tall. He is bigger by 4 inches than my brother. 5. We are going to Paris by car : it is the best means of making the journey. 6. We have many things to do, but we are determined to do them before to-morrow. 7. Paris is only two hundred kilometres from here. 8. She has bought the most beautiful house in the district. 9. Jean is the cleverest workman in the town. 10. She is determined not to sell this house which she likes better than the other. 11. The day when I saw him was the happiest of my life. 12. I noticed a crowd of tourists : they were going towards the castle, which is the finest in the country. 13. The policemen are looking for the thief who has taken my watch. 14. This road is bad, but the

other is yet worse. 15. He will not cross the river without falling into the water : which will be very amusing. 16. There are many French soldiers in the town. I have seen them. 17. They say that this Englishman is not as intelligent as you think him. 18. You are going on horseback, I on foot : but I shall arrive before you. 19. I lost my watch, but I have found it without the least difficulty. 20. You dress less quickly than I.

LESSON XVII

PARTITIVE USE OF ARTICLE

The future of all the regular verbs is formed by adding to the present infinite the terminations of the verb *avoir*. In 4th Conj. the *e* is elided.

1st Conj.	*2nd Conj.*	*4th Conj.*
danser ai	finir ai	perdrai
,, as	,, as	perdras
,, a	,, a	perdra
,, ons	,, ons	perdrons
,, ez	,, ez	perdrez
,, ont	,, ont	perdront

The imperative second person plural (the only part you will require for a long time) is formed by adding to the stem of the verb the termination *ez* (including the *iss* in second conjugation)—*dansez, finissez, perdez*. *Donnez-moi du beurre* = give me some butter. *Finissez tout de suite* = finish at once. *Rendez-moi ce que vous avez* = give up to me what you have.

Du beurre illustrates an important use of the article called the *partitive* use. When we talk of a thing in general, and yet only refer to a part of it, we use this *partitive article*. It consists of the definite article and *de*.

Have you money? Here we are talking of money in general
—a part of money in general—yet no particular part.
The French is *avez-vous de l'argent?* Where is the cream?
= *où est la crème?*—for here we are referring to a particular
portion of cream. Have you any cream? = *avez-vous de la
crème?* Will you cut some wood? = *couperez-vous du bois?*

An important impersonal verb is *il s'agit*, the meaning of
which may be gathered from the following examples:
Il s'agit d'argent = it is a question of money. *S'agit-il
de moi?* = is it about me? *De quoi s'agit-il* = what is
it about?—*i.e.*, what is going on? *Il s'agissait de lui
donner du pain* = it was a matter of giving him bread.

lait, milk.	*désirer*, desire, want.
œuf, egg.	*jaune*, yellow.
vache, cow.	*vert*, green.
chien, dog.	*marché*, market.
chat, cat.	*pluie*, rain.
moment, moment.	*quelque*, some.

tout, toute = all, every.

Translation III

Le lendemain de mon arrivée à Paris je me suis levé de
bonne heure. Ayant pris le petit déjeuner, qui consistait
en une tasse de café avec du pain et du beurre, je suis sorti
de l'hôtel, où j'étais descendu, pour aller faire une promenade en ville. En suivant les rues les plus fréquentées
j'arrive enfin à une grande place au milieu de laquelle se
dresse une colonne. C'est la Place de la Bastille. Ce qui
m'étonne un peu c'est de voir de tous côtés des baraques où
des marchands se sont installés. Un monsieur à qui je
pose une question, dans mon meilleur français, me dit que
ce n'est pas un marché ordinaire mais une foire. Il paraît
qu'il n'y a aucun arrondissement de Paris qui n'a (pas) à
quelque saison sa foire. L'ayant remercié de son explica-
tion je fais le tour des baraques. On y vend toute sorte de

choses : de la viande, des légumes, des oiseaux en cage, des chaussettes, des bas de soie artificielle. Outre les marchands j'ai remarqué un prestidigitateur, des acrobates et un vendeur de billets de loterie. En écoutant bien les marchands qui proclamaient à haute voix la qualité supérieure de leur marchandise, j'ai réussi à augmenter de quelques mots pittoresques mon vocabulaire français. Comme je n'avais dans ma poche qu'une dizaine de francs je n'ai rien acheté, mais je me suis beaucoup amusé. Il est vrai que j'étais seul. Mais je ne me suis pas ennuyé, car il y avait tant de choses intéressantes à voir. Il avait fait d'abord un temps magnifique. Vers midi, cependant, le ciel s'assombrit et en quelques minutes une légère pluie tombait. J'ai décidé donc de rentrer à l'hôtel.

Exercise 17

1. Having had milk, the cat desired cream. 2. It thunders and there is much rain. I think that I shall stay in my room. 3. If you do not listen you will hear nothing. 4. They have gone to see whether it is still raining. 5. It is a matter of getting up early. 6. He has seen nothing, for he had gone out with his friends. 7. All that he will lose will be some cows. 8. I bought at the market a dozen eggs and some meat for lunch. 9. He was wearing a green hat and a yellow coat which I did not like. 10. We have decided to go and see him at the hotel where he has put up. 11. Has the cow given any milk? 12. He has not yet succeeded in doing his work, for he has so many things to do. 13. Without looking at the visitor he went out of the room. 14. I went to see her but she had gone out. 15. Have you any butter? Yes. I have a pound. 16. He likes milk, but he likes eggs better. 17. Without working you will receive nothing. 18. She has gone to Paris for five weeks. 19. I would have given you some money if you had worked better. 20. I have only bought a score of eggs and some handkerchiefs.

LESSON XVIII

POSSESSIVE PRONOUNS—VOICI AND VOILA

There are two cases in which the rule about the partitive is broken. The article is omitted if (1) the word is used with a negative verb or (2) the word is *preceded* by an adjective. Do not give the boys money = *ne donnez pas d'argent aux garçons*. Give me some good milk = *donnez moi de bon lait*. But: Give me some good pure white milk = *donnez-moi du lait bon, pur et blanc*.

The distinction between *my* and *mine* is that *my* is never used without a noun, and *mine* never with one (old forms— *mine* ease, *mine* inn, *mine* host—must be neglected). *My* we know as *mon, ma, mes; mine* introduces a new set of words. We cannot do better than make our old friends introduce those new words.

Masculine.

		Sing.	Plur.	
mon	my	le mien	les miens	mine
ton	thy	le tien	les tiens	thine
son	his or her	le sien	les siens	his or hers or its
notre	our	le nôtre	les nôtres	ours
votre	your	le vôtre	les vôtres	yours
leur	their	le leur	les leurs	theirs

Feminine.

Sing.	Plur.	
la mienne	les miennes	mine
la tienne	les tiennes	thine
la sienne	les siennes	his or hers or its
la nôtre	les nôtres	ours
la vôtre	les vôtres	yours
la leur	les leurs	theirs

There are two very useful little words in French—*voici*

and *voilà*. They are really verbs, but since they have got mixed up with other words they have lost the right to have subjects. *Vois* is the singular imperative of the verb *voir* and therefore is the command *see!* If now we add *ici*, it runs *vois ici* = see here. If on the other hand we add *là*, it runs *vois là* = see there. The shortened forms are *voici* = here is, or behold; *voilà* = there is. Though they have lost the right to have a subject they retain their right to an object. *Voilà un garçon* = there is a boy. *Voici mon père* = here is my father. The same rules about pronouns hold here as in the case of the ordinary verb—the object comes before the verb. *Me voici* = here I am. *Nous voici encore* = here we are again. *Te voilà* = there you are. *Me voilà* = there I am (or *was*).

We must distinguish carefully between the two meanings of the English sentence : *There is a house.* It is ambiguous as it stands, for it may be rendered *il y a une maison* or *voilà une maison*. The former is the general form, the latter the demonstrative. If you are in doubt which to use, ask yourself whether you can point with your finger as you say *there*. If you can, then use *voilà*. *Voilà* and *voici* always imply a pointing finger.

Since they always point out, they may as well point out many things as one. Hence *voici* and *voilà* may mean *here are*, or *there are*, just as well as *here is* or *there is*.

You will learn the use of these new forms much more readily by using them than by any number of rules about them. Here is his book, where is mine? = *voici son livre, où est le mien?* I have my watch, have you yours? = *j'ai ma montre, avez-vous la vôtre?* His watch is good, but thine is better = *sa montre est bonne, mais la tienne est meilleure.* There are my horses beside yours = *voilà mes chevaux auprès des vôtres.* The best of mine is worse than the worst of his = *le meilleur des miens est pire que le pire des siens.* This is the key of your house, where is the key of mine? = *voici la clef de votre maison, où est la clef de la mienne?* Our cows are bigger than theirs = *nos vaches sont plus grandes que les leurs.* Their boxes are smaller than ours = *leurs boîtes sont plus petites que les nôtres.* Our letters are longer than yours = *nos lettres sont plus longues que les vôtres.* She has sent more books to my aunt than to yours = *elle a envoyé plus de livres à ma tante qu'à la vôtre.* They gave water to your horses and to mine = *ils ont donné de l'eau à vos chevaux et aux miens.* The price of your horse and of mine = *le prix de votre cheval et du mien.* From all these examples you will gather that the article of *le mien,* etc., is treated exactly as if it stood alone in respect of contracting with *à* and *de.*

Jean, John.	*utile,* useful.
Angleterre, England.	*difficile,* difficult.
encre (f.), ink.	*facile,* easy.
plume (f.), pen.	

Translation IV

Je vous ai dit déjà que j'ai eu l'intention de rentrer à mon hôtel. Mais on se trompe facilement de route en essayant de revenir sur ses pas surtout dans une grande ville où l'on se promène pour la première fois. Après quelques minutes il n'y avait plus de doute. Je m'étais égaré. On a quelquefois de bonnes idées et, apercevant une papeterie, j'y suis entré à la recherche d'un plan de Paris. Le propriétaire du magasin comprend aussitôt que je suis anglais et il essaye, par politesse, de me parler dans ma langue maternelle. Je m'obstine à employer la sienne. Le résultat est très drôle et nous rions, l'un et l'autre. Mais je n'ai aucune difficulté à acheter mon plan et nous nous félicitons poliment l'un l'autre de notre connaissance d'une langue étrangère. Puis je quitte le magasin et je me mets à consulter mon plan. En quelques instants j'ai réussi à m'orienter. Je suis dans la Rue St. Antoine. En la suivant je gagnerai la Rue de Rivoli. Heureusement la pluie cesse bientôt de tomber et c'est sous un ciel redevenu serein que je parcours les rues animées de la capitale. Des passages cloutés indiquent au piéton la route qu'il faut prendre pour traverser les rues. Ça et là je vois des enseignes portant les mots *entrée interdite, sens unique,* et je comprends que, malgré la largeur considérable de beaucoup de rues parisiennes, le problème de la circulation des véhicules est aussi difficile à résoudre à Paris qu'à Londres. Vers midi je me trouve dans la Place du Palais Royal. Mon hôtel n'est qu'à deux pas de là, ce qui est loin de me déplaire, car j'ai bien faim.

Exercise 18

1. Here is my watch. I have not seen his. 2. There is the hat which you are looking for. Give me back mine. 3. His car goes more quickly than yours. 4. Those two boys would not hit one another if you spoke to them. 5. I would give you some good coffee for your breakfast, but I have no milk. 6. If you do not work better you will not receive any money at the end of the week. 7. Have you seen my hat? Yours? Yes. There it is on the table. 8. There are not many people whom I don't like. 9. She has gone to the market in order to buy some good white bread : but we have much of it already. 10. I am sure that they will not find one another. 11. Here you are at last. I was going to look for you. 12. Do not give any money to that young man. He will spend it at once. 13. I was trying to retrace my steps. 14. There is your key, but I have lost mine. 15. No, I wasn't hungry, I was cold. 16. We shall have some fine fruit this year. 17. I tried not to laugh. 18. We intend to go out this evening if it doesn't rain. 19. We haven't any dogs, for my father doesn't like them. 20. You will notice on the left the castle and some old houses.

LESSON XIX

CE AND CELUI

This child is good. Here *this* is a demonstrative adjective pointing to *child*. *This is a good child.* Here *this* is an indefinite pronoun, and takes the place of *child* in the mind till the word child is mentioned. The first sentence runs in French *cet enfant est bon;* the second *c'est un bon enfant.*

This little pronoun *ce* will give you a great deal of trouble. We have already used it a good deal without saying much about it. What you have = *ce que vous avez.* It is the same *ce* that gathers up a whole sentence into a subject for a verb. *Elle acheta de la viande, ce qui était bon pour les enfants.* The English for this is ambiguous : *She bought meat, which was good for the children.* If this means that the particular kind of meat was good for the children, it would have to run in French *elle acheta de la viande qui était bonne pour les enfants.*

The verb that goes with *ce* must always be third person, but it need not be singular. *C'est le soldat,* but *ce sont les soldats; c'était le Français,* but *c'étaient les Français.*

But *ce,* with the help of two little additions, turns itself into two very useful words; *ci* is short for *ici* = here; and *là* = there. When these are joined to *ce* we have *ceci* = this here, and *cela* = this there, or shortly, *ceci* = this, *cela* = that. *Ceci* means the nearer one, *cela* means the more distant one. Notice that *cela* has no accent on the *a*.

Observe that *ceci* and *cela* are very independent little words. They must never be used joined on to a noun or pronoun. They always stand alone. If you look at a tree and wish to speak of it without naming it, you call it *ceci*; if you refer to another tree, it is *cela*. You put your hand into your pocket and pull out anything, you may then say *j'ai trouvé ceci dans ma poche*. Suppose this object is placed on the mantelpiece, you may by-and-by refer to it as *cela*.

On the other hand we frequently wish to refer to a noun previously used. *John's watch is better than that of his uncle.* Here *cela* is of no use; we need a new word, the masculine of which is *celui*, the feminine *celle*. We use the feminine here: *La montre de Jean est meilleure que celle de son oncle.* Mary's book is longer than Jane's = *le livre de Marie est plus long que celui de Jeanne.*

The plural of *celui* is *ceux*, of *celle*, *celles*. My horses are stronger than the general's = *mes chevaux sont plus forts que ceux du général.* Kings' crowns are bigger than queens' = *les couronnes des rois sont plus grandes que celles des reines.*

To these pronouns also we may add *ci* and *là*, when we speak of two objects or sets of objects. The *ci* indicates the near one, the *là* the one more remote. Speaking of two books *previously mentioned* you may ask which do you prefer, *celui-ci ou celui-là?* = this one or that? Continuing a conversation about watches, we may say *celle-ci est jolie mais celle-là est bonne* = this one is pretty, but that one is good. Speaking of pupils, we may say *ceux-ci sont attentifs, ceux-là sont habiles* = these are attentive, those are clever. Speaking of girls, *celles-ci sont gaies, celles-là sont prudentes.*

habit, coat.	*déchirer*, to tear.
manche, sleeve.	*longtemps*, long (of time only).
toujours, always.	*maintenant*, now.

Translation V

L'hôtel, dont il s'agit, n'était pas très grand. C'était à vrai dire un établissement assez modeste et ce fut pour cette raison que je l'avais choisi. Mais les hôtels à Paris, même ceux dont les clients ne payent que des prix modérés,

vous offrent tout confort moderne, chauffage central,
ascenseur, eau courante, etc. Chez nous, au contraire,
surtout en province, les hôtels laissent beaucoup à désirer.
Ce jour-là j'ai déjeuné mieux que je n'aurais fait à Londres
au même prix.   Le repas terminé je suis allé au salon où je
me suis amusé à lire les journaux.   Les journaux français,
à en juger par celui que j'avais devant les yeux, ne sont pas
aussi bons que les anglais.   Ils sont mal imprimés et le
papier n'est pas de très bonne qualité.   Jusqu'alors je
n'avais jamais lu de journal étranger.   Naturellement il y
avait beaucoup de mots que je ne comprenais pas, mais
j'ai réussi sans peine à saisir le sens général des articles, ce
qui m'a rendu fort content.

Après ma longue promenade du matin j'étais un peu las.
Mais je n'avais pas de temps à perdre, car je n'allais rester
que six jours à Paris, et il y avait tant de choses intéressantes à voir.   Je consulte de nouveau mon plan, au revers
duquel je trouve toutes sortes de renseignements indispens-
ables aux touristes, les routes d'autobus, les lignes du Métro-
politain, etc.   Je décide enfin d'aller visiter l'église du Sacré
Cœur, exemple remarquable du style byzantin.   De plus,
comme elle est située au sommet de Montmartre, on y
jouit d'un panorama magnifique.   Selon une tradition très
répandue c'est près de cet endroit qu'on a coupé la tête
à Saint Denis, saint patron de la France sous l'ancien régime:
d'où vient le nom du mont des martyrs, ou Montmartre.

Exercise 19

1. This is good, that is bad.   2. Of these two books this
will last longer than that.   3. She is older than you think.
4. Our house is smaller than the general's.   5. I have four
books, of which you have read two.   6. That gave them
much pleasure.   7. This is the coat of which the sleeve is
torn.   8. She will never more be happy.   9. We ate
an excellent meal.   10. See what I have for your lunch.
11. When one gets home one is tired.   12. There are the

two cars : this one is his, that one is yours. 13. He no longer eats, but he says he isn't hungry. 14. My car goes faster than the tourist's. 15. The Paris streets are wider than those of London. 16. To tell the truth, we went to your uncle's house, but he had gone out. 17. At my aunt's there are two little boys. 18. I will not give you this watch, but you shall have that (one). 19. In the French army there are clever soldiers, of whom General X is one. 20. I never hear what he says : he speaks yet worse than his brother.

LESSON XX

LEQUEL AND DONT

If you take up an old English book you will find among the old-fashioned forms the expression *the which*. In modern English we do not use the article at all with the relative pronoun, but in French we still use it just as we used to do in English. The French form is *lequel* and *lesquels* when masculine, and *laquelle* and *lesquelles* when feminine. This form is used after prepositions. The chair in which you are seated = *la chaise dans laquelle vous êtes assis*. The boxes in which I found the handkerchiefs = *les boîtes dans lesquelles j'ai trouvé les mouchoirs*. The pen with which I write = *la plume avec laquelle j'écris*. The book of which you speak = *le livre duquel vous parlez*. The boys to whom you gave apples = *les garçons auxquels vous avez donné des pommes*.

In passage V of our translation we found the word *dont* doing duty for *of which*. As a matter of fact, *of which*, *of whom*, and *whose* may be all translated by either *dont* or *duquel, de laquelle, desquels*. Le livre $\begin{Bmatrix} dont \\ duquel \end{Bmatrix}$ vous parlez. La rue $\begin{Bmatrix} dont \\ de\ laquelle \end{Bmatrix}$ j'ai entendu parler = the street of which I heard. (Note that *entendu* is not feminine, because *dont* or *de laquelle* is not the direct object.)

It is to be noted that if *of which, of whom, whose* are interrogative, they must not be rendered by the word *dont*. Of whom do you speak? = *de qui parlez-vous?* Whose hat is this? = *à qui ce chapeau?*

Occasionally the word *where* is misleading in English, for it sometimes really means *in which*. The house where I was born = *la maison où je suis né* or *la maison dans laquelle je suis né.*

Quoi = what or which, can only refer to things. It can be used as an exclamation as in English, or it may be used after a preposition. You have something to eat = *vous avez de quoi manger.* To what good? = *à quoi bon?*

Remember that *qui* is the subject, and must be placed as near as possible to the noun to which it refers. *Que* is the object. *Qui* must be close to the verb; *que* is usually separated from the verb by several words. A very important rule is that *que* must *never* be omitted in French, though it may be omitted in English. The man I saw = *l'homme que j'ai vu.* The book I shall buy = *le livre que j'achèterai.*

après, after.	*hier,* yesterday.
sage, wise, good.	*église,* church.
secret,[1] secret.	*dent* (f.), tooth.
avoir peur, to be afraid.	*ciel,* heaven.
oreille, the ear.	*s'avancer,* to advance.
île (f.), island.	*prêter,* to lend.

Translation VI

Vers trois heures de l'après-midi je sors de l'hôtel et je me dirige vers la station du Métro la plus proche. C'est celle du Palais Royal. Je descends les escaliers et je me trouve dans une longue galerie souterraine. Je ne vois ni

[1] In this word the *c* is sounded like *g* :—*s'grey.*

ascenseur ni escalier roulant. Sans doute il n'y a pas besoin d'en avoir dans la plupart des stations, car la voie n'est pas construite à la même profondeur qu'à Londres. Je m'approche du guichet et je demande un billet pour le parcours du Palais Royal à la station de Barbès. Mais l'employé me regarde d'une façon un peu dédaigneuse et je comprends que j'ai fait une gaffe. Il me demande si je désire un billet de première ou de deuxième classe. Je prends un billet de première et l'employé m'explique qu'il n'y a que deux prix selon la classe dans laquelle on voyage. Ce n'est pas comme à Londres où le prix des billets varie selon le parcours. Muni de son billet on peut changer de train autant de fois qu'on le désire et le billet ne cesse d'être valable que quand on aura dépassé la barrière pour remonter à la surface.

Le train arrive aussitôt. Il se compose de cinq voitures, dont la troisième est de première classe. Ayant consulté encore mon plan—que je suis bien aise de l'avoir !—je descends à la Gare de l'Est pour prendre un train correspondant et quelques minutes plus tard, en remontant les escaliers je me trouve à l'extrémité du Boulevard Barbès. Je ne saurais dire si le système parisien est plus pratique que le nôtre. Evidemment pour celui qui est obligé de faire des parcours considérables le système comporte des avantages : de plus c'est un moyen de transport assez rapide : mais si on veut aller, par exemple, du Palais Royal à la Place de la Concorde, on ferait mieux de prendre l'autobus : on jouirait ainsi du grand air, tout en faisant de petites économies.

Exercise 20

1. The castle which we are approaching is the biggest in the province. 2. Here is the knife with which I always cut the bread. 3. The men to whom I was speaking yesterday have already departed (partir). 4. How glad I am to see you ! 5. She advanced as far as the island. 6. This is the house in which she was born. 7. This island

is bigger than that you spoke of. 8. What ! Are you afraid of going in there alone ? 9. He told me the story of a man who lost all he had. 10. I cannot enter a house of which the doors and windows are shut. 11. Neither he nor she will be here to-morrow. 12. There is no need to take any money. I have all that is necessary. 13. I do not like the way in which he looks at me. 14. To whom did you give my watch? I have need of it. 15. The churches to which we are going are the most interesting in the town. 16. The cows at which you are looking have been already sold. 17. Will you give me back the book I lent you ? 18. What are these two men talking about? I understand neither the one nor the other. 19. The island I saw has a secret. 20. How fat those men are !

LESSON XXI

THE INDEFINITE PRONOUNS

We have already had two of what are called the indefinite pronouns. These are *on* and *l'un l'autre*. There are six others that we must now learn :—

autrui = others, other people.	*personne* = nobody.
chacun (m.) } = each one or	*quelqu'un* = somebody
chacune (f.) } everyone.	*quiconque* = whoever.

Autrui is used after a preposition. He depends on others = *il dépend d'autrui*. Other people's property = *le bien d'autrui*.

Chacun is always used in the masculine unless there is a particular reason for putting it in the feminine. *Chacun pour soi* = everyone for himself. Each one has his turn = *à chacun son tour*. Give to everyone his own = *rendez à chacun ce qui lui appartient*. They approached, each according to his rank = *ils s'approchèrent, chacun selon son rang.* The ladies will have each her share = *les dames auront chacune sa part.*

When *each* or *every* is an *adjective* it is rendered by *chaque.* Each went home = *chacun alla chez soi.* But : Each soldier went home = *chaque soldat alla chez lui.*

Personne when used as a noun, meaning *person*, whether applied to a male or female person, is feminine. Thus if we refer to a man as a person, we must say *cette personne.* The noun can be used in the plural like other nouns. Here are persons of distinction = *voici des personnes de condition.*

But when *personne* is used as an indefinite pronoun it is *always* singular and *always* masculine. Further, it always insists upon its verb having *ne* but no *pas.* Nobody has seen him = *personne ne l'a vu.* There is nobody in my room = *il n'y a personne dans ma chambre.* Who is there? Nobody = *Qui est là? Personne.* That is not good for anybody = *cela n'est bon pour personne.*

Quelqu'un and *quiconque* present no difficulty. They are always used as masculine. Someone has said = *quelqu'un a dit.* Whoever has told you that has deceived you = *Quiconque vous a dit cela vous a trompé.* I shall receive whomsoever he sends = *je recevrai quiconqu'il enverra.*

Certain adjectives if used without a noun are treated as indefinite pronouns. These are :—

nul (m.), *nulle* (f.)	= no one.
aucun (m.), *aucune* (f.)	= none.
tel (m.), *telle* (f.)	= such a one.
tout (unchangeable)	= all.

Nul and *aucun* demand a *ne* with the verb (but no *pas*) just like *personne.* I shall send you none = *je ne vous en enverrai aucun.* No one knows them = *nul ne les connaît.*

Tel as an adjective is differently placed with regard to the article in French. We say *such a man*, the French *un tel homme;* so, such a house = *une telle maison.* There is a peculiar use of *tel* : Mr. So-and-so = *Monsieur un tel* ; Mrs. So-and-so = *Madame une telle*.

Dans and *en* both mean *in*, but *dans* refers to a more limited space. In this room = *dans cette chambre* ; in Ireland = *en Irlande*. *Dans* and *en* are also used in connection with time. Generally speaking, when there is any qualifying word used (even the article) *dans* is preferred.

Translation VII

Il faut avouer qu'en m'approchant de la basilique du Sacré Cœur j'ai éprouvé une légère déception. Au premier aspect le style byzantin, dans lequel l'édifice est construit, m'a paru lourd. Ce n'est qu'après quelques minutes que je me suis rendu compte des nobles proportions et de la dignité de cette vaste construction, dont le clocher atteint une hauteur de plus de cent mètres. Il faisait assez sombre à l'intérieur, mais cette obscurité relative m'a rendu d'autant plus sensible à la beauté éblouissante du panorama de Paris qui s'est déroulé devant mes yeux, quand je suis venu me promener sur la terrasse devant la basilique, d'où on jouit d'une vue merveilleuse. Il est vrai que Montmartre a perdu son caractère original. Ce n'est plus le rendez-vous des vrais artistes, qui fréquentent plutôt le quartier de Montparnasse sur la rive gauche de la Seine. Les ateliers de Montmartre sont devenus des cabarets ou des boîtes de nuit. Malgré tout, cependant, Montmartre m'a séduit, et pendant plus d'une demi-heure je parcours les rues étroites en regardant les vieilles maisons de cette butte, si célèbre, qui domine la ville. Enfin je suis obligé de m'arracher à la contemplation de cette vue charmante, car il est temps de rentrer à l'hôtel. Je me sers encore de mon plan et je prends un chemin qui me mène à la Place Pigalle. Il y a tout près une station du Métro, mais je n'y entré pas, ayant pris le parti de rentrer en autobus. Je m'approche d'un arrêt où plusieurs personnes attendent déjà. J'en vois une qui prend un des billets numérotés qui sont fixés à un réverbère. Je fais de même sans savoir bien pourquoi. A l'arrivée de l'autobus, cependant, je comprends, car le receveur demande leurs numéros aux personnes qui veulent y monter et l'on y entre selon le numéro que l'on a. C'est très pratique, surtout pendant les heures d'affluence, car on évite d'être bousculé par ceux qui se battent pour obtenir une place. Mais cette fois je n'ai pas de chance. L'autobus est au complet et je me résigne à attendre encore quelques minutes.

Exercise 21

1. No one has seen Mrs. So-and-so. 2. Someone has used my book. 3. All is lost but no one is killed. 4. Is there nobody in the house? 5. He says that he has not seen anyone. 6. Each day I am obliged to wait for the bus, which annoys me very much. 7. Each of those ladies has all that is necessary to make (render) her happy. 8. No woman loves such a man. 9. Whoever arrives will have much to do. 10. No one has taken the pen which you use. 11. More than 50 visitors have arrived at the hotel since yesterday. 12. I will ask him not to borrow the money from this poor old woman. 13. No wise man will spend all his money. 14. I will not remain here more than 20 minutes. 15. Do not speak to him in such a scornful fashion (a fashion so scornful). 16. The pen of which you have made use is mine. 17. Someone shut the door of the house as I was approaching it. 18. I will ask the conductor for a ticket. 19. I have forgotten the story he told me. 20. There is someone, but I don't know him.

LESSON XXII

THE CARDINAL NUMBERS

The following are the numbers from 21 to 40 :—

21. vingt et un.	31. trente et un.
22. vingt-deux.	32. trente-deux.
23. vingt-trois.	33. trente-trois.
24. ving-quatre.	34. trente-quatre.
25. vingt-cinq.	35. trente-cinq.
26. vingt-six.	36. trente-six.
27. vingt-sept.	37. trente-sept.
28. vingt-huit.	38. trente-huit.
29. vingt-neuf.	39. trente-neuf.
30. trente.	40. quarante.

Beginning with 41 (quarante et un) write out all the numbers up to 69. This is quite easy, as the numbers follow exactly the above pattern. All you require to know is that 50 is *cinquante*, and 60 *soixante*.

At 70, however, a change is made. Instead of having a separate word for 70, we go right on from sixty-nine to sixty-ten, sixty-eleven, and so on up to 80.

69. soixante-neuf.	75. soixante-quinze.
70. soixante-dix.	76. soixante-seize.
71. soixante et onze.	77. soixante-dix-sept.
72. soixante-douze.	78. soixante-dix-huit.
73. soixante-treize.	79. soixante-dix-neuf.
74. soixante-quatorze	80. quatre-vingts.

From 81 (*quatre-vingt-un*), 82 (*quatre-vingt-deux*), the numbers go on regularly through 90 (*quatre-vingt-dix*) up to 99 (*quatre-vingt-dix-neuf*) and 100 (*cent*).

Notice that *et* is never used in French numbers except in 21, 31, 41, 51, 61, 71. For example, 91 is *quatre-vingt-onze*, 101 is *cent un*.

D

The numbers *vingt* and *cent* are the only two that can have the plural *s*, and that only if they are not followed by any other number. Thus *quatre-vingts* = four twenties, *i.e.*, 80; but the *s* is lost in all the other numbers up to and including 99 because these all have other numbers following the *vingt*. So we have 400 = *quatre cents*; 700 = *sept cents*; but 710 = *sept cent dix*; 405 = *quatre cent cinq*.

Mille is the French for 1,000. It never has the *s* of the plural. In dates it is written in the short form *mil*: thus 1870 = *mil huit cent soixante-dix*.

The following examples of numbers will illustrate the French usage :—

        175 cent soixante-quinze.
        493 quatre cent quatre-vingt-treize.
      1,101 mille cent un.
     10,517 dix mille cinq cent dix-sept.
    100,000 cent mille.
  1,000,000 un million.
    456,723 quatre cent cinquante-six mille sept cent vingt-
              trois.
  3,594,971 trois millions cinq cent quatre-vingt-quatorze
              mille neuf cent soixante et onze.

Observe that *million* is treated as a collective noun and has the *s* of the plural. In the exercise on p. 100 express all the figures in French words.

Translation VIII

C'est en première que je réussis enfin à obtenir une place. M'étant assis, je me dispose à acheter mon billet, sans savoir au juste, cependant, comment m'y prendre. Un monsieur, bien poli, auprès de qui je cherche à me renseigner, me conseille d'acheter, moyennant payement de huit francs, un carnet, dont le receveur détachera autant de billets qu'il faut. "La route se divise en sections," ajoute-t-il, "et le nombre de billets qu'il vous prendra dépend de la longueur du parcours." "Je veux aller jusqu'au Palais Royal," lui dis-je. "En ce cas il détachera quatre billets. Si vous aviez une place de seconde classe il ne lui en faudrait que trois."

Je suis son excellent conseil, et une vingtaine de minutes plus tard j'arrive à ma destination. Je suis sur le point de rentrer directement à l'hôtel quand, en regardant ma montre-bracelet, je constate que ce n'est pas encore l'heure du dîner. "Si j'allais prendre un apéritif au Café de la Régence, qui est tout près," me dis-je. "Voilà une bonne idée, car il est bien agréable de s'asseoir à une petite table en plein air et de regarder les passants."

Beaucoup de personnes sont déjà en train de déguster leurs boissons et ce n'est pas sans difficulté que je trouve une petite table de libre. Il n'y a pas besoin de dire que ce n'était pas celle où Bonaparte jouait aux Échecs. Le garçon m'a montré cette fameuse table, mais naturellement il est défendu aux consommateurs de s'y asseoir. Tout en buvant à petits coups le Cinzano que j'ai commandé je regarde les flâneurs. En me rappelant plus tard les détails de ma visite à Paris, j'ai été convaincu que, toute réflexion faite, les heures que j'ai passées à prendre un café crème ou un apéritif au dehors d'un des innombrables cafés, ont été les plus délicieuses de mon séjour dans la capitale. On est, pour ainsi dire, au cœur même de Paris.

Ce soir-là, en très peu de temps, j'ai vu passer toute sorte de gens : de bonnes familles bourgeoises, des hommes d'affaires, des vendeurs de tapis, des femmes élégantes. J'aime beaucoup le théâtre. Assis sur la terrasse d'un café on assiste à un spectacle de la vie réelle : ce qui est plus intéressant que n'importe quelle comédie. Bref je me suis fameusement amusé, et c'est avec peine que je me décide enfin à rentrer à l'hôtel.

Exercise 22

Express the following numbers in French words. (a) 10,001. (b) 327. (c) 18,504. (d) 1,000,101. (e) 437,610. (f) 19,896. (g) 4,836,997. (h) 61. (i) 98. (j) 1000. (k) 400. (l) 50,000. (m) 60,060. (n) 71,171. (o) 83,180. (p) 16,000. (q) 1331. (r) 333,333.

1. This man has bought 81 horses and 70 cows. 2. This house is 65 feet high. 3. I was born in 1919. 4. There are in Paris more than 3,000,000 people. 5. I had 460 francs but I have spent 39. 6. This church was built in 1643. 7. He lived in this house in 1928. 8. 2560 soldiers have been killed. 9. In 1921 I was only 2 years old. 10. 43 boats have crossed the river. There is another !

LESSON XXIII

ORDINAL NUMBERS AND TIME

When numbers are used in the ordinary way they are called *cardinal* numbers. All our last lesson was about cardinal numbers. But when we wish to express the *order* in which things have to be taken we use the *ordinal* numbers, as *first, thirty-second, hundred and twelfth* *Th* is the usual ending of the ordinals in English—four*th*, fif*th*, six*th*, etc. The French equivalent is *ième*, as *quatrième, cinquième, sixième*, etc.

First = *premier* (m.), *première* (f.).

Second = *second* (m.), *seconde* (f.). In this word the *c* is pronounced as *g*.

Another form of *second* is *deuxième*.

The other ordinals are quite regularly formed by adding *ième* to the cardinals, omitting the *e* if there is one before the *ième*, as in *quatorze, quatorzième* The *f* of *neuf* becomes *v, neuvième*. The following examples are helpful :—

18th, dix-huitième.   100th, centième.
105th, cent cinquième.   213th, deux cent treizième.
60th, soixantième.   93rd, quatre-vingt-treizième.
    1431st, mille quatre cent trente et unième.
    10,022nd, dix mille vingt-deuxième.

Sometimes we wish to say *how many times* a thing has happened. To express this we use the word *fois* along with the proper cardinal :—

    once, une fois (*une* is f. of *un*).
    twice, deux fois.
    thrice, trois fois.
    four times, quatre fois.
    twenty times, vingt fois.
    101 times, cent une fois.
    the twentieth time, la vingtième fois.
    the 101st time, la cent unième fois.
    the first time, la première fois.
    the last time, la dernière fois.

Fois thus means *time* answering to the question *how often ?* (*combien de fois ?*)

To answer the question *how long ?* we must use the word *temps* (*combien de temps ?*). While dealing with numbers we may as well explain the French way of expressing the time of day. You can never go wrong if you follow the method of our railway time-tables, *i.e.*, name the hour and add the number of minutes.

Two o'clock = deux heures.
Quarter past three = trois heures quinze.
Five minutes to six = cinq heures cinquante-cinq.

If you like, however, you can take the hour which is nearest to the time you speak of and either add or subtract the minutes, thus :—

Quarter past five = cinq heures et quart.

Quarter to six = six heures moins un quart.

Half-past one = une heure et demie.

Noon is *midi* and midnight is *minuit*. Corresponding to our A.M. is the word for morning (*matin*), and for P.M. the word for evening (*soir*). Thus 6.0 in the morning (evening) = *six heures* DU *matin* (*soir*). In time-tables, the 24-hour system is used, *e.g.* 3.35 P.M. = *15.35*; 11 P.M. = *23 heures*.

Exactly when used about time is represented by the adjective *précise*, which agrees with the *heures* in question.

Quelle heure est-il ? = what o'clock is it?

Il est une heure précise = it is one o'clock exactly.

When minutes are added, the adverb *juste* (or *tout juste*) is used.

Il est tout juste trois heures vingt = It is twenty past three o'clock exactly.

About with regard to time is *vers* and may have the article before the hour. About seven o'clock = *vers* (*les*) *sept heures*.

Translation IX

Avant mon départ de Londres on m'avait dit qu'un moyen admirable d'étendre ma connaissance du français ce serait d'assister à la représentation d'une bonne comédie. Chez nous il n'y a pas de théâtre national, quoiqu'on en parle depuis longtemps. Mais à Paris on trouve plusieurs théâtres, subventionnés par l'État, dont le mieux connu est la Comédie Française, la fondation de laquelle remonte au dix-septième siècle.

Après dîner j'ai donc consulté le bulletin des spectacles dans le journal pour savoir ce qu'on jouait en soirée au Français. C'est *Le Malade Imaginaire*. Heureusement j'avais lu déjà cette belle pièce de Molière qui compte à juste titre parmi les chefs d'œuvre du théâtre français.

Cette comédie a été représentée pour la première fois le dix février 1673. Mais elle porte toujours, car c'est une pièce vécue.

Mon hôtel n'était qu'à quelques pas de la Comédie Française et il y avait encore vingt minutes avant le lever du rideau. Mais je suis parti aussitôt, car je n'avais pas retenu ma place, et il y aurait sans doute beaucoup de monde. En effet j'ai remarqué à l'entrée du théâtre une foule de personnes, dont quelques-unes (étaient) en grande toilette. En arrivant au guichet j'ai demandé à l'employé une place dans la deuxième galerie. " Une seule ? " me dit-il. " Bon. Il y a le numéro soixante-sept au troisième rang. C'est un peu de côté, mais vous verrez bien la scène." " Eh bien, ça fera mon affaire," lui dis-je. " Ça fait quinze francs, monsieur. Merci."

Mon billet à la main, je suis entré dans la salle et une ouvreuse m'a conduit à ma place. Le théâtre était bondé. Il n'y avait pas une place de vide au parterre. C'est avec la plus vive impatience que j'attends le commencement de la pièce, car je sais bien que les rôles à la Comédie Française sont tenus par les meilleurs acteurs de Paris. Enfin on frappe les trois coups traditionnels. Il se fait dans la salle un silence profond. Le rideau se lève et les acteurs entrent en scène.

Exercise 23

1. He knocked at the old woman's door at 8 o'clock in the morning.[1] 2. At what hour did they depart for the theatre? 3. It is certain that she will arrive about ten o'clock. 4. How many times have I asked you not to wait for me? 5. Since when have you been waiting for the bus? Since half past five. I am beginning to think it will never come. 6. It is exactly ten past four by (à) my watch.

[1] *Note.*—In the morning—*le matin*. But, preceded by some hour of the day, it is turned into " of " the morning, e.g. *onze heures du matin*. So also : *sept heures du soir*, etc.

7. I will not fail to (manquer de) wake you at a quarter to seven. 8. My first house was not as good as my second. 9. That is the eleventh time that he has told me this story. 10. The train will start (partir) at twenty-five minutes past five. 11. At midday he set to work. 12. His house is the eighth on the right. 13. I have spoken to him for the last time. 14. The train will arrive at Havre at a quarter past two. 15. She arrived at the theatre three minutes before the rise of the curtain. 16. Lunch is at half-past one. 17. I always used to get up before eight. 18. There he is in the fifth row of the pit. 19. I shall be home at exactly three o'clock. 20. We have been looking for you for two hours.

LESSON XXIV

DATES, SEASONS, ETC.

In speaking of days of the month the French use the cardinal, not the ordinal numbers: thus the *fifteenth of May* is written *le quinze mai*. The same is true about the numbers applied to kings or chapters or pages. Henry the Eighth = *Henri Huit*; Chapter XIV = *Chapitre quatorze*. To this rule *premier* is an exception. James I = *Jacques Premier*.

The following are the French names for the months. They are all masculine. Note that they have no capitals.

January, *janvier*.	May, *mai*	September, *septembre*.
February, *février*.	June, *juin*.	October, *octobre*.
March, *mars*.	July, *juillet*.	November, *novembre*.
April, *avril*.	August, *août*.	December, *décembre*.

The days of the week are also all masculine and have no capitals.

Monday, *lundi*.	Wednesday, *mercredi*.	Friday, *vendredi*.
Tuesday, *mardi*.	Thursday, *jeudi*.	Saturday, *samedi*.

Sunday, *dimanche*.

The seasons are also all masculine, and have no capitals.

Spring, *le printemps.*	Autumn, *l'automne.*
Summer, *l'été.*	Winter, *l'hiver.*

Note the use of the article. In spring = *au printemps ;* but the other three seasons take *en* for *in* : thus, *en été* = in summer, *en hiver* = in winter, *en automne* = in autumn.

Before the days of the week the French omit the *on* that we use in English. I saw him on Thursday = *je l'ai vu jeudi.* He arrived on Sunday = *il est arrivé dimanche.*

When a thing happens habitually on a certain day we do not use the plural, but the singular with the article *le.* We have a market on Fridays = *nous avons un marché le vendredi.* If we wish to say *every day*, we write *all the days*, i.e. *tous les jours.* He shaves every day = *il se rase tous les jours.* He sleeps every night = *il dort toutes les nuits.* He goes home every Sunday = *il va chez lui tous les dimanches.* He is in Paris every month = *il est à Paris tous les mois.*

In writing a date the French use the article : June 24th = *le vingt-quatre juin.* At the heads of French forms we often find printed le..................19.........

There are two forms of the following words :—

an	or	*année* = year.
jour	,,	*journée* = day.
matin	,,	*matinée* = morning.
soir	,,	*soirée* = evening.

The distinction is that the termination *ée* indicates that we speak of the whole period in question; *journée* = a whole day or the duration of a day ; *jour* = day in general.

saison = season.	*Noël* = Christmas.
mois = month.	*pâque* or *pâques* = Easter.
semaine = week.	*le jour de l'an* = New Year's Day.
temps = time or weather.	*congé* = holiday, or leave.

Translation X

L'intrigue du *Malade Imaginaire* est peu compliqué. Il s'agit d'un bourgeois, qui s'obstine à croire qu'il est atteint d'une grave maladie. Il s'entoure de médecins qui lui prodiguent leurs soins. Mais, comme vous l'aurez deviné, ils ne lui donnent pas des consultations gratuites, et Argan— c'est le nom du soi-disant malade—se lasse enfin de leur payer de grosses sommes d'argent. Il décide donc de marier sa fille avec un médecin, pour qu'il paye moins cher à l'avenir les remèdes dont il croit avoir besoin. Sa fille est amoureuse d'un jeune homme, mais le père veut absolument qu'elle épouse un médecin pédant et ridicule. Il ne réussit pas cependant à accomplir son dessein. Les personnes à qui il se fie le trahissent et il se rend compte enfin des belles qualités de la fille dont il a failli sacrifier le bonheur. C'est une pièce des plus amusantes et les acteurs ont parlé si clairement que j'ai tout compris.

Dans la plupart des théâtres parisiens, sauf les music-halls, il est défendu au public de fumer. Aussi ai-je quitté ma place à l'entr'acte pour aller fumer une cigarette au foyer. Beaucoup de personnes ont fait de même. L'entr'acte n'a duré que dix minutes, mais il m'a semblé de beaucoup trop long, car il me tardait de voir les derniers actes.

A la fin de la pièce la salle a croulé sous les applaudissements de l'assistance enthousiasmée et je suis sorti du théâtre en proie à une vive émotion. " Voilà une représentation," me dis-je, " que je n'oublierai jamais."

Il était presque minuit, mais je n'avais aucune envie de me coucher. Les étoiles brillaient et il soufflait une légère brise comme je me suis dirigé au clair de lune le long de l'Avenue de l'Opéra jusqu'au Café de la Paix. Là, en buvant à petits coups mon café crème je me suis mis à penser à la pièce que je venais de voir jouer d'une façon si magistrale. A une table voisine deux messieurs parlaient affaires. " Que pensez-vous de la situation financière ? "

" Très mauvaise. Cela empire de jour en jour." De l'autre côté de moi deux jeunes gens se parlaient à voix basse. Evidemment ils ne se souciaient guère de l'accroissement artificiel de la circulation fiduciaire. Ni moi non plus. J'étais encore sous le charme de Molière.

Exercise 24(a)

1. Le vingt-deux décembre. 2. A la Noël il ne fait pas beau temps. 3. Au mois de mai il fera beau temps. 4. Il a travaillé toute la journée. 5. Il travaillera tous les jours. 6. Le printemps est la plus belle des quatre saisons. 7. François Premier ne gagna rien cette fois. 8. Charles Deux aimait bien ses plaisirs. 9. Il viendra ici tous les matins. 10. Il y a sept jours dans la semaine et quatre semaines dans un mois. 11. Je reviendrai le jour de Noël. 12. La semaine de Pâques était bien triste pour lui. 13. Il me l'a donné le trente août mil neuf cent trente-sept. 14. Les soldats ont congé le dimanche. 15. En été nous avons des fruits, mais au printemps nous avons de belles fleurs. 16. Jacques Deux, roi d'Angleterre, demeura longtemps en France. 17. Nous avons eu une soirée bien agréable. 18. Il fait mauvais temps cette semaine. 19. Le premier janvier s'appelle ordinairement le jour de l'an. 20. Février est un mois bien triste.

Exercise 24(b)

1. We get up every morning at seven o'clock. 2. I often think of her. 3. I see him from time to time. 4. I nearly missed the train this morning. 5. I went to her house, but she had just gone out. 6. He always comes to see me on Mondays. 7. It's very cold here in winter. 8. I have just dined with him. 9. Most people don't work all day. 10. I used to go home every Friday. 11. We shall start for America on July 21st. 12. He is going to marry a widow. 13. Of what are you thinking? 14. He nearly

fell into the water. 15. We go to Paris every two months. 16. Louis XIV was king of France for (pendant) 72 years. 17. Napoleon I was the uncle of Napoleon III. 18. I forbid you to speak to him. 19. She has just crossed the street. 20. We are surrounded on all sides.

LESSON XXV

VERB BUILDING

Up till now we have used the Table of Irregular Verbs mainly to identify words we come across in our French reading. We must now see how we are to use it in turning English into French. You will observe that in most cases only five parts are given : the pres. infinitive, the pres, part., the past part., the pres. ind, and the past historic. This is so because these five parts are called the *primitive* parts, since all the rest can be built out of these. Taking them in the order they occur, we shall see what we can build out of each of the primitive parts.

Pres. Infinitive. From this we form (1) the *future* by simply adding the terminations *ai, as, a ; ons, ez, ont*.

(2) The *conditional present* by adding the terminations *ais, ais, ait ; ions, iez, aient.*

Pres. Participle. Three parts are formed from this. In all cases we cut off the *ant* and work from the stem which is left.

(1) The *plural* of the *present indicative* by adding *ons, ez, ent*.

(2) The *imperfect ind*. by adding *ais, ais, ait ; ions, iez, aient.*

(3) The *pres. subj.* by adding *e, es, e ; ions, iez, ent.*

Past Participle.	From this are formed *all compound tenses*, as we have found in our exercises, by the help of *avoir* and *être*.
Pres. Indicative.	From this we form the *imperative* by simply doing away with the pronoun.[1]
Past Historic	By taking the second pers. sing. of this tense we can form the complete *imperfect subjunctive* by adding *se, ses, t* (before adding this *t* we must cut off the *s*, and, besides, we must add a circumflex accent over the vowel before the *t*) ; *sions, siez, sent.*

To give meaning to these rules we must apply them to our Table of Irregular Verbs (p. 209). This Table is drawn up in such a way as to give no information that you can find out for yourself. Take the first verb *absoudre* and write out in full the pres. ind. All the help we get are the two words *j'absous*. But we know that the second person ends in *s* and the third in *t*. So we can confidently add *tu absous, il absout*. For the plural we are a little at sea. We are inclined to write *nous absouons* till we remember that the plural of the pres. ind. is always formed from the present participle. Accordingly we take *absolv* from the present participle and write *nous absolvons, vous absolvez, ils absolvent*. To write the future we have only to put down the *infinitive*, and add *ai, as*, etc. But here a little rule must not be forgotten. If the infinitive ends in *e*, the *e* must be cut out before adding *ai, as*, etc. Thus we have *j'absoudrai, tu absoudras, il absoudra ; nous absoudrons, vous absoudrez, ils absoudront*.

---

[1] *Avoir* and *être* are exceptions, their imperatives having the same form as their present subjunctives, namely, *aie* and *sois* respectively.

Now we want the present subjunctive. It also comes from the present participle and runs easily. *J'absolve, tu absolves, il absolve ; nous absolvions, vous absolviez, ils absolvent.*

Sometimes, however, the future and the subjunctive are not so good-natured. They have peculiarities, and then we must give you a hint in our Table. The future of *venir*, for example, should be *venirai*, but if you look up your Table you will find it *viendrai*. Once you get this start all goes well, for the word runs quite smoothly : *Viendrai, viendras, viendra ; viendrons, viendrez, viendront.* There is still a worse case with *aller*. Its future ought to be *allerai*. Instead of that you find *irai*, a totally different word. Yet here again the heart is everything : *Irai, iras, ira ; irons, irez, iront.*

With the present subjunctive things do not go quite so smoothly. So it is sometimes not enough to give only the first singular as in the future. The *singular* of the present subjunctive never gives any trouble ; if you get the first person, the other two have exactly the same stem. If *boive* is the first person, then you may be absolutely sure that the second and third are *boives, boive.* It is the plural that introduces doubt. If the Table gives only the first singular, then there is no difficulty. Under *courir* we get *coure*, so we proceed *coure, coures, coure ; courions, couriez, courent.* Let us now go back to *boive.* Here we have the two forms *boive* and *boivent.* If you get it fixed in your mind that *this Table gives nothing that can be discovered from your rules*, you will see that *boivent* is the exception in this verb. The singular of course runs *boive, boives, boive ;* by the rule the plural is formed from the stem of the present participle and must run *buvions, buviez, buvent.* It is because the third plural does not follow the rule that we find *boivent* in the Table. If you look down the list of present subjunctives, you will find a good many third plurals given. This means that first and second plurals are according to rule.

The imperfect subjunctive is very easily formed, and is free from the changes that afflict the third plural of present subjunctive. Take the second singular past historic of *venir*. This is *vins*. Now add our terminations : *Vinsse, vinsses, vînt ; vinssions, vinssiez, vinssent.* The circumflex over the *i* in third singular distinguishes *vînt* the subjunctive from *vint* the past historic.

In doing the following exercises follow your rules blindly, unless exceptions are given in the Table. Do not trouble to put in pronouns.

Exercise 25(a)

Give the English meaning of each of the following words :
1. Bu, cru, crû, dû, eu, lu, mû, pu, su, tu, vu. 2. Qu'il vînt. 3. Que nous battissions. 4. Qu'il faille. 5. Il but. 6. Tu cours. 7. Il valut. 8. Elles tiennent. 9. Nous enverrons. 10. Il écherra. 11. Qu'il dorme. 12. Que faites-vous là? 13. Il fallut. 14. Haï. 15. Fleurissant, florissant. 16. Elle a lui. 17. Tu mets. 18. Qu'il lût. 19. Nui. 20. Je les suis.

Exercise 25(b)

Write out each of the following tenses in full : 1. Present subjunctive of *aller*. 2. Future of *conclure*. 3. Present subjunctive of *venir*. 4. Present indicative of *mourir*. 5. Imperfect subjunctive of *écrire*. 6. Present indicative of *pouvoir*. 7. Imperfect subjunctive of *aller*. 8. Present subjunctive of *devoir*. 9. Present indicative of *mouvoir*. 10. Present indicative of *devoir*. 11. Present subjunctive of *faire*. 12. Past historic of *vivre*. 13. Future of *voir*. 14. Present indicative of *voir*. 15. Present indicative of *croître*. 16. Present indicative of *croire*. 17. Present indicative of *vouloir*. 18. Present indicative of *connaître*. 19. Present subjunctive of *envoyer*. 20. Present indicative of *haïr*.

Exercise 25(c)

As a special exercise write out in full all the simple tenses of *avoir* and *être* (pronouns as well) using the Table of Irregular Verbs and the rules for forming tenses.

LESSON XXVI

THE SUBJUNCTIVE

Up till now we have said nothing about the Subjunctive Mood, about which so much is written in French grammars. Far too much is made of this mood in proportion to its importance in actual use.

When a statement is made plainly without any conditions we are said to use the *indicative* mood. When we add a condition or state a thing doubtfully or guardedly we are told to use the *subjunctive*. Perhaps the best way to put it is to say that when we state a fact, or what we are convinced is a fact, we use the indicative; in other cases, the subjunctive. Subject to this principle the subjunctive may be said to be used in the following cases :—

1. After verbs expressing any emotion : *Je ne m'étonne plus qu'il craigne de me voir* = I am no longer astonished that he is afraid to see me.

2. After impersonal verbs : *Il faut qu'il parte* = he must set out. *Il est possible qu'il soit innocent* = it is possible that he is innocent.

3. After the negative and interrogative form : *Il ne prétend pas qu'elle soit morte* = he does not maintain that she is dead. *Pensez-vous qu'ils soient coupables ?* = do you think they are guilty?

4. After the relative pronouns, the superlative of adjectives and words equal to the superlative, as *l'unique* = the only; *le seul* = the only; *le premier* = the first and *le dernier* = the last. *C'est le premier que nous ayons*

trouvé = it is the first we have found. *Je cherche un homme qui soit honnête et poli* = I am looking for a man who is honest and polite.

5. After certain conjunctional phrases, such as :—

afin que = in order that.
à moins que = unless.
avant que = before.
bien que = although.
de crainte que }
de peur que } = for fear that ; lest.
de façon que }
de manière que } = in such a way ; so that.
de sorte que }
loin que = far from.

pour que = in order that.
pourvu que = provided that.
quel que = whatever.
qui que = whoever.
quelque . . . que = however ; whatever.
quoique = although.
sans que = without.
jusqu'à ce que = until.

Do not confound the conditional with the subjunctive mood. The former is nearly always formed by adding the terminations *ais, ais, ait, ions, iez, aient* to the present infinitive. The conditional corresponds to what used to appear in our grammars under the name of the potential mood. It is translated *might, could, would* or *should* love.

aimerais   aimerions
  ,,   ais   ,,   iez
  ,,   ait   ,,   aient

This is the *present* conditional; the past conditional is made up of the conditional of *avoir* and the past participle of the verb—*j'aurais aimé, tu aurais aimé,* etc.

In the old-fashioned English grammars *if* was the mark of the subjunctive mood; the queer thing in French is that *si* is NEVER used with the subjunctive—except with auxiliary verbs.

When *if* means that if one thing happens another will necessarily follow, we use *si* with the indicative : *Si vous venez j'irai* = if you come I will go. *S'ils vous frappaient ils seraient punis* = if they should strike you they will be punished.   In both these cases there is no doubt as to the connection between the two parts.   We are not sure about the *coming* in the one case and the *striking* in the other; but we are quite sure that if the *coming* takes place the going will necessarily follow; that if the *striking* takes place the punishment is certain.

When *si* = *whether* it may be translated by either the future or the conditional, according to circumstances.   I don't know whether I shall see him = *je ne sais pas si je le verrai.*   You wished to know whether he could do it = *vous vouliez savoir s'il pourrait le faire.*

The conditional is also used to throw the responsibility of a statement upon someone else : *Selon lui la maison aurait coûté bien cher* = according to him the house cost dear.

There is another use of the subjunctive that must not be lost sight of—the *jussive* use, or the use as command. In all the above cases the subjunctive is used in a subordinate clause, and depends upon something else.   But it can stand along with its *que*.   *Qu'il vienne* = let him come. *Que le garçon le fasse* = let the boy do it.   *Que la chandelle soit maudite* = let the candle be accursed.

Translation XI

Quand je m'éveillai le lendemain matin, il pleuvait à verse.   On se moque volontiers du climat anglais, mais il n'est pas, à mon avis, plus capricieux que celui de la France. J'avais voulu passer la deuxième journée de mon séjour à Paris à visiter la rive gauche.   Il était évident, cependant, que je devrais renoncer à ce projet, car j'aurais été trempé jusqu'aux os, si j'avais eu l'imprudence de faire une longue promenade par un temps pareil, et je n'avais aucune envie de m'enrhumer.   Heureusement je me trouvais au plein centre de Paris.   L'entrée du Louvre n'était qu'à deux cents mètres et je tenais à visiter ce musée célèbre.

L'ancien palais des rois de France, qui sert maintenant de musée, est la construction la plus vaste qu'on puisse s'imaginer. Il ne reste que très peu du donjon primitif et la partie centrale du palais date du seizième siècle, car Catherine de Médicis adopta le Louvre comme résidence royale et fit construire la Petite Galerie, achevée plus tard sous le règne de Henri Quatre. Louis Quatorze ne s'intéressa guère au Louvre. Il s'établit à Versailles à quinze kilomètres de Paris, et le Louvre, qui logeait déjà l'Académie Française, donna asile à une foule de parasites dont les baraques encombrèrent la cour. Accaparé sous la Révolution par des journalistes et des boursiers, le Louvre fut restauré sous le premier Empire et transformé en Palais des Arts.

Pendant le cours des siècles beaucoup de choses d'un grand intérêt se sont passées au Louvre. C'est de là que sortait Coligny quand il fut arquebusé par Maurevert, deux jours avant le massacre de la Saint-Barthélemy, qui eut lieu le 24 août, 1572. C'est dans l'ancienne salle des gardes que Molière joua pour la première fois devant le roi. Il présenta une tragédie de Corneille, qui fut médiocrement goûtée, et une farce de sa façon, dont le monarque, alors âgé de vingt ans, fut ravi.

En face du Louvre se trouve l'Eglise St. Germain l'Auxerrois, fondée au septième siècle, détruite par les Normands et rebâtie. C'est du clocher actuel qu'on fit sonner le tocsin qui donna le signal du massacre, auquel j'ai fait allusion ci-dessus. C'est une des églises les plus intéressantes de Paris.

Exercise 26(a)

1. Supposons qu'il réussisse. 2. Il importe que vous gardiez ce secret. 3. Il s'ensuit de là que vous avez tort. 4. Il veut que je vienne. 5. J'ignorais qu'elle fût folle. 6. L'Angleterre compte que chaque homme fera son devoir. 7. Je ne vois rien là qui puisse vous blesser. 8. Je suis

le seul qui vous connaisse. 9. C'est le plus jeune qui a remporté un prix. 10. C'est le plus jeune qui ait remporté un prix. 11. Je n'en ferai rien à moins que vous [1] ne me payiez d'avance. 12. Vous avez pris ma montre afin de vous en servir vous-même. 13. N'est-il pas juste que nous défendions nos droits? 14. Pensez-vous qu'il vienne? 15. Je doute si vous viendrez à bout de cette affaire. 16. Tout éloquent qu'est cet orateur, il n'est pas écouté parce qu'il n'est pas estimé. 17. Il fallait que les poètes fussent bien rares dans votre siècle. 18. Il est possible qu'elle soit en retard. 19. Il est certain que nous arriverons à temps. 20. Dieu soit loué !

Exercise 26(b)

1. If two and two make four, four and ten make fourteen. 2. He did not know whether she was dead. 3. The first man who enters this room will find the watch. 4. I am to go to his house. 5. This man must go to bed. 6. He began to drink in order to forget his anxiety. 7. He is working although he is tired. 8. Is it evident that he has spoken? 9. It is evident that he has spoken. 10. He has come in order to sell the meat. 11. Let him be punished. 12. She had just hidden the money lest the thief should arrive. 13. Although I am poor I shall work till I am rich. 14. I am looking for a man who knows French. 15. Let her remain here until her friends have arrived. 16. I do not wish that you should speak to him. 17. According to the newspapers many soldiers were killed. 18. Although we got up early we shall be late. 19. Is it possible that she is not dead? 20. It was necessary that the man should depart at once in order not to miss the train.

[1] The conjunctions *à moins que*, *de peur que*, and *de crainte que* in addition to taking a subjunctive require the insertion of a *ne* before the verb in the dependent clause.

LESSON XXVII

POSITION OF THE ADJECTIVE—VERBS LAISSER AND FAIRE

In English and in French alike the adjective may be placed either before or after the noun, but in English most adjectives are placed before the noun, in French most are placed after. As usual, the pleasantness of sound has a good deal to do with whether the adjective comes before or after in French. Little adjectives come naturally before, big adjectives after. If the noun begins with a vowel, a plural adjective comes naturally before, as the *s* of the adjective runs smoothly into the vowel of the noun.

On the other hand, in the following cases the adjectives usually follow :—

1. When more than one adjective is used.

2. When the adjective contains more syllables than the noun.

3. Most present participles, and all past participles, when used as adjectives.

4. Adjectives representing colour, nationality, or physical qualities.

When all this has been said, there remains a long list of adjectives which are sometimes used before and sometimes after a noun, and the trouble is that the meaning in these cases varies with the position. Thus *un homme grand* is a tall man, *un grand homme* a great man ; *un cher ami* is a friend whom I love dearly, *un ami cher* a friend who has cost me dear ; *un pauvre peintre* is one who cannot paint very well, *un peintre pauvre* is a painter who is hard up. The list of such varying meanings is too long and depressing to give. We must try rather to find some general principle on which the difference of meaning depends.

Speaking generally, when there is a difference of meaning the adjective following the noun retains its literal meaning, the adjective preceding takes a metaphorical meaning.

Another principle at work in this matter is illustrated in the following case : A man was writing to a lady regretting his inability to be present at the marriage of her daughter. He was in doubt whether to write *les noces de votre aimable fille* or *fille aimable*. On asking several Frenchmen he found that they all recommended *aimable fille*; and further investigation showed that to have written *fille aimable* would have been an insult to the mother. It would have meant that he would not have cared whether he had been absent from the wedding of any other of her daughters, but he was sorry to miss the wedding of the amiable one. In other words—of course we speak generally here—an adjective indicating a quality inherent in the noun is placed before it, and an adjective that indicates something special to the individual in question is placed after. If we call Huxley *un savant professeur* we compliment him, and at the same time compliment all professors by taking it for granted that they are learned. If we call him *un professeur savant* we still compliment him, but at the expense of all other professors.

It is clear that no one of these rules and principles is absolutely true, but if you keep them all in view while reading French, you will find no difficulty in deciding in each case that arises the proper place of the adjective.

The verb *faire* is one of the most useful and troublesome verbs in the French language. We have already found it in a number of idioms : *Il fait beau temps* (fine), *il fait froid* (cold), *il fait chaud* (hot), *il fait du vent* (wind), but its ordinary use is still more important, especially in connection with the infinitives of other verbs. The verb *laisser* = to allow, let, or permit, follows the same rules as *faire* in this respect.

1. These verbs allow no object word, whether noun or pronoun, to come between them and the infinitive they govern. He lets time slip by = *il laisse passer le temps.* He made the Arabs run = *il fit courir les Arabes.*

2. In these cases the dependent infinitive is intransitive (*i.e.* has no object). When the infinitive has one object and *faire* or *laisser* seems to have an object too, then the apparent object of *faire* or *laisser* is treated as an indirect object. He made the boy sing = *il fit chanter le garçon.* Here there is no difficulty, but when we say : he made the boy sing a song, we have this peculiar construction, *il fit chanter une chanson au garçon.* The ogre let him kill the pig = *l'ogre lui a laissé tuer le cochon.* A coat must be made for him = *il faut lui faire un habit. Faire faire* here equals to *cause to make.* Make the little one go to school = *Faites aller le petit à l'école.*

Translation XII

De retour à l'hôtel je demandai mon courrier et parmi les lettres que le concierge me remit il s'en trouva une qui portait un timbre-poste français. L'adresse était écrite d'une main que je connaissais bien. C'était l'écriture d'un de mes amis qui avait trouvé quelques mois auparavant un emploi dans une grande maison de commerce, dont le siège social était situé Boulevard Haussmann. Dans cette lettre il m'invita à aller le voir le lendemain matin et me pria de lui téléphoner dès que j'aurais lu sa communication.

En entrant dans la cabine téléphonique de l'hôtel c'est avec une certaine hésitation que je décroche le récepteur, car voici la première fois que j'essaye de me servir du téléphone en France.

Je n'entends d'abord qu'une friture formidable, à laquelle succède un silence relatif interrompu par la voix de la téléphoniste qui dit d'un ton funèbre : " J'écoute."

Je jette un coup d'œil sur la lettre que je viens de recevoir pour vérifier le numéro d'appel que je veux demander.

"Donnez-moi, s'il vous plaît," dis-je en m'adressant à la demoiselle invisible, "Taitbout zéro-cinq-trente-deux."

Mais celle-ci reste implacable.

"Veuillez répéter le numéro. Parlez plus près de l'appareil." Sans me laisser déconcerter, je redemande le numéro. Cette fois elle paraît plus contente de moi, mais je ne suis pas encore à bout de mes peines. Le signal "pas libre" résonne et je dois raccrocher.

Au bout de quelques minutes j'essaye de nouveau. Cette fois tout va bien et je demande à être mis en relation avec mon ami. Il vient aussitôt à l'appareil et, en reconnaissant sa voix, je pousse un soupir de soulagement.

"Allô ! C'est toi, Jean ? "

"Oui, c'est moi qui parle. J'ai eu du mal à t'avoir, tu sais. Mais n'importe. Tout est bien qui finit bien. Comment ça va ? "

"Pas trop mal. Alors tu as reçu mon bout de lettre ? "

"Oui, tout à l'heure. Et on se verra demain."

"Bien sûr. Viens ici vers les onze heures. J'ai des tas de choses à te raconter. J'espère bien que nous pourrons déjeuner ensemble. Et je te ferai voir les postes de T.S.F. qu'on fabrique chez nous. Si j'ai bonne mémoire, tu t'intéresses à la téléphonie sans fil."

"Oui, je crois me connaître en tout ce qui concerne la radio-diffusion."

"C'est bien. Mais je suis très occupé en ce moment et——"

"Et je te dérange, hein ? Alors, mon vieux, à demain."

Exercise 27(a)

1. Mon ancien professeur m'a donné quelque chose à faire. 2. Un simple soldat n'est pas toujours un homme simple. 3. Ce n'est qu'un franc scélérat. 4. Le roi Harold était à la fois un grand homme et un homme grand. 5. C'est une histoire véritable. 6. C'est une véritable histoire. 7. Voilà un cruel raconteur. 8. Voilà une noire

action. 9. Néron était un empereur cruel. 10. Il a fait là un faux pas. 11. Elle m'a envoyé un triste cadeau. 12. Nous n'avions qu'une bouteille pleine de vin. 13. Il s'est fait faire un nouveau complet. 14. Le garçon triste a bu ce que vous lui avez laissé. 15. Il m'a parlé de certaines affaires auxquelles il s'intéresse. 16. En plein hiver il se lave toujours avec de l'eau froide. 17. Un grand homme est quelquefois un petit homme mais jamais un homme petit. 18. C'est le résultat d'un pur accident. 19. Voilà un pauvre acteur qui a beaucoup d'argent. 20. Ma chère amie se plaint toujours de la vie chère.

Exercise 27(b)

1. They made him follow the long way. 2. I shall go and see how he is. 3. He sent her a dear book. 4. A damp house is not good enough for me. 5. They will make him cut some bread. 6. This eloquent and honest orator will speak for the French soldiers. 7. I shall let the old woman do what she likes. 8. The learned doctor has written a long, important and dreary book. 9. Where are you making her go? 10. A hat must be made for the boy. 11. I am going to get a house built. 12. I will come as soon as I have finished my work. 13. I will make the boy do what I want. 14. Do you think he is trying to deceive you? 15. The king had the thief killed. 16. You ought to go home. 17. You have made me wait an hour. 18. It is an affair which will interest you, I am sure. 19. You must be at the theatre at 7 o'clock. 20. He let the letter fall.

LESSON XXVIII

CERTAIN VERBS—WHAT

There are certain verbs which, while not irregular, have special rules about their accents. These rules must be attended to if we wish to write French accurately.

1. If there is an *e* mute or an *é* in the last syllable of the *stem* of a verb, that *e* or *é* is changed into *è* before the terminations *e, es, ent*.

Thus from *men-er* = to lead, we have *mène, mènes, mènent* in indicative, and *que je mène, que tu mènes, qu'il mène, qu'ils mènent* in the subjunctive.

So from *répét-er* we have *répète, répètes, répète, répètent,* and the same for the subjunctive.

If the verb has the *e* mute, the future and conditional take the grave accent, as *mènerai,* etc., *mènerais,* etc. But when the verb has the *é,* the acute is retained in these tenses, *répéterai,* etc., *répéterais,* etc.

2. Verbs ending in *cer* require the cedilla below the *c* whenever the *c* is followed by *a* or *o,* to show that the *c* is sounded soft like *s*.

Thus *sucer* has *suçais, suçons,* etc.

3. Most verbs ending in *eler* and *eter* double the *l* or *t* before terminations beginning with *e*.

Thus from *appeler* = to call, we have *j'appelle, tu appelleras, qu'ils appellent.* From *jeter* = to throw, we have *il jette, que tu jettes, il jettera*.

4. Verbs ending in *ger* keep the *e* before any termination beginning with *a* or *o*. Thus *nager* = to swim, gives *nageant, nageai, nageons,* etc. The *e* is kept in to soften the *g*. It is a *very* common error to omit this *e*.

5. Verbs ending in *uyer* or *oyer* change *y* into *i* before a mute syllable. This change is optional with verbs in *ayer*. *J'appuie, J'emploierai. Je paye* (or *je paie*). But : *nous employons : j'appuyais*.

WHAT. This word is so troublesome to translate that it deserves a section to itself. As an exclamation it is rendered *quoi !* After a preposition it is also usually rendered *quoi. What are you thinking of* may be put into French by *à quoi pensez-vous ?* We have already had the expression *de quoi manger,* and the word *why* is really made up of a preposition and *quoi* in *pourquoi*.

As an interrogative *what* is frequently rendered *que :
Que voulez-vous ?* = what would you have? *Qu'avez-vous fait ?* = what have you done? *Que pensez-vous ?* = what do you think?

As a compound relative *what* is rendered by *ce qui* or *ce que*, according as it is subject or object. What is good for the State is good for the king = *ce qui est bon pour l'Etat est bon pour le roi.* He did what he could = *il a fait ce qu'il a pu.*

As an adjective *what* is rendered by *quel.* What cat's averse to fish? = *quel chat n'aime pas le poisson ? Quelle femme !* = what a woman !

It is said that a barber once placed this notice in his window : What do you think I'll shave you for nothing and give you a drink. He carefully avoided punctuating it, and thus left it ambiguous. The simple customer who entered understood it to mean *Qu'en pensez-vous ? Je vous raserai pour rien et je vous donnerai à boire.* The barber's rendering was different. Turned into French it would read : *Quoi ! Pensez-vous que je vous rase pour rien et vous donne à boire ?*

Ambiguities of this kind are much less common in French than in English. The English relative is frequently ambiguous, as in *The duke yet lives that Henry shall depose.* The moment this goes into French, only one of the meanings remains. The two forms are : *Le duc vit encore qui déposera Henri,* and *Le duc vit encore qu'Henri déposera.*

Translation XIII

This passage is written in familiar style, with *tu* and *toi* replacing the formal *vous* and *votre.* It includes also some colloquial phrases.

Il n'y a pas besoin de dire que mon ami me fit, le lendemain matin, l'accueil le plus cordial, et, moi, je fus ravi de revoir mon ancien camarade d'école. En effet pendant quelques moments c'était à qui jaserait le mieux. Mais enfin il me coupa la parole.

" En voilà assez," me dit-il, en souriant. " Il paraît que nous avons, tous les deux, la langue bien pendue. Au déjeuner nous aurons le temps de causer. En attendant je voudrais te faire voir quelques-uns de ces postes, dont je t'ai parlé hier. Ils sont vraiment superbes. Tiens, voici un de nos modèles les plus récents."

Il indiqua de l'index un poste à six lampes, orné de deux larges barres en métal chromé avec pieds assortis.

" Ce poste te captera l'Amérique et tu obtiendras une audition parfaitement claire. J'ai écouté moi-même le signal horaire et le journal parlé diffusés hier par la station de Schenectady."

" Mais ce poste doit être assez cher."

" Au contraire. Ce poste ne peut être égalé par aucun autre d'un prix approchant. Ce modèle ne coûte que deux mille huit cents francs, ou on peut l'avoir à crédit en payant cent cinquante francs par mois. C'est un prix dérisoire, tu sais. Avec ce poste on se moque de parasites et de l'hétérodynage. Le morse qui intervient au dessous de ta station préférée, quand tu essaies d'écouter un programme de choix, ce sifflement continu qui accompagne l'émission de certaines stations—en te servant de ce poste tu n'auras pas à te plaindre de ces inconvénients, qui troublent quelquefois toute une bande.

" De plus, regarde ce contrôle qui rend le réglage du poste si facile. Son index lumineux et son éclairage indirect permettent de lire clairement et avec précision la longueur d'onde ou la station recherchée."

" Voilà qui est trop fort," lui dis-je. " Aie pitié de moi je t'en prie. Tu sais bien que je n'ai chez moi qu'un méchant poste portatif et tu me fais venir l'eau à la bouche en me parlant ainsi.

" D'ailleurs tu perds ton temps. A t'entendre parler on croirait que tu t'efforces de me faire acheter un de ces modèles. Evidemment tu me crois plus riche que je ne le suis. Si tu étais vraiment gentil tu m'en ferais cadeau ! "

" Et, toi, tu veux me faire flanquer à la porte ! Allons déjeuner, imbécile ! "

Exercise 28

1. What ! Do you repeat what he said? 2. He always throws his burdens on me. 3. They lead the horses to the water. 4. I must repeat the story which you have just told me. 5. He was swimming with his friends. 6. What are you thinking about? 7. What do you say (what is it that you do say)? 8. What do you think about it? 9. What man could do it? 10. What has been done must be forgotten. 11. While advancing to the house he was thinking of what he must say. 12. Let her repeat what she has said. 13. He was only 2 years old but he was beginning to talk. 14. I am going to his house in order that I may receive the present he has bought me. 15. Which of these ladies did you see this morning? 16. Of what ladies are you talking? 17. I used to eat some fruit every day. But I have given it up now. 18. I have been employing him for six months : he is a clever workman. 19. If I receive the money I am waiting for I will pay you at once. 20. I don't trust that man. He used to call himself Dupont. Now he calls himself Simon.

LESSON XXIX

THE ADVERB—CERTAIN TERMINATIONS

The rules for the place of the adverb are clearer than for the place of the adjective. Adverbs are placed usually after the verb in simple tenses. *Je le crois bien* = I well believe it. *Vous m'aimez beaucoup* = You love me much.

In compound tenses the adverb comes between the

auxiliary and the past participle : *J'ai souvent marché jusqu'à Londres* = I have often walked as far as London. *Ils ont beaucoup travaillé* = they have worked much.

Sometimes an adverb may begin a sentence : *Enfin je vous ai trouvé* = at last I have found you. *Ici on parle Français* = French is spoken here.

But adverbial phrases, two or three adverbs together and long adverbs generally come after the verb, not between the auxiliary and the verb. *Je l'ai fait sur le champ* = I did it at once. *Vous l'avez fait bien et vite* = you have done it quickly and well. *Vous avez agi sagement* = you have acted prudently. If several adverbs come together, the adverb of time is put last. *Vous avez parlé discrètement et éloquemment aujourd'hui* = you spoke discreetly and eloquently to-day.

The rule which English people most frequently break is : *The adverb must never come between the subject and the verb.* He dearly loves a duke = *il aime bien les ducs.* The English immediately yielded = *les Anglais cédèrent aussitôt.*

As in English we change an adjective into an adverb by adding *ly,* so in French we change an adjective into an adverb by adding *ment.* Clever, cleverly = *habile, habilement.* So long as the adjective ends in a vowel we have only to add *ment : Triste, tristement ; vrai, vraiment.*

If the adjective ends in a consonant the *ment* is added to the feminine : *Froid, froidement ; franc, franchement ; sec, sèchement.*

Above we used *éloquemment.* This comes from *éloquent,* according to the rule that adjectives in *ent* and *ant* drop the *nt* and add instead *mment : Elégant, élégamment ; savant, savamment ; innocent, innocemment ; décent, décemment.*

Gentil makes *gentiment, présent* makes *présentement* and *lent* (= slow) makes *lentement.* The great value of this termination *ment* makes us look for other useful endings.

It is not proposed to give lists of these, for lists are dreary things and do not do much good after all. It is better to give several examples, and thus direct the student to be on the lookout for similar aids in increasing his vocabulary.

Note first the endings which indicate abstract nouns, showing what grammars call " state of " or " quality of " in combin*aison* = state of being combined, autor*ité* = quality of authority. Similarly, grand*eur*, mis*ère*, un*ion*. These terminations, you remember, are all feminine.

Then we have endings indicating the person who does something or is something. Charret*ier* = carter; musi-*cien* = musician; trait*eur* = a wine-house keeper; traît*re* = a traitor; command*ant* = a commander.

The ending *oir* when added to the stem of a verb has two meanings :—

1. The place where the action of the verb is carried on. Compt*oir* (= a counting house) comes from *compter*, to count. Parl*oir*, or talking place (parlour), comes from *parler*. *Fumer*, to smoke, gives *fumoir*, a smoking-room. *Bouder* means to sulk, which is not a pleasant derivation for *boudoir* = a lady's room.

2. The thing with which to do the action of the verb. *Raser*, to shave, gives ras*oir* = a razor; *gratter* means to scrape, gratt*oir* is a scraping knife, or scraper.

The termination *âtre* means *ish*, and is applied to colours. It is added to the adjective of colour. *Jaunâtre* = yellow-ish; *bleuâtre* = bluish; *noirâtre* = blackish; *blanchâtre* = whitish; *grisâtre* = greyish; *verdâtre* = greenish.

You may find several meanings for the same termina-tion. Thus we have seen that *oir* has two meanings; and in addition to those there is the ending of certain verbs. So with *ier*. Certain verbs end thus, and we have seen that this termination also means the *actor* or *doer*. Still further when added to the name of a fruit it indicates the tree on which that fruit grows. *Pomme* = apple, *pommier* = apple tree; *châtaigne* = chestnut, *châtaignier* = chestnut-tree. So with *poire* (pear), *poirier*; *amande* (almond), *amandier*; *cerise* (cherry), *cerisier*.

The terminations *ule, tte, lle* and *ceau* are diminutives: *particule* = a little part; *clochette* = a little bell; *ruelle* = a little street, a lane; *lionceau* = a little lion.

The point of all this is the hint given to pay particular attention to the endings of words, as they frequently give help in placing a word. It is quite a common thing for students who pay no attention to this point to try to construe an apple-tree as an infinitive of the first conjugation.

Translation XIV

Je crois avoir dit déjà quelque chose au sujet du Café de la Régence. Depuis ma première visite j'y suis rentré plusieurs fois et j'ai fini par vouloir avoir là-dessus de plus amples renseignements. Un soir, un monsieur assis près de moi me demanda du feu pour allumer sa cigarette et, après lui avoir tendu mon briquet, je profitai de l'occasion pour aborder le sujet du Café, en lui demandant de me dire quelque chose de son histoire. Il ne se fit pas prier. Pendant plus d'une demi-heure il m'a entretenu des Cafés de Paris, sujet dont il paraissait avoir une connaissance approfondie. C'était, comme on dit, une encyclopédie vivante.

" Savez-vous," me dit-il, " que Jean-Jacques Rousseau fréquentait le Café de la Régence et lorsqu'il y parut la police fut obligée de lui interdire de se montrer dans les lieux publics, parce que sa présence attirait une foule prodigieuse. C'est Grimm qui a noté ce fait dans un des dix-sept volumes de sa ' Correspondance littéraire.' De nos jours un philosophe passe inaperçu. Il faut une étoile de cinéma pour faire attrouper la populace !

" Mais de tous les cafés du dix-huitième siècle," reprit-il, " le plus célèbre était le Procope, dont la clientèle se composait surtout de gens de lettres. Là aussi Rousseau fut acclamé. Voltaire allait quelquefois au Procope. Une

fois il se déguisa en ecclésiastique et se blottit dans un coin
obscur du café afin de connaître l'opinion des habitués
sur une de ses tragédies, qui venait d'avoir sa ' première.'
Les dramaturges d'aujourd'hui supporteraient avec moins
de patience les jugements de critiques trop francs !

"A la veille de la Révolution les discussions littéraires
cédèrent peu à peu la place aux disputes politiques. Le
Procope était infesté d'espions, ce qui devait éloigner
Voltaire. Ayant passé quelques mois en prison dans sa
jeunesse, il n'avait aucune envie de se voir arrêter de
nouveau."

" Et le Café Procope existe toujours, monsieur ? "

Mon compagnon secoua la tête.

" Non. Sous le Second Empire on y avait installé le
gaz, mais les jeunes gens préférèrent des cafés plus neufs,
plus bruyants. Sa vogue tomba. Alors "—il haussa les
épaules—" encore une partie du vieux Paris qui a disparu."

Il vida son verre, me fit un petit signe de tête amical et
sortit.

Exercise 29

1. He does it badly.   2. They were already near their
father's house.   3. You will do it quickly at least.   4. He
immediately asked me to come with him.   5. After
arresting one thief, the policeman set to work immediately
to look for the other.   6. I have sometimes walked as
far as Paris.   7. Having lost much money he began by
selling his house.   8. I think I have already read this book.
9. I think she saw us.   10. I see him from time to time,
but he often goes to London.   11. He was making his way
slowly towards the castle.   12. You always ask me
ridiculous questions.   13. He was wearing a yellowish
hat.   14. Get into the train quickly lest it should start.
15. I should very much like to go there by boat.   16. How
many times have I told you not to walk so fast ?   17. I
shall have to cut (down) the pear-tree to-morrow.   18. I

E

will take advantage of the fine weather to come and see you. 19. If you disguise yourself as a workman no one will recognise (reconnaître) you. 20. He sadly shook his head.

LESSON XXX

EMPHASIS—QUELQUE

To indicate emphasis in French it is necessary to depend upon a change in the order of the words, as it is against the genius of the language to lay stress on words in speaking.

Any word used in any unusual place becomes naturally emphatic. Thus in modern French poetry emphasis is sometimes gained by placing an adjective of colour *before* its noun. Ordinary people may not imitate the poets, but here is a convenient little expression that enables us to single out nearly any word, and point to it as specially important. This finger-post is *c'est*. Its use you will readily see from the following examples. The idea we wish to convey is : My cousin sets out for London on Tuesday evening at 8.40. In plain French this reads : *Mon cousin part pour Londres mardi soir à huit heures quarante*. Now we shall give it with the emphasis indicated by *c'est*.

Emphasis on *Cousin* : *C'est mon cousin qui part pour Londres*, etc.

„ *London* : *C'est pour Londres que mon cousin part*, etc.

„ *Tuesday* : *C'est mardi que mon cousin*, etc.

„ *Evening* : *C'est le soir de mardi que mon cousin*, etc.

„ 8.40 : *C'est à huit heures quarante que mon cousin*, etc.

The possessive pronouns are emphasised in a somewhat

different way by repeating the corresponding disjunctive pronoun with *à*. *My* cousin = *mon cousin à moi*. So, *our* house = *notre maison à nous*. *His* book = *son livre à lui*.

Sometimes emphasis is gained by the simple expedient of repeating a word—*c'était un attentat horrible, horrible* = It was a *horrible* attempt. This plan is practically confined to spoken language.

The finger-post *c'est* is frequently inverted to make questions a little more vivacious. *Etes-vous malade ?* = are you ill? This is the regular form; but it is often (particularly in common speech) lengthened into *est-ce que vous êtes malade ?* = is it that you are ill? As we have seen, this interrogative finger-post can be put before almost any question, but it should be reserved for quick, vivacious questions.

Quelque (pl. *quelques*) is an adjective and means *some*. *Some apples* may be expressed in two ways—*des pommes* and *quelques pommes*. The difference is that the former is more general, the latter conveying rather the idea of the individual apples. When we say : *There are some men in the street*, and mean merely *there are men in the street*, we say *il y a des hommes dans la rue*. But if our meaning is rather *there is a man or two in the street*, we say *il y a quelques hommes, etc.* In other words, when we use *quelques* we have in our minds the notion of the objects referred to as units. If there is a large number of units, we use instead of *quelques* the adjective *plusieurs*.

Quelque may be used in the singular : Some enemy has done it = *quelque ennemi l'a fait*.

Quelque may be used along with *que* and a verb to mean whatever : Whatever secrets he has he tells to his wife = *quelques secrets qu'il ait il les dit à sa femme*.

When the noun qualified by *quelque* is subject to the verb *être*, the *quel* or *quelle* is used separately from the *que*. Whatever your hopes may be he will never return =

quelles que soient vos espérances, il ne reviendra jamais.
Whatever the years may be he complains = *quelles que soient les années il se plaint.*

With an adjective or an adverb *quelque* is invariable and is equivalent to the English *however*. However clever you are you cannot escape = *quelque habile que vous soyez vous ne pouvez échapper.* However eloquently you spoke you did not deceive them = *quelque éloquemment que vous ayez parlé vous ne les avez pas trompés.* Good as you are he is better = *quelque bon que vous soyez, il est meilleur.*

Translation XV

En descendant au salon le lendemain matin je me suis arrêté un moment au bureau de réception de l'hôtel. " Je suis à court d'argent français," dis-je à l'employé, " voulez-vous me changer cinq livres sterling en argent français ? "

" Mais certainement, monsieur. Aujourd'hui le cours du change est de cent quarante-six francs. Je prélève une commission d'un franc, ce qui fait cent quarante-cinq. Voici donc un billet de cinq cents francs, deux de cent francs, une pièce de vingt francs, et une de cinq."

" Merci. Mais ne pourriez-vous pas me donner de petite monnaie ? J'en serais très reconnaissant, car j'ai quelques toutes petites emplettes à faire."

" Très bien. Je vous reprends la pièce de vingt francs et voici dix pièces de deux francs. Cela vous convient ? "

" Parfaitement. Et je veux aussi des timbres-poste. Veuillez me donner deux timbres d'un franc cinquante."

" Malheureusement, il ne m'en reste absolument plus, monsieur. Mais je puis vous donner six timbres de cinquante centimes. Cela fera également bien votre affaire, n'est-ce pas ? "

" Merci bien."

" C'est tout, monsieur ? "

" Oui. Ah, j'y pense. Il me faut des cigarettes. Voulez-vous avoir la bonté de me dire s'il y a un bureau de tabac près d'ici ? "

" Bien sûr, monsieur. Il y en a un à deux minutes de l'hôtel. Vous n'avez qu'à tourner à gauche en sortant et vous le verrez en face."

" Bon jour, monsieur, qu'y-a-t-il pour votre service ? " me dit poliment le marchand de tabac, dès que j'eus franchi le seuil de son débit.

" Est-ce que vous vendez des cigarettes anglaises ? "

" Mais, oui, monsieur. Nous avons toutes les meilleures marques."

" Bon. Alors donnez-moi un paquet de vingt Gold Flake. Qu'est-ce que ça coûte, ça ? "

" Huit francs, soixante-quinze, monsieur."

" Mon Dieu ! ça revient cher. Je vois bien que je devrai m'habituer à fumer les cigarettes françaises."

" Vous y prendrez facilement goût, monsieur. On fait maintenant de très bonnes cigarettes en France. Voici des Gitanes, c'est une marque très recommandable et qui se vend trois francs cinquante le paquet."

" Bien, j'en prendrai deux."

" Merci, monsieur. Et en fait de tabac——"

" Non, je vous remercie. Je ne fume pas la pipe."

J'ai passé ensuite chez le chemisier pour acheter des faux-cols doubles et mous.

" Quelle est votre encolure, monsieur ? " me demande l'employé.

Voilà une question bien difficile et je ne savais pas comment me tirer d'affaire.

" Je ne sais pas la mesure française," lui dis-je enfin, " mais en Angleterre je porte des faux-cols de quinze pouces."

" Pour trouver la mesure française il faut diviser par deux et multiplier par cinq. Voyons un peu "—il fait un calcul rapide—" Oui, cela nous donne trente-huit centimètres."

" Bon.   Je veux des faux-cols blancs en percale."

" Bien, monsieur, j'ai justement votre affaire.   Combien vous en faut-il ? "

" J'en prendrai trois.   Cela me suffira, vu que je dois rentrer à Londres samedi."

" Et vous ne voulez rien d'autre, monsieur? "

" Merci.   J'ai tout ce qu'il me faut."

So far as general composition goes, a letter is pretty much like any other piece of writing : it is a little more familiar in style and personal in matter than an essay, but that is all.   It is the beginning and ending that demand attention.   The date and address are put in the right-hand top corner; notice that the *le* has no capital.

27 Rue Richelieu,
Paris : *le 11 novembre*, 1937.

To begin an English letter with *sir* is very stiff, *dear sir* is more friendly, *my dear sir* still more friendly.   In French *monsieur* is not regarded as stiff at all, *cher monsieur* is very friendly, while *mon cher monsieur* is not used at all.

The endings of French letters are much more complicated than ours.   We say *yours very truly* or *yours faithfully* and have done.   The following are some of the roundabout ways the French have of ending their letters :—

Agréez,[1] madame, mes compliments empressés, et l'assurance de mes sentiments distingués.

Agréez, monsieur, l'assurance de ma considération distinguée.

Acceptez, monsieur, mes salutations respectueuses.

Recevez, monsieur, mes salutations empressées.

[1] *Agréer* = to receive or accept.

Exercise 30(a)

Turn the following short letter into French :—

27 PATERNOSTER ROW,
LONDON : 14*th March*, 1937.

Messrs. JARGEAU & CO.,

Dear Sirs,

I hope you have received the book I sent you on Saturday. I have some boxes at home which I can give you in order that you may send back the others. Whatever doubts you may have, I assure you that the money will be paid when you ask it. My *father* has promised, and however angry he may be he will not fail to pay.

I am,

Yours faithfully,

JOHN SMITH.

Exercise 30(b)

1. However clever he may be he will not succeed unless he works well. 2. As soon as the soldiers had entered the castle they killed the king. 3. He came to see us, but we had gone out. 4. Whatever letters he receives he shows them to his brother. 5. When he had sold his car, he bought another. 6. He has lost all his money, hasn't he? Yes. He has gone bankrupt. 7. I saw him some time ago. 8. Will you cut me some bread, please? 9. Be so kind as to open the window. It's very hot. 10. What have you in the way of fruit this morning?

LESSON XXXI

ORDER OF PRONOUNS—THE IMPERATIVE

When a verb has two pronouns as objects, one direct and the other indirect, they must occur in the order of their person—1st person before 2nd—2nd before 3rd. *Il me l'envoie* = he sends it to me. *Ils vous la mèneront* =

they will lead her to you, though this would usually be rendered *ils la mèneront à vous.*

If *both* object pronouns are third person, the direct comes before the indirect : *Je le lui donne* = I give it to him (to her). *Vous le leur donnerez* = you will give it to them.

If *y* occurs along with object pronouns, it comes *after* them. I shall give it to you there = *je vous l'y donnerai*. But if *en* also occurs, it must come last of all. Talking of food and a man in prison we might say : We shall send him some there = *nous lui en enverrons là-bas.*

The imperative must now be more fully treated. There are two real imperative forms. The first comes from the present indicative[1] by omitting the *je*, and the second from the present indicative omitting the *vous*. Thus we have *parle* = speak (thou), and *parlez* = speak (you). In the same way by omitting the *nous* of the present indicative we get *parlons* = *let us speak*. To get the remaining forms *let him speak* and *let them speak* we must fall back upon the third pers. of the pres. subj., *qu'il parle* and *qu'ils parlent.*

1st Conj.	2nd Conj.
marche	agis
qu'il marche	qu'il agisse
marchons	agissons
marchez	agissez
qu'ils marchent	qu'ils agissent

3rd Conj.	4th Conj.
reçois	perds
qu'il reçoive	qu'il perde
recevons	perdons
recevez	perdez
qu'ils reçoivent	qu'ils perdent

[1] Note (see footnote to p. 109) that the imperatives of *avoir* and *être* are identical in form with their present subjunctives : *aie, ayons, ayez : sois, soyons, soyez.*

When a pronoun is in the objective after an imperative, it comes *after* as in English. *Tuez-le* = kill him (note the hyphen); *attrapez-les* = catch them. If the first or second person is used, the disjunctive form takes the place of the conjunctive. Help me = *aidez-moi*. Amuse thyself = *amuse-toi*. Here also the direct object comes first. Give it to me = *donnez-le-moi*. Take her to him = *menez-la-lui*.

If *en* is used, then the personal pronoun comes first in the *conjunctive* form, and *me* and *te* are contracted into *m'* and *t'*. Send me some of it = *envoyez-m'en*, *va-t'en* = get away; *allez-vous-en* = go away. (The last two are forms of an important verb, *s'en aller* = to go away.)

Note specially that all this about the imperative and its object pronouns applies only to the imperative *affirmative*. The imperative *negative* follows all the usual rules. Do not say it to him = *ne le lui dites pas*. Do not give it to me = *ne me le donnez pas*. Do not send me some = *ne m'en envoyez pas*. Do not go away = *ne vous en allez pas*. Do not kill him = *ne le tuez pas*.

Translation XVI

Paris est si plein d'intérêt que c'était à peine si je me décidai à m'absenter de la ville pendant quelques heures pour en visiter les environs. Mais avant mon départ de Londres mon ancien professeur de français m'avait prié de ne pas manquer de faire une excursion à Versailles. J'avais promis de faire ce qu'il me demandait et je ne voulus pas lui manquer de parole. D'ailleurs, après avoir fait la visite de ce palais somptueux, j'ai compris pourquoi il tenait à ce que j'y allasse. Car Versailles est une des merveilles du monde.

Au commencement du dix-septième siècle Versailles n'était qu'un petit village. En 1624 Louis XIII, grand amateur de la chasse, se fit bâtir sur le sommet de la butte, qui dominait le village, un château modeste en pierre et brique. Son successeur, qui se sentait mal à l'aise au Louvre, songea à transférer à Versailles le siège de la cour et du gouvernement. Il chargea les meilleurs architectes du royaume de remanier et d'embellir la construction ancienne, et les dépenses totales des travaux s'élevèrent à plus de soixante millions de livres, soit environ vingt millions de livres sterling. Sous Louis XIV, dont le règne dura soixante-douze ans, le château de Versailles fut à l'apogée de sa gloire. Mais les beaux jours passent.

En 1789 la foule envahit le château, massacre les gardes et ramène à Paris le roi Louis XVI, la reine Marie Antoinette et leurs enfants. Cet événement marque la fin de l'ancien régime.

Pendant la guerre de 1870 les Allemands firent de Versailles le centre de leurs opérations contre Paris et c'est dans la Galerie des Glaces que le roi Guillaume était proclamé empereur d'Allemagne. Dans cette même galerie était signé, quarante-huit ans plus tard, le traité de Versailles qui restituait à la France les provinces perdues en 1871.

J'essaye de me mettre au courant de l'histoire du château en consultant mon guide, avant de prendre le tramway qui fait le trajet entre Paris et Versailles. Mais le château est trop vaste pour qu'on se fasse dans une seule visite une bonne idée de sa splendeur. Il me tarde de m'y rendre de nouveau. Malheureusement ce n'est pas possible, car mon séjour à Paris touche à sa fin.

Exercise 31(a)

The student will probably find this letter difficult. But it will be good practice.

Hôtel de l'Univers,
    Place du Palais Royal,
        Paris, *Sep. 15th*, 1937.

My Dear Edward,

Before crossing the Channel I had promised to inform you of all which happened to me during my stay in

Paris. I know only too well that I have broken my word, for I shall be back in London on Saturday and this is the first letter I address to you. However, I beg you not to cherish a grievance against me (me tenir rigueur de) for my negligence. I have been so busy since the moment of my arrival that I have hardly had time to write to my father and mother.

Very regretfully I went this morning to Cook's to reserve my seat in the train which leaves the Gare du Nord daily at noon. I hope I shall have a fine crossing, for I am not a good sailor. I will give you a ring on Saturday evening about 8.0. You can count on it, for I am longing to see you again. By the way, I had lunch the day before yesterday with Peter. He asked me to give you his regards. Well, this is enough from

Your affectionate friend,
JOHN.

In private correspondence the beginnings and endings of letters may be as varied as in English. Mon ami; mon cher ami; mon cher Tompkins; mon cher Edouard; chère tante; très chère cousine; mon bien cher papa; ma bonne petite Marie; ma sœur bien aimée, and so on.

The endings are equally varied : à vous de cœur; tout à vous; bien à vous; je vous serre cordialement la main; bien cordialement à vous; votre bien dévoué; votre (or ta) cousine affectionnée.

Exercise 31(b)

1. Do not lend him those books. He will never give them back to you. 2. I do not like that book. I hope you will speak of it no more. 3. Go away, if you don't want to be killed. 4. Don't give it to him, give it to me. 5. You say he didn't go to the station, but I saw him there myself. 6. He has plenty of money, but he never gives me any. 7. This affair is boring, let us not think about it any more.

8. If I had known that you had lost your watch I would never have asked you for it.   9. This boy has been looking for my father for an hour. Take him to him.   10. If you haven't a watch I will buy you one.

LESSON XXXII

SOME HINTS TO HELP IN THE TRANSLATION OF DIFFICULT PASSAGES

1. Make up your mind that the passage contains *some* meaning, that the words must make sense. This seems an elementary truth, but the reading of many examination papers convinces one that it is not always accepted. Perhaps it does not seem very helpful either, but it is something to know that it is not enough to put down all the English words for French in a given passage. A " sort of meaning " is not enough.

2. As soon as you find a passage making nonsense, see that you are not taking a *qui* for a *que* or *vice-versâ*. This is perhaps the most common source of nonsense in translation.

3. Next take a general look at the agreement in number and person and gender of the various words. Frequently confusion is detected by disagreement among the words in this way.

4. It is assumed that before you have treated the passage as nonsense, you have looked up every new word in it. If now it still refuses to make sense, you must look up all the words you *think* you know. Sometimes you find a word has a special meaning that you have not yet come across. If even this fails, you must look up and examine even the commonest words, such as the everyday conjunctions and auxiliary verbs.

To illustrate, take the following four lines from Béranger :—

> Vous qu'afflige la détresse,
> Croyez que plus d'un héros,
> Dans le soulier qui le blesse,
> Peut regretter ses sabots.

Experience shows that this passage generally produces nonsense. Students look up all the words they do not happen to know, and set down something like : " You who afflict distress believe that more of a hero in the shoe which hurts him is able to regret his wooden shoes." This is unpromising, so we examine the *qui's* and *que's*. We at once find that we have been making the second word into *qui*, forgetting that the *i* of *qui* is never cut away. " You whom distress afflicts " is better, but the rest gives only a " sort of meaning." We next examine the concords among the words, and find nothing amiss. Then we look at the less common words, and then at the commoner. It seems hopeless to look at *vous* and *la* and *plus* and *un* and *dans*. Yet the key of the problem lies in the word *un*, which means *one* as well as *a*. Now the whole thing makes sense. " You who are oppressed by poverty believe that more than one hero," etc.

" Les poutres étaient la maison " once gave a sleepless night to a teacher of French who found the words in the middle of an extract his class was reading. At first he thought it was a misprint, but when he compared the extract with the original, he found the words were accurate enough. He knew every one of the words, and the grammar was all right, but there was no sense in " the beams were the house." It was only when he had given up grammar and fallen back on common sense, and had asked himself what beams had to do with houses, that he thought of making *étaient* a transitive verb. It is, as a matter of fact, not the imperfect of *être*, but the present of *étayer*, which means to *shore up* or *support*.

In translating French verse these are the two main

difficulties :—1. The use of peculiar words and words used in a peculiar sense. 2. The peculiar construction common to poetry in all languages. These difficulties must be met by a corresponding care in looking up and arranging words. But there is one special form of inversion that is so common in French poetry as to demand a note to itself. In prose *the hope of my life* runs *l'espoir de ma vie*; in verse it would almost certainly run *de ma vie l'espoir*.

Il fallait employer cette pénible voie
Pour briser des rameaux et pour y recueillir
Le feu que des cailloux mes mains faisaient jaillir,
Des glaçons dont l'hiver blanchissait ce rivage
J'exprimais avec peine un douleureux breuvage.
Enfin, cette caverne et mon arc destructeur
Et le feu, de la vie heureux conservateur,
Ont soulagé du moins les besoins que j'endure,
Mais rien n'a pu guérir ma funeste blessure.

Here you have the inversion of *de* three times in nine lines : at line 3, 4, and 7. The whole passage is translated in Part II.

Translation XVII

Le jour fixé pour mon départ arriva. Ayant pris le petit déjeuner, j'allai faire un dernier petit tour par les rues du quartier. En longeant la Rue de Rivoli je regardai d'un œil inquiet les arbres aux jardins des Tuileries. Pas une branche ne remuait et je poussai un soupir de soulagement. La mer serait calme. J'allai jusqu'à la Place de la Concorde, mais le temps passait vite et je dus bientôt revenir sur mes pas. Je réglai la note et le concierge fit descendre mes bagages, pendant que le chasseur allait chercher un taxi.

Vingt minutes plus tard je descendis à la Gare du Nord.

Le train partit à midi juste et à cinq heures moins dix je débarquai à Douvres.

J'ai bien soif. Il y a encore quelques minutes avant le départ du rapide, aussi vais-je au buffet de la gare.

" Quoi ! De la bière ? A cette heure ? " me dit l'employée d'un ton plein de reproche.

" Ah ! Pardon," lui dis-je. " Je pensais être encore à l'étranger. Mais je vois bien maintenant que je suis dans mon pays natal ! "

Moralité

On ne s'afflige point d'avoir beaucoup d'enfants,
    Quand ils sont tous beaux, bien faits et bien grands.
       Et d'un extérieur qui brille ;
    Mais si l'un d'eux est faible, on ne dit mot,
    On le méprise, on le raille, on le pille :
Quelquefois, cependant, c'est ce petit marmot
Qui fera le bonheur de toute la famille.

CONCLUSION

The student is now in a position to advance on his own account. The first thing to do is to read a great deal of French so as to fix thoroughly by practice all that he has already learnt. This involves the purchase of a dictionary and one or two French books. In the " Teach Yourself Series " there is also a very handy English–French and French–English dictionary in one volume. Cassell & Co. issue a larger dictionary which will supply him with all the information he is ever likely to require, even if he goes on to a very thorough mastery of the language.

As to the books to read, there are many cheap, well-printed little books published under the name of the *Classiques Illustrés* or *Classiques Garnier*. These may be purchased from Libraire Française Hachette, of 127 Regent Street,

London W.1. There are, doubtless, other collections. The following dozen volumes contain some of the most notable performances of the great prose stylists, and may be recommended to students with a literary turn of mind who desire to make rapid progress in reading French. Two plays of Racine: if you prefer comedy let it be *Les Plaideurs*, if tragedy then *Iphigénie*, but best try them both. Extracts from Voltaire's *Histoire de Charles XII* or *Lettres choisies* can be profitably studied together with *Pages choisies* from Rousseau. They should be followed by Flaubert's *Contes* and George Sand's *La Mare au Diable*. The great historian Michelet is represented by *Pages choisies* and *Jeanne d'Arc*. Molière and Beaumarchais each demand your attention. *Le Barbier de Séville* and *Le Malade imaginaire*, are capital plays to start with. The final volume is *Pages choisies* of Chateaubriand.

These volumes, supplemented by such others as your taste may suggest, will afford you an insight into French literature in its most typical developments. Famous French novels may be had from Librairie Hachette or other foreign booksellers at a somewhat higher price, but within the means of most students. Any of Dumas' works will prove interesting: *Les Trois Mousquetaires* is a general favourite, and *La Tulipe Noire* is equally popular. The first three volumes of *Monte Cristo* are absorbing in their interest. Anything by Edmond About is well worth reading. Lastly, the works of Anatole France deserve mention. He was a great stylist and master of irony. Second-hand French novels may be bought in large variety from several booksellers in Charing Cross Road. Also, buy a French newspaper occasionally. *France-Soir*, *Le Figaro*, or *Le Monde* are available in London and most large towns. You might try translating paragraphs from English newspapers into French, and compare your style with that of foreign periodicals.

The great thing is to read much, and to read for the sake

of the matter, not merely for the words. The words and the constructions and all the rest come, if only there is enough reading. Before you are aware of it, you will find yourself thinking in French.

If, however, the student has special reasons for attending to grammatical constructions, let him buy from a French bookshop a French translation of some standard English work (say the first vol. of *Le Ministre de Wakefield* or the first vol. of *Robinson Crusoe*), translate from the English copy into French, paragraph by paragraph, and then compare his French with that in the French version. To work through a whole volume is a big undertaking, but the result will be a very accurate knowledge of French construction.

By the time the student has reached this stage, he is in a position to discover for himself the best way of further extending his requirements in view of his special circumstances, and in his further work we wish him Godspeed.

PART II

PART II

KEY TO EXERCISES AND TRANSLATIONS

Exercise I

(*a*) 1. Nous. 2. tu. 3. ils (elles). 4. vous. 5. ils (elles). 6. nous. 7. tu. 8. tu. 9. vous. 10. vous.

(*b*) 1. aimes. 2. étaient. 3. courons. 4. marchez. 5. marches. 6. tenons. 7. parles. 8. craignaient. 9. aimions. 10. tranchiez.

(*c*) 1. vous portez. 2. vous porterez. 3. je porterai. 4. Je porte. 5. ils (elles) portent. 6. nous porterons. 7. tu portes. 8. vous porterez. 9. il porte. 10. il portera.

(*d*) 1. je porte. 2. nous porterons. 3. vous porterez. 4. nous portons. 5. il (elle) porte. 6. tu portes. 7. ils (elles) portent. 8. tu porteras. 9. je porterai. 10. ils (elles) porteront.

Exercise 2

1. Sa maison. 2. La Cathédrale. 3. Ma terre. 4. Sa clémence.[1] 5. Ta beauté. 6. Sa femme. 7. La charrette. 8. Ma mélancolie. 9. Ton terrain. 10. La misère. 11. Ton courage. 12. Sa pitié. 13. Sa rumeur. 14. Ta capote. 15. La boue. 16. Son médecin. 17. Sa marche. 18. Ta preuve. 19. La fève. 20. La molécule.

Exercise 3(a)

1. The streets are wide. 2. The big town is interesting. 3. The house is small. 4. We are young. 5. The little houses are interesting. 6. I am sure that the tourists will visit the castle. 7. We are sure that our friends will visit

[1] All French nouns ending in " ence " are feminine except *le* silence.

the town. 8. Our friend is in the little house. 9. Their friends are young. 10. The young tourist gets into his car. 11. The little boy will carry the table. 12. Our young friends will get into our car. 13. She is sure that her brother will visit the house. 14. The houses in our town are interesting. 15. His (Her) Majesty will visit the castle. 16. They are sure that my friend and his cousin are small. 17. The streets in our town are wide. 18. The tourists will get into their big car.

Exercise 3(b)

1. La sentinelle est grande. 2. Sa maison est intéressante. 3. Ils sont petits. 4. Mon frère visite la maison. 5. Les petits garçons portent leur table. 6. Je suis sûr que son frère visitera la ville. 7. Les touristes montent dans leur voiture. 8. Elle est sûre que je visiterai le château. 9. Ses jeunes amis monteront dans sa grande voiture. 10. Ils sont sûrs que nous visiterons la grande maison. 11. Les rues dans notre ville sont larges. 12. Sa Majesté visitera la petite ville. 13. Notre voiture est petite. 14. Les petits garçons sont dans la grande maison. 15. Nous sommes sûrs que la ville est intéressante. 16. Les touristes sont dans leur petite voiture. 17. Ils porteront leur frère dans la maison. 18. Les touristes visiteront le grand château.

Exercise 4(a)

1. The Emperor's soldiers arrive at the castle. 2. The men of the emperor's army are young but big. 3. The workman works in the big street. 4. The soldiers will march towards the town. 5. The emperor will speak to the soldiers. 6. We listen to the lark : it sings in the woods. 7. The workmen are in the little house. 8. Honour and money are (belong) to the clever workmen. 9. The five children of the workmen walk towards the castle of the great emperor. 10. We shall eat the fruit. 11. You have

the money, but you speak and we work. 12. I am sure that the emperor will arrive at the castle. 13. The emperor's soldiers sing and we listen to their voices. 14. The tourists speak to the workman's little child. 15. Twenty soldiers march towards the great emperor's castle. 16. We are sure that the larks sing in the woods. 17. Five tourists arrive at the castle in their big car. 18. The children walk towards the castle of His Majesty and speak to the sentries.

Exercise 4(b)

1. Nous écoutons[1] les alouettes : elles chantent aux bois (better, really, than *dans les bois*). 2. J'ai l'argent des ouvriers : ils sont au château. 3. Les fruits de l'année sont bons. 4. Le porteur de l'argent parlera aux ouvriers. 5. Je parlerai de la sentinelle à l'empereur. 6. Les hommes écoutent les écureuils aux bois. 7. Les petits enfants de l'empereur visiteront le château. 8. Le touriste mangera dans ma maison, mais les ouvriers mangeront dans la rue. 9. Les soldats de l'empereur marcheront vers le château. 10. Les enfants de l'empereur parlent à la sentinelle. 11. Ils ont une jeune alouette et un écureuil. 12. Les jeunes enfants des ouvriers sont à la maison. 13. Je suis sûr que vous avez l'argent de l'ouvrier. 14. Le frère de sa Majesté arrivera avec les soldats. 15. Elle est jeune mais grande. 16. Nous porterons l'argent à l'empereur. 17. J'écoute la voix du jeune homme dans la rue. 18. Elle est à la maison de son ami. 19. Les larges rues de la ville sont intéressantes aux touristes.

Exercise 5(a)

1. The general's child crossed the river. 2. Her husband was very poor. 3. My friend's husband carried the money

---

[1] In English we say *listen to* : but in French *écouter* means the whole thing—*listen-to*. One French word equals the two English words.

to her cousin. 4. The soldiers who arrived at the big town were very young. 5. If he crosses the street he will arrive at the emperor's castle. 6. The tourists who visit the town are very numerous. 7. The wood which the soldiers were cutting is good. 8. His affairs are very bad. 9. The fruit(s) which the little boys like is (are) there. 10. If you speak to my lark she (it) will sing. 11. The poor animals carried the burdens. 12. The castles which the tourists visit are very interesting. 13. If you arrive here to visit the emperor's castle you will speak to the sentry. 14. The boys who loved the fruit were in the wood. 15. The burdens which he carries to the castle are great. 16. The boats which crossed the river are here. 17. If she gets into my car she will arrive at the house. 18. The general's horses were crossing the streets of the town. 19. I will speak to the sentries if they are there. 20. The child she was carrying was the workman's small boy.

Exercise 5(b)

1. Les affaires de son mari étaient mauvaises. 2. Le chapeau du touriste était dans les eaux du fleuve. 3. Les touristes qui visitaient le château étaient très nombreux. 4. Les chevaux des soldats portaient leur fardeau à la ville. 5. Les enfants qu'elle aimait étaient ici. 6. Si elle traverse la rue elle arrivera à la maison d'un ouvrier. 7. Les garçons qui coupaient le bois sont les enfants du jeune soldat. 8. S'il arrive, il traversera le fleuve pour visiter le château. 9. Je mangerai le fruit s'il est ici. 10. L'homme qui était là coupait le bois. 11. L'ouvrier qui coupait le bois est le cousin de Jean. 12. Nos bateaux traversaient le fleuve. 13. Les soldats qui avaient les chevaux marchaient vers le fleuve. 14. Si vous chantez il écoutera. 15. La maison était son affaire. 16. Sa Majesté la Reine visitera la ville. 17. Si vous parlez de l'affaire à Jean, il écoutera. 18. Si nous montons dans leur voiture nous arriverons à la ville. 19. Ils traversaient

le fleuve pour parler aux petits garçons au bois. 20. Les ouvriers qui étaient ici sont très habiles.

Exercise 6(a)

1. The tourist gives the money to the skilful workman. 2. The boys who have been punished are the children of the merchant. 3. The men who (have) killed your horse are in the wood with my friend. 4. The book which you (have) sold to the merchant was very interesting. 5. We are sure that the soldiers have been punished. 6. If the general gives up the town his soldiers will cross the river with their horses. 7. We have been at the castle with the workmen who cut the wood. 8. I am sure that her husband has been killed by the soldiers. 9. The woman who sang is in the house. 10. The small boys who lost their books have been punished. 11. I listened to the girls who sang. 12. The tourists sold their car to the merchant. 13. I have finished the book which you have given to my cousin. 14. The tables have been polished. 15. The horses which crossed the line were killed by a train. 16. The train killed two men. 17. The book which he lost is here. 18. If we cross the line we shall arrive at the castle. 19. The general will visit the castle which the queen has given up. 20. I noticed a tall young man who was speaking to your husband.

Exercise 6(b)

1. Sa fille est perdue. 2. Ses livres ont été donnés aux pauvres. 3. La grande maison du marchand a été vendue. 4. Nous avons remarqué la sentinelle qui parlait aux ouvriers. 5. Je suis sûr que les chevaux sont perdus. 6. Nous avons perdu l'argent qu'il a donné à la femme. 7. Si vous marchez vers la ville vous traverserez la voie. 8. Le touriste qui montait dans le train a perdu son chapeau. 9. Les enfants qui ont été tués étaient les petites filles du

marchand. 10. J'ai remarqué le garçon qui a coupé le bois. 11. Ils ont rendu la ville aux soldats de l'empereur. 12. Sa mère a marché vers la maison avec son mari. 13. Il a perdu l'argent, mais ses frères ont été punis. 14. La table a été polie par les ouvriers. 15. Le train a tué les chevaux qui traversaient la voie. 16. Ils ont vendu leurs bateaux au jeune frère du soldat. 17. La pauvre femme qui était au bois avec ses enfants a été tuée. 18. Nous sommes sûrs que les livres sont perdus. 19. Nous avons remarqué la fille qui chantait dans la rue. 20. Le cheval que j'ai remarqué a été vendu.

Exercise 7(a)

1. He filled his pocket with money. 2. She gently shut the door of her room. 3. She was finishing her work. 4. The evenings are very sad in his house. 5. We heard the general speak. 6. I noticed a small boy who was filling his pockets with fruit. 7. The street is filled with horses. 8. The tourists were walking quickly towards the town in order to visit the castle which I noticed. 9. They broke the windows of the workman's house. 10. He had the money in his pocket. 11. We quickly finished our work. 12. We gave the money to the young man who was visiting my cousin. 13. We hear the voice of the merchant who sells books. 14. We were listening to the larks in the wood. 15. They filled the room with men. 16. If you go up into my room you will notice a book on the table. 17. If you have finished your work I will give your books to the merchant's son. 18. We noticed the tourist (who was) getting into the train. 19. The window which he was shutting was broken by a small boy. 20. His pockets are filled with (full of) fruit.

Exercise 7(b)

1. Elle finit son travail. 2. Nous avons fini notre travail. 3. Il remplissait ses poches. 4. Ils ont cassé les

fenêtres de la maison du marchand. 5. Les soirées avec mon père étaient tristes. 6. Il a entendu parler le garçon. 7. Nous avons entendu chanter un homme dans votre chambre. 8. Nous traversions la voie pour arriver vite à la ville. 9. Ils remplissaient leurs poches d'argent. 10. Cinq chambres dans la maison sont pour les garçons. 11. J'ai entendu l'homme qui fermait doucement la porte de sa chambre. 12. Nous avons perdu le livre que vous avez donné à mon cousin. 13. Vous remarquerez que la fenêtre de ma chambre est cassée. 14. Le touriste vend sa voiture au fils du marchand. 15. Les rues sont remplies de soldats : ils marchent vers le château. 16. Si vous écoutez, vous entendrez le train qui traverse le fleuve. 17. Nous donnerons l'argent au garçon que vous avez remarqué dans la rue. 18. Nous avons parlé à la sentinelle à la porte du château. 19. Les garçons qui ont cassé la fenêtre ont été punis. 20. Il avait dans sa poche l'argent que vous avez perdu.

Exercise 8(a)

1. Life is not sad. 2. You do not speak gently. 3. The boys will not cut the wood to-morrow. 4. The general has not given up the town. 5. The horses have not been killed. 6. The animals were not led here. 7. I have killed the rabbit but I have not killed the lark. 8. We were not looking at your books, we were looking for my hat which I have left in your room. 9. If you do not listen you will not hear his words. 10. I did not like the life which he was leading. 11. I am sure (that) she is not here. 12. I will not look for the money which you have lost. 13. If you do not get into the train quickly we shall not arrive. 14. His watch is not of a very good make. 15. I haven't noticed the animals (which) you are looking for. 16. They spoke quickly and I did not hear a word. 17. I am sure we owe the merchant much. 18. We shall not receive the money which he owes. 19. The soldiers

did not lead their horses to the water. 20. The workmen have not cut the wood : they are working in the fields.

Exercise 8(b)

1. Le train n'arrivera pas. 2. Vos livres ne sont pas ici. 3. Je ne suis pas sûr si elle visitera le château. 4. Il n'écoutera pas un mot. 5. Les fenêtres n'ont pas été cassées. 6. Vous n'entendrez pas sa voix, si vous n'écoutez pas. 7. Les touristes n'arriveront pas demain. 8. Les animaux n'ont pas été menés à l'eau. 9. Je ne cherchais pas mon argent, je cherchais sa montre. 10. Si elle ne monte pas vite dans le train elle n'arrivera pas à la ville. 11. Le lapin de l'enfant n'a pas été tué. 12. Les touristes qui doivent l'argent à mon père montent dans leur voiture. 13. Si vous fermez la porte il n'entendra pas un mot. 14. Les affaires de son mari ne sont pas très bonnes. 15. La vie qu'il menait n'était pas intéressante. 16. Je n'ai pas remarqué les bateaux qui traversaient le fleuve. 17. Le château n'a pas été rendu. 18. Nous chercherons demain l'argent que vous avez perdu. 19. Nous sommes sûrs qu'il ne remplissait pas ses poches d'argent. 20. Je ne donnerai pas à l'ouvrier l'argent que vous devez au marchand.

Exercise 9(a)

1. She has been happy. 2. He has had a short and joyous life. 3. We have not had much fruit. 4. The streets of our little town are not very long. 5. Having walked much she is weary. 6. We noticed a pretty little girl who was walking with the widow. 7. He carried (or wore) a new coat and a white hat. 8. I am sure that his wife is mad. 9. The animal you are looking at is the emperor's favourite horse. 10. I am listening to the girl who is singing in the street : she has a fine voice. 11. The general has finished his public life. 12. I have sold my car : it is not new, but it's good. 13. The doors of the

castle are very thick. 14. Having lost his favourite
daughter he is very sad. 15. Before the death of his dear
wife he led an active life. 16. The rooms of the old houses
are very low. 17. The old woman who is crossing the line
is the widow of the former (or "ex") merchant Dubois.
18. I shall sell my house : it is not dry. 19. We shall
arrive before to-morrow in a new car. 20. Life (living) is
very dear and I owe much money.

Exercise 9(b)

1. Il fut là avant le soir. 2. Ayant une maison neuve
son épouse est heureuse. 3. La maison blanche est basse
mais belle. 4. La fille du gros homme monta dans le
train. 5. Sa longue vie fut vive et heureuse. 6. La
vieille femme a été tuée par un train. 7. Les années de
la vie d'un homme ne sont pas longues, mais brèves.
8. Le cheval portait un gros fardeau. 9. Vous n'entendrez
pas parler la vieille femme : elle est muette. 10. L'ancien
général visitera Sa Majesté avant demain. 11. Elle est
lasse mais elle cherchera demain le chapeau neuf qu'elle
a perdu. 12. Les deux vieux châteaux ont été vendus à
la veuve du marchand. 13. J'ai remarqué dix soldats
qui traversaient le fleuve. 14. Ayant laissé son chapeau
au château le touriste a parlé à la sentinelle à la porte.
15. Elle était vive et heureuse avant la mort de son mari.
16. Elle est très vieille mais elle n'est pas immortelle !
17. Les portes épaisses du château étaient fermées aux
touristes. 18. Sa voiture neuve était d'une belle marque.
19. Sa vie n'a pas été heureuse, mais il recevra beaucoup
d'honneur à sa mort. 20. Nous avons donné une livre de
beurre frais à la pauvre veuve.

Exercise 10(a)

1. The lady is here : you have seen her. 2. We have
seen them. 3. My aunt is a sad but kindly lady. 4. The

box was lost but my uncle has found it. 5. The box was filled with books. 6. I have lost my books, but she has found them. 7. While the old woman was crossing the line the train killed her. 8. I am sure she was there, because I saw her. 9. The merchant has not bought the car : he has sold it. 10. I think that the shops in the town are very good. 11. We spoke to the sentry : he listened to us. 12. You are looking for the fruit : I am sure that the little boy has eaten them (it). 13. I knocked at the door of the house because it was shut. 14. You are looking for your books? Your uncle has sold them. 15. The hats were lost but I have found them and I have left them on the table in your room. 16. We had a fine chair but we have sold it. 17. The lady was speaking to the officer : I noticed her. 18. He found his house filled with soldiers. 19. He crossed the street whilst I was polishing the table. 20. I thought that we should visit the castles : but they are shut.

Exercise 10(b)

1. Il m'a frappé. 2. Je l'ai frappée. 3. Nous les avons vus. 4. Elle nous a vus. 5. Je regardais la fenêtre : vous l'avez cassée. 6. J'avais sept livres mais je les ai perdus. 7. Leur chaise est ici : ils l'ont polie. 8. Elle a chanté et nous l'avons écoutée. 9. Les soldats ont marché vers le château et nous les avons regardés. 10. Je l'ai remarquée pendant que je parlais au touriste. 11. J'ai frappé à la porte : elle était fermée. 12. J'avais une montre mais je l'ai vendue à un de mes amis. 13. Son père le frappera parce qu'il a rempli ses poches de fruits. 14. Nous avons trouvé une montre et je l'ai donnée à sa tante. 15. Nous ne traverserons pas le fleuve : les bateaux sont remplis d'eau. 16. Je pense que nous l'avons vue avec mon oncle. 17. Ils montaient dans leur voiture : je les ai entendus. 18. Il a donné sa montre au garçon et il le frappera s'il l'a perdue. 19. Le marchand n'a pas acheté la chaise : il l'a vendue. 20. Si le magasin est fermé nous frapperons à la porte.

Exercise 11(a)

1. It is he who struck me. 2. As for me I will find her in spite of you. 3. They in the palace and I in the shop ! 4. You and she will find the street on your left hand. 5. It is I who have the money, because I am clever. 6. They and we have broken the box. 7. You saw them ? So did I. 8. He and they are poor. 9. It is you who sold it. 10. I saw the sentry : he was before the castle gate. 11. I looked to right and left but I did not see her. 12. Your hat ! It was she who lost it and I who found it. 13. In spite of you I shall arrive before her at the town. 14. I, strike him ! It's ridiculous ! 15. If we walk quickly, you and I, we shall arrive at the castle before them. 16. As for the old lady, she has been killed. 17. It is not he, it is she who sold her watch. 18. We also have seen her : she was crossing the street with her uncle. 19. It was the left hand which was cut. 20. He walks quickly : he will arrive before us at the station.

Exercise 11(b)

1. Quant à elle, il l'a tuée. 2. Malgré lui je vendrai ma voiture. 3. C'était elle qui était au-dessus. 4. Eux et moi, nous ne sommes pas heureux, parce que nous sommes pauvres. 5. C'était lui qui a laissé son chapeau dans le train. 6. Moi, remplir mes poches d'argent ! C'est ridicule ! 7. Le garçon et moi, nous les avons vus. 8. Vous remarquerez la maison à droite. 9. Lui et eux ne sont pas avec mon oncle. 10. Quant à eux, ils sont très heureux. 11. Malgré moi, il l'a frappée. 12. Votre fenêtre ! C'était lui qui l'a cassée. 13. Qui les a vus ? Moi. 14. Lui, elle et moi, nous sommes las. 15. Leur automobile était devant la gare : je l'ai remarquée. 16. Quant à l'argent, je l'ai perdu. 17. Eux, je ne parlerai pas d'eux. 18. C'était elle qui marchait vers le fleuve. 19. J'étais là avec lui : elle aussi. 20. Vous et elle, vous avez beaucoup d'argent.

Exercise 12(a)

1. Has not the emperor lost his horses? 2. When will she be at the house? 3. How will she find her? 4. When did the officer give you the money? 5. Has he not yet spent the money which I gave him? 6. Hasn't the tourist missed the train? 7. Where are the poor people? They are picking up the money which the merchant let fall (dropped). 8. The stories which he tells are long. 9. Will the soldiers march again to the castle? 10. When will your cousin arrive? 11. The castle is there. Have you not yet visited it? 12. How are his affairs going? Has he lost much money? 13. I will leave you here: but are we not losing our time? 14. Wasn't the officer speaking to the sentry when you saw him? 15. Will you remain here long? An hour. 16. Won't he miss the train if he does not walk quickly? 17. Are not the pleasures of life great? 18. Has she not yet told you the story of her husband's death? 19. Has the tourist spent much? 20. Haven't the workmen lost (wasted) their time?

Exercise 12(b)

1. Les soldats dépensent-ils beaucoup d'argent? 2. Ne marche-t-elle pas vite? 3. Comment dure l'argent? (Comment l'argent dure-t-il?) 4. A-t-il encore manqué le train? 5. Ne ramassiez-vous pas le bois? 6. Ne resterons-nous pas ici une heure? 7. Comment les garçons passent-ils leur temps? 8. L'officier, ne sera-t-il pas ici? 9. N'avez-vous pas entendu l'histoire qu'il racontait? 10. Les gens de la ville, n'ont-ils pas regardé les soldats qui passaient? 11. Madame votre tante, ne vous donnera-t-elle pas l'argent? 12. Votre cousin, n'a-t-il pas encore trouvé son argent? 13. Ne parlaient-ils pas à l'officier quand je les ai vus? 14. Comment l'avez-vous trouvée? 15. Ne marcherons-nous pas vers la gare? 16. La vieille dame n'a-t-elle pas été tuée? 17. Est-ce que les touristes

dépensent beaucoup d'argent dans cette ville? 18. Ne les avez-vous pas vus? 19. La dame, n'est-elle pas votre tante? 20. Ne me raconterez-vous pas l'histoire?

Exercise 13(a)

1. Now I'm going to bed. 2. He escapes. 3. I will save him. 4. I will cut the bread myself. 5. He is in haste to become rich. 6. Isn't he going to bed? 7. We are not dressing ourselves. 8. He amuses us very much. 9. We shall amuse ourselves. 10. In spite of me they amused themselves. 11. Isn't the boy waking up? 12. Where is this man hiding himself? 13. Is this table in your house? 14. When will you go to bed? 15. I am sure that you are mistaken. 16. I will wake him myself. 17. We will dress quickly. 18. Haven't you noticed this fine shop, these old houses and this hotel? 19. I will hasten to get up. 20. We will hide under the table. 21. We shall find him (it) ourselves. 22. She is tired: she will not awake before to-morrow.

Exercise 13(b)

1. Ce soir elle s'éveillera. 2. Vous lavez-vous? 3. Il ne se trompe pas. 4. Quand vous levez-vous? 5. Les enfants ne se hâteront-ils pas? 6. Où vous cachez-vous? 7. Ne vous coucherez-vous pas? 8. Je m'habillerai. 9. Je l'habillerai moi-même. 10. Ce marchand ne s'enrichira pas. 11. Il se glissa dans la maison pour se sauver. 12. Ces livres vous amusent-ils? 13. Votre argent? Il le glissait dans sa poche. 14. Ils se glissaient dans la maison. Je les ai vus. 15. Je lui parlerai moi-même. 16. Son père le frappa mais il se leva. 17. Ils l'ont caché eux-mêmes. 18. Vous vous trompez si vous pensez que j'ai parlé à cet homme. 19. Ce marchand ne vous trompera pas. 20. Quand cet officier s'éveillera-t-il?

F

Exercise 14(a)

1. She has fallen in the street. 2. He lost his money three months ago. 3. He will be here to-morrow : I am glad (of it). 4. We have not gone to bed. 5. Haven't you read this book? No. But I have heard (tell) of it. 6. I haven't many books, but I shall sell five. 7. They were living in this street 6 months ago. 8. There are seven days in a week and Monday is one. 9. My cousins had arrived at the house before the death of their father. 10. We have remained here an hour because our car won't go. 11. Have you seen that house? We live in it. 12. He told me a very interesting thing : I will speak to you of it. 13. We have made a mistake : I am sure that his house is not in this street. 14. If you don't like this book, I will give you another. 15. This officer is very rich. He has two cars and now he is going to buy another. 16. How long will you stay here? An hour or two. I'm not sure. 17. I do not trust that man. 18. There were two sentries at the castle gate : now there are three. 19. If she had not walked fast she wouldn't have fallen. 20. They have not yet got up.

Exercise 14(b)

1. Mes cousins Pierre et Guillaume sont arrivés. 2. Où sont les couteaux? Il y en avait deux sur la table. 3. Nous sommes bien las. Nous ne nous sommes pas couchés cette semaine. 4. Je n'aime pas cette femme, parce que je ne m'y fie pas. 5. Les garçons, ne se sont-ils pas cachés dans la rue? 6. J'avais cinq livres, mais je lui en ai donné un. 7. Il y a quatre ans nous demeurions dans une grande maison. 8. Votre mari, ne s'est-il pas encore levé? 9. Elle est tombée dans l'eau pendant qu'elle traversait le fleuve. 10. Avez-vous remarqué cette maison à gauche? Mon oncle y demeure. 11. Moi-même, j'ai vu l'homme qui s'est tué. 12. Si vous ne travaillez pas vous ne vous

enrichirez pas. 13. Elle est arrivée et j'en suis bien aise. 14. Si vous avez lu ce livre nous vous en donnerons un autre. 15. J'étais sûr qu'elle s'était trompée. 16. Il se levait mais il ne s'était pas habillé. 17. Serait-elle tombée si elle n'avait pas marché vite? 18. Je vous donnerai mon livre si vous n'en avez pas un. 19. Nous avons visité le château et nous y sommes restés une heure. 20. Elle a beaucoup travaillé, mais elle ne s'est pas enrichie.

Translation I

LITERAL VERSION. My elder brother had not but 18 years when he has visited Paris for the first time, and that which has much impressed him, it is the animation and the breadth of the streets. At London, the streets even the more big had not but 60 feet of wide and the small had not but 20 of them. At Paris, especially in the beautiful quarters of the town, it was quite different. The streets were wide and well lighted and it is not without justice that one has called Paris the " town light." At this period the motor-cars were still little numerous : indeed one saw scarcely of them and the pedestrians had no difficulty to cross the streets. One could stroll without mistrust : that which is no more possible.

FREE VERSION. My elder brother was only eighteen (years old) when he paid his first visit to Paris, and what impressed him very much was the liveliness and spaciousness of the streets. In London even the biggest roads were only 60 feet wide and the small only 20. In Paris, especially in the fashionable parts of the town, it was quite different. The streets were wide and well lighted, and it is not without justice that Paris has been called the " City of Light." At this period motor-cars were still very few : in fact one saw scarcely any and pedestrians had no difficulty in crossing the streets. One could stroll about without mistrust—which is no longer possible.

NOTES. *N'avait que. Ne . . . que* means *only.* But NOT *not only,* which is *ne . . . pas seulement.*

Ce n'était que mon père—it was only my father.

Pouvoir does not require the *pas* in negatives. Other verbs that can do with *ne* only, omitting the *pas,* are *cesser* = to cease, *oser* = to dare, *savoir* = to know. *Je ne saurais dire* = I couldn't say.

A Londres. Note that " to," " in," or " at " before names of towns is generally rendered in French by *à ;* except those towns where an article forms part of the name—*e.g. Le Hâvre,* Havre. In Havre, naturally, is—*Au Hâvre.*

Ce qui. In English the relative can have a whole clause for its antecedent, *e.g.* he was very little, which annoyed his mother. The French relative will not stand this treatment : it demands an antecedent all to itself. Thus, the above sentence would run—*il était fort petit, ce qui chagrinait sa mère.*

On l'a appelé. On is here used for people in general. *On dit* = people say. This construction is frequently used in French where a passive would be used in English. He was quickly surrounded = *On l'entoura vite.*

Fois. Note that *fois* is used for a number of times, *temps* for a space of time. *Deux fois* = twice. *Combien de temps ?* = How long ?

Exercise 15

1. Ce garçon est jeune : il n'a que huit ans. 2. Un des touristes pouvait monter dans le train. 3. On dit qu'il a acheté une automobile qui va très vite. 4. Ce qui me chagrine, c'est que j'ai perdu mon argent. 5. On dit que la dame qui demeurait dans cette vieille maison s'est tuée. 6. En avez-vous vu ? 7. Il vendit son cheval qui avait dix ans. 8. Il tomba dans le fleuve, ce qui était très amusant (drôle). 9. Cette fenêtre a trois pieds de large, mais l'autre n'en a que deux. 10. L'animation de la ville les a beaucoup impressionnés. 11. J'avais beaucoup

de livres, mais maintenant je n'en ai que sept. 12. Le cheval tomba et ne pouvait (pas) se lever. 13. Les rues ici, ne sont-elles pas bien éclairées? 14. Regarder les magasins, c'est amusant. 15. Je regardais les nombreuses automobiles qui passaient. 16. J'ai lu un livre que je n'aime pas. 17. Ecouter ses histoires, ce n'est guère amusant. 18. On dit qu'elle s'est cachée dans mon magasin : ce qui n'est pas possible. 19. Je les ai vus ce soir pour la première fois. 20. Je n'ai acheté que deux livres de beurre.

Translation II

LITERAL VERSION. All the world knows very well that London is the biggest city of Europe. Paris is far from being as big as the capital of England. But, if it is less vast, it is in revenge, at least to the opinion of the French, of much more agreeable. And, to judge of it by the great number of tourists who visit the town, it is evident that foreigners realise the beauty of Paris. The Exhibition, one of the most large and varied which one has seen since the end of the war, has attracted crowds of visitors. For the tourists who dread the crossing of the Channel the best means of to go to Paris, it is to make the journey by aeroplane : but it is not the least dear. The people who have more leisure would not know how to do better than to go there in car. The roads are good : one sees well the country : in following the national road it is almost impossible to lose his way. And one can easily do the journey in two days, seeing that Paris is only at three hundred kilometres from Calais. In France, as in most countries of the world, the vehicles hold the right, but the intelligent tourist will accustom himself without the least difficulty to this rule. He has only to say to himself : " I am determined not to forget it," and in a few minutes he will laugh at the anxiety which has tortured him from the moment when, from the deck of the boat, he has perceived the French coast.

FREE VERSION. Everyone knows very well that London is the largest city in Europe. Paris is far from being as large as the capital of England. But, if it is less vast, it is, to make up for it, at least in the opinion of the French, much nicer. And, judging by the large number of tourists who visit the city, it is evident that foreigners realise the beauty of Paris. The Exhibition, one of the biggest and most varied which have been seen since the end of the war, attracted crowds of visitors. For tourists who dread the Channel crossing the best means of going to Paris is to make the journey by air : but it is not the cheapest. People who have more leisure could not do better than go there by car. The roads are good : one can see something of the country : by following the main road it is almost impossible to lose one's way. And one can easily do the journey in two days, seeing that Paris is only 300 kilometres from Calais. In France, as in most countries of the world, vehicles keep to the right, but the intelligent tourist will accustom himself to the rule without the least difficulty. He has only to say to himself : " I am determined not to forget it," and in a few minutes he will laugh at the anxiety which has tortured him from the moment when, from the deck of the boat, he caught sight of the French coast.

NOTES. The article is seldom required in French before the names of towns. But, save in exceptional circumstances, the article is inserted before names of countries and continents. Most of these are feminine. We have seen that in Paris is *à Paris*. But with countries, etc., *en* is used *without* the article—*e.g.*, *en France*; *en Allemagne* (Germany).

Loin d'être. In English, far from being. Note that in French after *all* prepositions except *en* the infinitive is used instead of the participle. *Sans hésiter* = without hesitating : but *en entrant* = on entering.

Français. Nouns of nationality are written in French with a capital letter, adjectives of nationality with a small letter. *Les Anglais*, but *un village allemand*.

Foule. Remember the rule given in a previous footnote. Nouns and adverbs of quantity require in French the insertion of *de* or *d'*, when followed by a noun.

De beaucoup. Note this construction : *Il est plus grand que moi de six pouces* = he is 6 inches taller than I.

En automobile. Similarly *en bateau* : but *à pied, à cheval, à bicyclette* (bicycle).

Sauraient. The conditional of *savoir* (to know) is freely used instead of the present tense of *pouvoir* (to be able).

Campagne = the country as opposed to the town. *Le pays* = any country or district. *La patrie* = one's native land.

Il est impossible de. Impersonal constructions preceded by *il est* translate the English *to* by *de* before an infinitive (not by *à*).

A trois cents kilomètres. Note the *à* untranslated in English.

De ne pas oublier. Certain verbs require *de* after them followed by an infinitive : *résoudre* is one of them. Others require *à*. Note that in a negative *infinitive*, both *ne* and *pas* precede the verb.

Le moment où. When is *quand*, but if preceded by a noun of time it is translated by *où* in French.

Pont. Ordinarily a bridge : but, of ships, the deck.

La côte française. Note that adjectives of nationality always *follow* the noun in French.

Exercise 16

1. Elle est vieille mais elle chante mieux que sa fille. 2. Vous travaillez mal, mais je suis sûr que vous travaillerez mieux avant la fin de l'année. 3. Il est le plus grand homme du pays. 4. Pierre est grand. Il est plus grand de quatre pouces que mon frère. 5. Nous allons à Paris en auto(mobile) : c'est le meilleur moyen de faire le voyage. 6. Nous avons beaucoup de choses à faire, mais nous sommes résolus de les faire avant demain. 7. Paris n'est

qu'à deux cents kilomètres d'ici.   8. Elle a acheté la plus belle maison du pays.   9. Jean est le plus habile ouvrier de la ville.   10. Elle est résolue de ne pas vendre cette maison qu'elle aime mieux que l'autre.   11. Le jour où je l'ai vu était le plus heureux de ma vie.   12. J'ai remarqué une foule de touristes : ils allaient vers le château, qui est le plus beau du pays.   13. Les agents de police cherchent le voleur qui a pris ma montre.   14. Cette route est mauvaise, mais l'autre est encore pire.   15. Il ne traversera pas le fleuve sans tomber dans l'eau : ce qui sera très amusant.   16. Il y a beaucoup de soldats français dans la ville.   Je les ai vus.   17. On dit que cet Anglais n'est pas aussi intelligent que vous le pensez.   18. Vous allez à cheval, moi à pied, mais j'arriverai avant vous.   19. J'ai perdu ma montre, mais je l'ai trouvée sans la moindre difficulté.   20. Vous vous habillez moins vite que moi.

Translation III

LITERAL VERSION. The next day of my arrival at Paris I have got up early. Having taken the breakfast, which consisted in a cup of coffee with some bread and some butter, I have gone out of the hotel where I had descended, in order to go to make a walk in town. In following the most-frequented streets I arrive at last at a big square in the middle of which stands a column. It is the Square of the Bastille. What astonishes me a little, it is to see on all sides some booths where some merchants have installed themselves. A gentleman to whom I put a question in my better French tells me that it is not an ordinary market, but a fair. It appears that there is no quarter of Paris which does not have at some season its fair. Having thanked him of his explanation I make the tour of the booths. One sells there every sort of things : some meat, some vegetables, some birds in cage, some socks, some stockings of artificial silk. In addition to the merchants I have noticed a juggler, some acrobats and a seller of lottery tickets. In listening well to the merchants who proclaimed at high voice the superior quality of their merchandise I have succeeded to increase of a few picturesque words my French vocabulary. As I had in my pocket only about ten of francs, I have bought nothing, but I have amused myself much. It is true that I was alone but I have not been bored, for there were so many interesting things to see. It had made at first a magnificent weather. Towards midday, however, the sky grew dark and in some minutes a light rain was falling. I have decided, therefore, to return to the hotel.

FREE VERSION. The morning after my arrival in Paris, I got up early. Having had breakfast, which consisted of a cup of coffee with bread and butter, I left the hotel where I had put up to go for a walk in the town. By following the busiest streets I arrived at last at a big square in the middle of which stood a column. It was the Place de la Bastille. What astonished me somewhat was to see booths on all sides in which traders had installed themselves. A gentleman, to whom I put a question in my best French, told me that it was not an ordinary market, but a fair. It appears that there is no quarter in Paris which does not have its fair at some season (of the year). Having thanked him for his explanation, I walked round among the booths. Every sort of thing was on sale : meat, vegetables, caged birds, socks, artificial silk stockings. In addition to the stallholders, I noticed a juggler, some acrobats and a seller of lottery tickets. By listening carefully to the vendors who were loudly proclaiming the superior quality of their wares, I succeeded in adding to my French vocabulary a few picturesque words. As I had only about 10 francs in my pocket, I didn't buy anything, but I enjoyed myself hugely. It is true that I was alone, but I wasn't bored, for there was so much of interest to see. It had been beautifully fine at first. About midday, however, the sky grew dark and in a few minutes it was drizzling. I decided, therefore, to go back to the hotel.

NOTES. *Le déjeuner* = lunch, *le petit déjeuner* = breakfast.

Une tasse. Note the *de.*

Sortir and *descendre*, used as intransitive verbs, require the auxiliary verb *être*, not *avoir*.

To go to see, or, to go and see—*aller voir.* No preposition after *aller* before an infinitive.

J'arrive. The French frequently use the present tense where in English we should use the past tense. This gives for the Frenchman an effect of vividness.

Demander = to ask, *poser une question* = to ask a question.

Arrondissement. This is the name given to each of the twenty municipal areas into which Paris is divided.

NOTE. *Remercier de* = to thank *for.*

En écoutant. Note again the use of the participle after *en.* With all other propositions the infinitive is required. The meanings of *en* are varied—by, in, on, etc.

Réussir à—to succeed *in.*

Une dizaine = about ten. So *une vingtaine, une douzaine.* English, a dozen, a score, etc. These words require *de* or *d'* when followed by a noun.

Ne . . . rien = nothing. Note that *pas* is not also required here.

Car = for (conj.) in sense of *since, because.* As preposition *pour* is used.

Tant = so much, so many. Note the *de* following a word of quantity. The French frequently use impersonal verbs in describing the weather. *Il fait beau*, it is fine. *Il fait froid*, it is cold. *Il pleut*, it rains. *Il tonne*, it thunders. *Il neige*, it snows.

To decide to. In French, *décider de.*

Exercise 17

1. Ayant eu du lait le chat désirait de la crème. 2. Il tonne et il pleut beaucoup. Je pense que je resterai dans ma chambre. 3. Si vous n'écoutez pas vous n'entendrez rien. 4. Ils sont allés voir s'il pleut encore. 5. Il s'agit de se lever de bonne heure. 6. Il n'a rien vu, car il était sorti avec ses amis. 7. Tout ce qu'il perdra ce sera des vaches. 8. J'ai acheté au marché une douzaine d'œufs et de la viande pour le déjeuner. 9. Il portait un chapeau vert et un habit jaune que je n'aimais pas. 10. Nous avons décidé d'aller le voir à l'hôtel où il est descendu. 11. La vache a-t-elle donné du lait? 12. Il n'a pas encore réussi à faire son travail, car il a tant de choses à faire. 13. Sans regarder le visiteur il sortit de la chambre. 14. Je suis allé la voir, mais elle était sortie. 15. Avez-vous du beurre? Oui, j'en ai une livre. 16. Il aime le lait mais il aime mieux les œufs. 17. Sans travailler vous ne recevrez rien. 18. Elle est allée à Paris pour cinq semaines. 19. Je vous aurais donné de l'argent si vous aviez mieux travaillé. 20. Je n'ai acheté qu'une vingtaine d'œufs et des mouchoirs.

Translation IV

LITERAL VERSION. I have already told you that I have had the intention of to return to my hotel. But one deceives oneself easily of route in trying to come back on one's paces above all in a large city where one walks for the first time. After some minutes there was no more of doubt. I had lost myself. One has sometimes some good ideas and, perceiving a stationer's shop, I entered there to the search of a plan of Paris. The owner of the shop understands immediately that I am English and he tries by politeness to speak to me in my maternal tongue. I persist to employ his. The result is very comic and we laugh, the one and the other. But I have no difficulty to buy my plan and we congratulate ourselves politely the one the other of our knowledge of a foreign language. Then I leave the shop and I begin to consult my plan. In some instants I have succeeded to take my bearings. I am in the Rue St. Antoine. In following it I shall join the Rue de Rivoli. Happily the rain ceases soon to fall and it is under a sky become again serene that I traverse the animated streets of the capital. Some nailed passages indicate to the pedestrian the route which it is necessary to take in order to cross the streets. Here and there I see some notices bearing the words " entry forbidden," " direction unique," and I understand that, in spite of the considerable breadth of many Parisian streets, the problem of the circulation of vehicles is as difficult to solve in Paris as in London. Towards midday I find myself in the Place du Palais Royal. My hotel is only at two steps from there, which is far from to displease me, for I have well hunger.

FREE VERSION. I have already told you that I intended to return to my hotel. But it is easy to mistake one's road in trying to retrace one's steps, especially in a large city in which one is walking for the first time. After a few moments there was no longer any doubt. I had lost my way. One has good ideas sometimes and, seeing a stationer's shop, I went in in search of a plan of Paris. The shopkeeper realised at once that I was English and tried, out of politeness, to speak to me in my mother tongue. I persisted in using his. The result was exceedingly comic, and we both laughed. But I had no difficulty in buying my plan, and we congratulated each other politely on our knowledge of a foreign language. Then I left the shop and set to work to consult my plan. In a few moments I had managed to get my bearings. I was in the Rue St. Antoine. By following it I should reach the Rue de Rivoli. Fortunately the rain soon stopped, and it was beneath a once more cloudless sky that I traversed the lively streets of the capital. Stud-marked crossings indicated the route the pedestrian should follow in crossing the streets. Here and there I saw notices bearing the words "no entry," "one-way street," and I realised that, despite the considerable breadth of many Parisian streets, the problem of traffic circulation was as difficult to solve in Paris as it was in London. About twelve o'clock I found myself in the Place du Palais Royal. My hotel was only a few yards from there, which was far from unwelcome to me, for I felt very hungry.

NOTES. *L'un l'autre* is used after reflexive verbs that imply reciprocal action. They love each other = *ils s'aiment l'un l'autre*. If *they* means more than two we must have *ils s'aiment les uns les autres* (if any of them are masculine) or *elles s'aiment les unes les autres* (if *all* are feminine).

If now we put in *et* between the two words, it makes them into *both*, and the words have no connection with reciprocal verbs. They both began to cry = *ils se mirent à pleurer, l'un et l'autre*. These ladies are both beautiful = *ces dames sont belles, l'une et l'autre*.

Où l'on se promène. The *l'* before *on* is not translated. It is inserted to avoid an ugly sound, always an important consideration in French.

De doute. Note *de* after the negative.

J'ai faim. Literally, I have hunger. So also *j'ai froid* (*chaud*), I am cold (hot). *Bien*, not *très*, is used for *very* in these expressions. Remember, by the way, that you cannot write *très beaucoup*. *Very much* is simply *beaucoup*.

Exercise 18

1. Voici ma montre : je n'ai pas vu la sienne. 2. Voilà le chapeau que vous cherchez. Rendez-moi le mien. 3. Son automobile va plus vite que la vôtre. 4. Ces deux garçons ne se frapperaient pas l'un l'autre, si vous leur parliez. 5. Je vous donnerais de bon café pour votre

petit déjeuner, mais je n'ai pas de lait. 6. Si vous ne travaillez pas mieux vous ne recevrez pas d'argent à la fin de la semaine. 7. Avez-vous vu mon chapeau? Le vôtre? Oui, le voilà sur la table. 8. Il n'y a pas beaucoup de gens que je n'aime pas. 9. Elle est allée au marché pour acheter de bon pain blanc, mais nous en avons déjà beaucoup. 10. Je suis sûr qu'ils ne se trouveront pas l'un l'autre. 11. Vous voici enfin. J'allais vous chercher. 12. Ne donnez pas d'argent à ce jeune homme. Il le dépensera aussitôt. 13. J'essayais de revenir sur mes pas. 14. Voilà votre clef, mais j'ai perdu la mienne. 15. Non, je n'avais pas faim, j'avais froid. 16. Nous aurons cette année de beaux fruits. 17. J'ai essayé de ne pas rire. 18. Nous avons l'intention de sortir ce soir s'il ne pleut pas. 19. Nous n'avons pas de chiens car mon père ne les aime pas. 20. Vous remarquerez à gauche le château et de vieilles maisons.

Translation V

LITERAL VERSION. The hotel, of which it is a question, was not very large. It was to say true an establishment modest enough and it was for this reason that I had chosen it. But the hotels in Paris, even those of which the clients only pay moderate prices, offer you all modern comfort, heating central, lift, running water, etc. At our home to the contrary, especially in the provinces, the hotels leave much to desire. That day I have lunched better than I should have done in London at the same price. The meal finished I went to the drawing-room where I amused myself to read the papers. The French papers, to judge of them by that which I had before the eyes, are not as good as the English. They are badly printed and the paper is not of very good quality. Up to then I had never read any foreign paper. Naturally there were many words which I did not understand, but I succeeded without difficulty to seize the general sense of the articles, this which has rendered me very content.

After my long walk of the morning I was a little tired. But I had not any time to lose, for I was only going to remain six days in Paris, and there were so many interesting things to see. I consult again my plan, at the reverse of which I find all sort of information indispensable to the tourists, the routes of buses, the lines of the Metropolitan, etc. I decide finally to go to visit the Church of the Sacred Heart, remarkable example of the Byzantine style. Of more, as it is situated at the summit of Montmartre, one enjoys there of a magnificent panorama. According to a tradition very widespread it was near this spot that one has cut the head to St. Denis, patron saint of France under the ancient régime : from where comes the name of the mount of martyrs, or Montmartre.

FREE VERSION. The hotel in question was not very big. It was, to tell the truth, a modest enough place, and it was for that reason that I had chosen it. But Paris hotels, even those whose guests pay only moderate prices, offer one every modern comfort—central heating, lift, running water, etc. With us, on the other hand, especially in the provinces, the hotels leave a good deal to be desired. That day I had a better lunch than I should have got in London for the same price. The meal over, I went into the lounge, where I amused myself by reading the papers. French papers, judging by the one before me, are inferior to English. They are badly printed and the paper is of poor quality. Until then I had never read a foreign paper. Naturally there were many words I could not understand, but I easily managed to grasp the general sense of the articles : which pleased me very much.

After my long morning walk I was rather tired. But I had no time to lose, for I was only going to stay in Paris six days, and there was so much of interest to see. I consulted my plan again, and found on the back of it all sorts of information indispensable to the tourist : bus routes, Underground lines and so on. I eventually decided to go and see the Church of the Sacred Heart, a remarkable example of Byzantine style. Moreover, as it stands on the summit of Montmartre, one can enjoy a splendid view from it. According to a very widespread tradition, it was near this spot that the head of St. Denis, patron saint of France under the old régime, was cut off : whence comes the name of the mount of martyrs, or Montmartre.

NOTES. *Jusque* = up to, is a useful word. *Jusqu'ici* = up to here. *Jusqu'à ma maison* = as far as my house. *Jusqu'alors* = until then.

Tout = all, every. Feminine is *toute*. Plural *tous* (m.), *toutes* (f.).

Ne . . . jamais means never. *Il ne fume jamais* = he never smokes. *Ne . . . plus* = no more, no longer. *Je n'ai plus d'argent* = I have no more money.

Chez = at the house of. *Chez moi* = at my house. *Chez mon oncle* = at my uncle's house. The word is often used in a wider sense : *chez les savants*—among learned men.

Dont is a pronoun meaning, *of which, of whom*, or *whose*.

Mieux que je n'aurais fait. There is a negative feel about this sentence : hence the *ne*, though there is no *pas*. This construction is used in comparison where a negation lies hidden. He dances better than he sings—*il danse mieux qu'il ne chante.*

Exercise 19

1. Ceci est bon, cela est mauvais. 2. De ces deux livres celui-ci durera plus longtemps que celui-là. 3. Elle est plus vieille que vous ne pensez. 4. Notre maison est plus petite que celle du général. 5. J'ai quatre livres dont vous avez lu deux. 6. Cela leur a donné grand plaisir. 7. Voici l'habit dont la manche est déchirée. 8. Elle ne sera plus jamais heureuse. 9. Nous avons mangé un excellent repas. 10. Voyez ce que j'ai pour votre déjeuner. 11. Quand on rentre chez soi on est las. 12. Voilà les deux automobiles : celle-ci est la sienne, celle-là est la vôtre. 13. Il ne mange plus, mais il dit qu'il n'a pas faim. 14.

Mon automobile va plus vite que celle du touriste. 15. Les rues de Paris sont plus larges que celles de Londres. 16. A vrai dire, nous sommes allés chez votre oncle, mais il était sorti. 17. Chez ma tante il y a deux petits garçons. 18. Je vous ne donnerai pas cette montre-ci, mais vous aurez celle-là. 19. Dans l'armée française il y a d'habiles soldats dont le Général X (est un). 20. Je n'entends jamais ce qu'il dit : il parle encore pis que son frère.

Translation VI

LITERAL VERSION. Towards three hours of the afternoon I go out of the hotel and direct myself towards the station of the Metro the most near. It is that of the Palais Royal. I go down the stairs and find myself in a long subterranean gallery. I do not see neither lift nor rolling stairway. Without doubt there is no need of to have them in most of the stations, for the track is not constructed at the same depth as in London. I approach myself of the booking office and I ask a ticket for the journey from the Palais Royal to the station of Barbès. But the clerk regards me of a fashion a little scornful and I understand that I have made an error. He asks me if I want a ticket of first or second class. I take a first and the clerk explains to me that there are only two prices according to the class in which one travels. It is not as at London where the price of tickets varies according to the journey. Provided with one's ticket one can change train as many times as one desires and the ticket ceases to be valid when one shall have passed the barrier in order to remount to the surface.

The train arrives immediately. It is composed of 5 coaches, of which the third is of 1st class. Having consulted again my plan—that I am well glad of to have it ! —I descend at the Gare de l'Est to take a corresponding train and some minutes later, by going up the stairs, I find myself at the end of the Boulevard Barbès. I would not know to say if the Parisian system is more practical than ours. Evidently for that one who is obliged to make some considerable journeys the system comports some advantages : moreover it is a means of transport enough rapid : but if one wishes to go, for example, from the Palais Royal to the Place de la Concorde one would do better to take the bus : one would enjoy thus the great air, all in making some little economies.

FREE VERSION. About three o'clock in the afternoon I left the hotel and made my way towards the nearest Tube station. It was the Palais Royal. I went down the stairs, and found myself in a long underground gallery. I saw neither lift nor moving staircase. Doubtless they are unnecessary in most stations, for the track is not laid at the same depth as in London. I went up to the booking-office and asked for a ticket for the journey from the Palais Royal to the Barbès station. But the clerk looked at me rather scornfully, and I understood that I had made a mistake. He asked me if I wanted a first- or second-class ticket. I took a first, and the clerk explained that there were only two prices, according to the class in which one travelled. It is not the same as in London, where the price of the tickets varies with the length of the journey. Provided with one's ticket, one can change as often as one likes, and the ticket only becomes invalid when one has passed the barrier to come up again to the surface.

The train arrived at once. It consisted of five coaches, the middle one of which was first class. Having again consulted my plan—how glad I was to have it !—I alighted at the Gare de l'Est to get a connecting train, and a few minutes later, by going up the stairs, I found myself at the end of the Boulevard Barbès. I can't say if the Parisian system is better than ours. Obviously for anyone who has to go considerable distances it entails advantages : moreover it's a fairly rapid means of transport ; but if one wants to go, for instance, from the Palais Royal to the Place de la Concorde, one would do better to take a bus : that way one would enjoy the fresh air and economise at the same time.

Notes. *Que je suis bien aise !* The usual way of expressing exclamations with verbs. How blue the sky is !—*que le ciel est bleu !* How good you are !—*que vous êtes bon.*

Neither . . . nor. Generally translated by *ni . . . ni.* If the phrase contains a verb, *ne* is required before it. Neither he nor I—*ni lui ni moi.* Neither one nor the other has gone out—*ni l'un ni l'autre n'est sorti.*

Exercise 20

1. Le château dont nous nous approchons est le plus grand de la province. 2. Voici le couteau avec lequel je coupe toujours le pain. 3. Les hommes à qui je parlais hier sont partis déjà. 4. Que je suis aise de vous voir ! 5. Elle s'est avancée jusqu'à l'île. 6. Voici la maison où elle est née. 7. Cette île est plus grande que celle dont vous avez parlé. 8. Quoi ! Avez-vous peur d'y entrer seul ? 9. Il m'a raconté l'histoire d'un homme qui perdit tout ce qu'il avait. 10. Je ne saurais entrer dans une maison dont les portes et les fenêtres sont fermées. 11. Ni lui ni elle ne sera ici demain. 12. Il n'y a pas besoin de prendre de l'argent. J'ai tout ce qu'il (nous) faut. 13. Je n'aime pas la façon dont il me regarde. 14. A qui avez-vous donné ma montre ? J'en ai besoin. 15. Les églises auxquelles nous allons sont les plus intéressantes de la ville. 16. Les vaches que vous regardez ont été déjà vendues. 17. Me rendrez-vous le livre que je vous ai prêté ? 18. De quoi parlent ces deux hommes ? Je ne comprends ni l'un ni l'autre. 19. L'île que j'ai vue a un secret. 20. Que ces hommes sont gras !

Translation VII

Henceforward only one rendering will be given. In the case of difficult phrases the literal translation will be inscribed between brackets *after* the free rendering of the passage concerned.

It must be confessed that, on approaching the basilica of the Sacré Cœur, I experienced a slight disappointment. At first sight the Byzantine style, in which the building is constructed, appeared to me heavy. It was only after a few minutes that I realised the noble proportions and dignity of this edifice, the belfry of which attains a height of more than a hundred metres. It was rather dark inside, but this comparative gloom made me the more sensitive (rendered me by as much more sensitive) to the dazzling beauty of the view of Paris which unfolded itself before my eyes when I came to walk on the terrace before the basilica, from which one enjoys a marvellous outlook. It is true that Montmartre has lost its original character. It is no longer the meeting-place of real artists, who frequent rather the Montparnasse quarter on the left bank of the Seine. The studios of Montmartre have become cabarets or night clubs.

In spite of all, however, Montmartre charmed me, and for more than half an hour I walked the narrow streets, looking at the old houses of this famous mound which dominates the city. At length I was obliged to tear myself away from the contemplation of this delightful view, for it was time to return to the hotel. I referred again to my plan (I made use again of my plan), and took a road which led me to the Place Pigalle. There was an Underground station quite close, but I didn't go in, having made up my mind (having taken the party) to go back by bus. I went up to a stop where several people were waiting already. I saw one of them take one of the numbered tickets which are fixed to a lamp-post. I did the same without knowing why. On the arrival of the bus, however, I understood, for the conductor asked the people who wanted to get on for their numbers, and entry depended on the number one had. It is very practical, especially in the " rush " hours, for one avoids being jostled by people fighting to get a place. But this time I had no luck. The bus was full, and I resigned myself to waiting a few minutes longer.

NOTES. *Plus de.* *Than* coming between *plus* or *moins* and a numeral is rendered by *de* or *d'*. More than ten = *plus de dix* : but, less than you = *moins que vous.*

To ask a person to do something = *demander à une personne de faire quelquechose.*

S'arracher à = to tear oneself away from. One would expect *de* rather than *à*, but many French constructions are derived from Latin, and the Latin prepositions *ad* and *ab* are both rendered in French by *à*. These particular verbs are mostly connected with the idea of taking. To buy from = *acheter à*, to steal from = *voler à*, to borrow from = *emprunter à.*

Se servir de = to make use of. *Je me sers de savon* = I use soap. *Il s'en est servi* = he has used it.

Exercise 21

1. Personne n'a vu Madame une telle. 2. Quelqu'un s'est servi de mon livre. 3. Tout est perdu mais personne n'est tué. 4. N'y a-t-il personne dans la maison ? 5. Il dit qu'il n'a vu personne. 6. Chaque jour je suis obligé d'attendre l'autobus : ce qui me chagrine extrêmement. 7. Chacune de ces dames a tout ce qu'il faut pour la rendre heureuse. 8. Nulle femme n'aime un tel homme. 9. Quiconque arrivera aura beaucoup à faire. 10. Personne n'a pris la plume dont vous vous servez. 11. Plus de cinquante visiteurs sont arrivés à l'hôtel depuis hier. 12. Je lui demanderai de ne pas emprunter l'argent à cette pauvre vieille femme. 13. Nul homme sage ne dépensera tout son argent. 14. Je ne resterai pas ici plus de vingt minutes. 15. Ne lui parlez pas d'une façon si dédaigneuse. 16. La plume dont vous vous êtes servi(s) [1] est la mienne. 17. Quelqu'un ferma la porte de la maison comme je

[1] Agreement of the participle depends on whether *vous* refers to one person or to two or more.

m'en approchais. 18. Je demanderai un billet au receveur.
19. J'ai oublié l'histoire qu'il m'a racontée. 20. Voilà
quelqu'un : mais je ne le connais pas.

Translation VIII

It was in the first-class seats that I managed eventually
to get a place. Having sat down, I got ready to buy my
ticket, without, however, knowing exactly how to set about
it. A very polite gentleman of whom I sought information
(near whom I sought to inform myself) advised me to buy
for the sum of (in consideration of payment of) eight francs
a booklet, from which the conductor would detach as many
tickets as were necessary. "The route is divided into
sections," he added, "and the number of tickets which he
will take from you depends on the length of the journey."
"I want to go as far as the Palais Royal," I told him.
"In that case he will tear off four tickets. If you were in
the second class, he would only need three."

I followed his excellent advice and about twenty minutes
later I arrived at my destination. I was on the point of
returning directly to my hotel when, looking at my wrist-
watch, I noted that it was not yet dinner time. "Suppose
I went and had an appetiser at the Café de la Régence,
close by," I said to myself. "That's an excellent idea, for
it is very pleasant to sit at a little table in the open air and
watch the passers-by."

Many people were already in the act of taking their
drinks, and it was not without difficulty that I found a
small free table. It is needless to say that it was not that
at which Napoleon played chess. The waiter showed me
this celebrated table, but naturally, customers are forbidden
to sit at it. While sipping the Cinzano I had ordered, I
looked at the people strolling about. On recalling later
the details of my visit to Paris, I was convinced that, all
things considered, the hours I spent drinking coffee with
milk or an appetiser outside one of the innumerable cafés

were the most delightful of my stay in the capital. One is, so to speak, in the very heart of Paris.

That evening, within a very short time, I saw all sorts of people go by : solid middle-class families, business men, carpet-sellers, smartly dressed women. I am very fond of the theatre. Sitting on the terrace of a café, one is present at a scene from real life : which is more interesting than any comedy you like (no matter what). In a word, I enjoyed myself enormously, and it was with difficulty that I at length decided to return to the hotel.

Exercise 22

(a) Dix mille (et) un.[1] (b) Trois cent vingt-sept.[2] (c) Dix-huit mille cinq cent quatre. (d) Un million cent un. (e) Quatre cent trente-sept mille, six cent dix. (f) Dix-neuf mille, huit cent quatre-vingt-seize. (g) Quatre millions, huit cent trente-six mille, neuf cent quatre-vingt dix-sept. (h) Soixante et un. (i) Quatre-vingt-dix-huit. (j) Mille. (k) Quatre cents. (l) Cinquante mille. (m) Soixante mille soixante. (n) Soixante et onze mille, cent soixante et onze. (o) Quatre-vingt-trois mille, cent quatre-vingts. (p) Seize mille. (q) Mille trois cent trente et un. (r) Trois cent trente-trois mille, trois cent trente-trois.

1. Cet homme a acheté quatre-vingt-un chevaux et soixante-dix vaches. 2. Cette maison est haute de soixante-cinq pieds. Or Cette maison a 65 pieds de haut. 3. Je suis né en mil neuf cent dix-neuf (or dix-neuf cent dix-neuf). 4. Il y a à Paris plus de trois millions de gens. 5. J'avais quatre cent soixante francs mais j'en ai dépensé trente-neuf. 6. Cette église fut construite en seize cent quarante-trois (mil six cent quarante-trois). 7. Il de-

[1] The et is usually left out, though The Thousand and One Nights is written Les Mille et une Nuits.
[2] Note that hyphens are only used in those parts of a number whose limits fall between 17 and 99, and then only where there is no et.

meura dans cette maison en dix-neuf cent vingt-huit. 8. Deux mille cinq cent soixante soldats ont été tués. 9. En dix-neuf cent vingt et un je n'avais que deux ans. 10. Quarante-trois bateaux ont traversé le fleuve. En voilà un autre !

Translation IX

Before my departure from London I had been told that an admirable means of extending my knowledge of French would be to witness a performance of a good comedy. With us there is no national theatre, although people have been talking about it for a long time. But in Paris you can find several State-aided theatres, of which the best known is the " Comédie Française," whose foundation goes back to the 17th century.

After dinner, therefore, I consulted the newspaper theatre guide to find out what was on that evening at the " Français." It was *Le Malade Imaginaire*. Fortunately I had already read this fine piece by Molière, which justly counts among the masterpieces of the French stage. This comedy was performed for the first time on February 10th, 1673. But it still draws, for it is true to life (a piece lived).

My hotel was only a few paces from the " Comédie Française," and there was still 20 minutes before the rise of the curtain. But I set out at once, for I had not reserved my seat, and there would doubtless be many people. Indeed, I noticed at the theatre entrance a crowd of people, of whom some were in evening dress. On getting to the booking-office, I asked the clerk for a seat in the second circle. " Single one ? " he said. " Right. There is number 67 in the third row. It's a little to one side, but you will see the stage well." " All right, that will suit me (that will make my affair)," I said. " That will be 15 francs (that makes 15 francs), sir. Thank you."

Ticket in hand, I entered the auditorium, and an attendant took me to my place. The theatre was packed. There was not a seat empty in the pit. It was with the liveliest impatience that I awaited the beginning of the play, for I knew well that the parts at the " Comédie Française " are played by the best actors in Paris. At last the three traditional blows were struck. A deep silence fell on the theatre. The curtain rose and the actors came on the stage.

NOTES. *Monsieur.* When used in addressing a person it means *sir.* When used by itself as a noun it means *gentleman. J'ai vu trois messieurs* = I saw three gentlemen. There is a word *gentilhomme,* but it generally means *nobleman* : anyway, it implies good birth.

On en parle depuis longtemps. Note this French construction. If a process began in the past but is not yet completed, the French use the present tense where we use the past—*e.g.* I have been waiting for him for ten minutes —*je l'attends depuis dix minutes* ; or, *il y a dix minutes que je l'attends.* Similarly, French imperfect for English pluperfect. I had been waiting for him for ten minutes —*je l'attendais depuis dix minutes* ; or, *il y avait dix minutes que je l'attendais.* But *Je l'ai attendu dix minutes ce matin*—I waited for him for ten minutes this morning. (But I am not still waiting. The process is entirely in the past.)

Exercise 23

1. Il frappa à la porte de la vieille femme à huit heures du matin. 2. A quelle heure sont-ils partis pour le théâtre ? 3. Il est certain qu'elle arrivera vers les dix heures. 4. Combien de fois vous ai-je demandé de ne pas m'attendre ? 5. Depuis quand attendez-vous l'autobus ? Depuis cinq heures et demie. Je commence à croire qu'il n'arrivera jamais. 6. Il est tout juste quatre heures dix à ma montre. 7. Je ne manquerai pas de vous éveiller à sept heures moins un quart. 8. Ma première maison n'était pas si bonne que ma seconde. 9. Voilà la onzième [1] fois qu'il

[1] Before onze, onzième, huit, huitième, the *e* or *a* of the article is not cut out.

m'a raconté cette histoire.   10. Le train partira à cinq heures vingt-cinq.   11. A midi il se mit à travailler. 12. Sa maison est la huitième à droite.   13. Je lui ai parlé pour la dernière fois.   14. Le train arrivera au Havre à deux heures et quart.   15. Elle est arrivée au théâtre trois minutes avant le lever du rideau.   16. Le déjeuner est à une heure et demie.   17. Je me levais toujours avant huit heures.   18. Le voilà au cinquième rang du parterre. 19. Je serai chez moi à trois heures précises.   20. Nous vous cherchons depuis deux heures.

Translation X

The plot of the *Malade Imaginaire* is simple.   It concerns a citizen who persists in believing that he is afflicted by a serious illness.   He surrounds himself with doctors who lavish their attentions upon him.   But, as you will have guessed, they do not give him free consultations, and Argan—that is the name of the self-styled invalid—wearies at length of paying them large sums.   He therefore decides to marry his daughter to a doctor, in order that, in future, he shall pay less dearly for the remedies which he fancies he needs.   His daughter is in love with a young man, but the father insists that she shall marry a pedantic and grotesque doctor.   He does not, however, succeed in executing his scheme.   The people in whom he trusts betray him, and at last he realises the noble qualities of the girl whose happiness he has all but sacrificed.   It is a most amusing piece, and the actors spoke so clearly that I understood everything.

In most Paris theatres, except the music-halls, the audience are forbidden to smoke.   So in the interval I left my seat to go and smoke a cigarette in the foyer.   Many people did the same.   The interval only lasted ten minutes, but it seemed to me much too long, for I was longing to see the last acts.

At the end of the play the place shook under the applause

of the enthusiastic audience, and I left the theatre a prey
to deep emotion. "That was a performance," I told
myself, "which I shall never forget."

It was close on midnight, but I had no desire to go to
bed. The stars were shining and a light breeze was blowing
as I made my way in the moonlight along the Avenue de
l'Opéra as far as the Café de la Paix. There, as I sipped
my coffee, I began to think of the piece which I had just
seen played (seen to play) in so masterly a manner. At a
neighbouring table two men were talking business. "What
do you think of the financial situation?" "Very bad. It
gets worse every day."

On the other side of me a young couple were talking in
low voices. Evidently they were scarcely worrying about
the artificial inflation of the currency. Neither was I. I
was still under the spell of Molière.

NOTES. *Venais de voir.* Literally " came from seeing."
Therefore the seeing was just finished. Hence we translate
as " I had just seen." So also *Je viens de le rencontrer* = I
have just met him.

S'entourer de = to surround with. Note the difference
between *s'entourer de médecins* and *s'entourer des médecins.*
The second would mean *with the doctors*, the first simply
with doctors.

Marier = to give in marriage or perform the ceremony.
Epouser means to take someone to husband or wife. *Se
marier* = to get married.

Faillir = lit. to fail. *Faire faillite* = to go bankrupt.
But the word also means " nearly to do something," *i.e.*
only just not to. *Il faillit tomber* = he nearly fell.

La plupart = most. Nearly all nouns or adverbs of
quantity require *de* when followed by a noun. *La plupart*
requires *du, de la,* or *des.* So also does *bien,* sometimes
used instead of *beaucoup,* i.e. *beaucoup de fois* or *bien des
fois* = many times.

Penser à. To think about, to have in one's mind. *Je*

pense à lui = I think of him.   *J'y pense* = I think of it.
Penser de = to have an opinion of.   *Que pensez-vous de lui ?* = What do you think of him?

De jour en jour = from day to day.   Similarly *de temps en temps, de plus en plus* (more and more), etc.

Exercise 24(a)

1. The 22nd of December.   2. At Christmas it is not fine.   3. In the month of May it will be fine.   4. He has worked all day.   5. He will work every day.   6. Spring is the most beautiful of the 4 seasons.   7. Francis I gained nothing that time.   8. Charles II liked his pleasures. 9. He will come here every morning.   10. There are 7 days in the week and 4 weeks in a month.   11. I will come back on Christmas Day.   12. Easter week was very sad for him. 13. He gave it me on August 30th, 1937.   14. The soldiers have a holiday on Sundays.   15. In summer we have fruit, but in spring we have beautiful flowers.   16. James II, King of England, lived for a long time in France.   17. We have had a very pleasant evening.   18. It's wet this week. 19. The first of January is commonly called New Year's Day.   20. February is a very dismal month.

Exercise 24(b)

1. Nous nous levons tous les matins à sept heures.   2. Je pense souvent à elle.   3. Je le vois de temps en temps. 4. J'ai failli manquer le train ce matin.   5. Je suis allée chez elle, mais elle venait de sortir.   6. Il vient toujours me voir le lundi.   7. Il fait bien froid ici en hiver.   8. Je viens de dîner avec lui.   9. La plupart des gens ne travaillent pas toute la journée.   10. J'allais chez moi tous les vendredis.   11. Nous partirons pour l'Amérique le vingt et un juillet.   12. Il va se marier avec une veuve.   13. A quoi pensez-vous?   14. Il faillit tomber dans l'eau.   15. Nous allons à Paris tous les deux mois.   16. Louis Quatorze fut roi de France pendant soixante-douze ans.   17. Na-

poléon Premier était l'oncle de Napoléon Trois. 18. Je
vous défends de lui parler. 19. Elle vient de traverser la
rue. 20. Nous sommes entourés de tous côtés.

Exercise 25(a)

1. Drunk, believed, increased, owed, had, read, moved,
been able, known, concealed, seen. 2. That he might
come. 3. That we might beat. 4. That it may be
necessary. 5. He drank. 6. Thou art running. 7. It
was worth. 8. They hold. 9. We shall send. 10. It
will fall due. 11. That he may sleep. (Let him sleep.)
12. What are you doing there? 13. It was necessary.
14. Hated. 15. Flourishing (literally, as a flower flourishes), flourishing (metaphorically, as a city or a person
flourishes.) 16. She has shone. 17. Thou placest. 18.
That he might read. 19. Injured. 20. I follow them.

Exercise 25(b)

1. Aille, ailles, aille; allions, alliez, aillent. 2. Con-
clurai, concluras, conclura; conclurons, conclurez, con-
cluront. 3. Vienne, viennes, vienne; venions, veniez,
viennent. 4. Meurs, meurs, meurt; mourons, mourez,
meurent. 5. Ecrivisse, écrivisses, écrivît; écrivissions,
écrivissiez, écrivissent. 6. Peux (*puis* is sometimes used),
peux, peut; pouvons, pouvez, peuvent. 7. Allasse, al-
lasses, allât; allassions, allassiez, allassent. 8. Doive,
doives, doive; devions, deviez, doivent. 9. Meus, meus,
meut; mouvons, mouvez, meuvent. 10. Dois, dois, doit;
devons, devez, doivent. 11. Fasse, fasses, fasse; fassions,
fassiez, fassent. 12. Vécus, vécus, vécut; vécûmes, vé-
cûtes, vécurent. 13. Verrai, verras, verra; verrons,
verrez, verront. 14. Vois, vois, voit; voyons, voyez,
voient. 15. Croîs, croîs, croît; croissons, croissez, crois-
sent. (Note the absence of the circumflex in plural, because
it is absent in present participle.) 16. Crois, crois, croit;
croyons, croyez, croient. 17. Veux, veux, veut; voulons,

voulez, veulent. 18. Connais, connais, connaît; connaissons, connaissez, connaissent. 19. Envoie, envoies, envoie; envoyions, envoyiez, envoient. 20. Hais, hais, hait; haïssons, haïssez, haïssent. (Note diæresis from present participle.)

Exercise 25(c)

Infinitive Present.	Infinitive Present.
être, *to be.*	avoir, *to have.*

Participle Present.	Participle Present.
étant, *being.*	ayant, *having.*

Participle Past.	Participle Past.
été, *been.*	eu, *had.*

Indicative Present.	Indicative Present.
je suis, *I am.*	j'ai, *I have.*
tu es.	tu as.
il (*or* elle) est.	il (*or* elle) a.
nous sommes.	nous avons.
vous êtes.	vous avez.
ils (*or* elles) sont.	ils (*or* elles) ont.

Imperfect.	Imperfect.
j'étais, *I was.*	j'avais, *I had.*
tu étais.	tu avais.
il (*or* elle) était.	il (*or* elle) avait.
nous étions.	nous avions.
vous étiez.	vous aviez.
ils (*or* elles) étaient.	ils (*or* elles) avaient.

Past Historic.	Past Historic.
je fus, *I was.*	j'eus, *I had.*
tu fus.	tu eus.
il (*or* elle) fut.	il (*or* elle) eut.
nous fûmes.	nous eûmes.
vous fûtes.	vous eûtes.
ils (*or* elles) furent.	ils (*or* elles) eurent.

Future.

je serai, *I shall be.*

tu seras.

il (*or* elle) sera.

nous serons.

vous serez.

ils (*or* elles) seront.

Future.

j'aurai, *I shall have.*

tu auras.

il (*or* elle) aura.

nous aurons.

vous aurez.

ils (*or* elles) auront.

Conditional Present.

je serais, *I would* or *should be.*

tu serais.

il (*or* elle) serait.

nous serions.

vous seriez.

ils (*or* elles) seraient.

Conditional Present.

j'aurais, *I would* or *should have.*

tu aurais.

il (*or* elle) aurait.

nous aurions.

vous auriez.

ils (*or* elles) auraient.

Subjunctive Present.

que je sois, *that I may be* or *that I be.*

que tu sois.

qu'il (*or* qu'elle) soit.

que nous soyons.

que vous soyez.

qu'ils (*or* qu'elles) soient.

Subjunctive Present.

que j'aie, *that I may have* or *that I have.*

que tu aies.

qu'il (*or* qu'elle) ait.

que nous ayons.

que vous ayez.

qu'ils (*or* qu'elles) aient.

Subjunctive Imperfect.

que je fusse, *that I might be.*

que tu fusses.

qu'il (*or* qu'elle) fût.

que nous fussions.

que vous fussiez.

qu'ils (*or* qu'elles) fussent.

Subjunctive Imperfect.

que j'eusse, *that I might have* or *that I had.*

que tu eusses.

qu'il (*or* qu'elle) eût.

que nous eussions.

que vous eussiez.

qu'ils (*or* qu'elles) eussent.

Imperative.

sois, *be (thou).*

soyons, *let us be.*

soyez, *be (you).*

Imperative.

aie, *have (thou).*

ayons, *let us have.*

ayez, *have (you).*

Translation XI

When I woke up next morning, it was raining in torrents. One laughs readily at the English climate, but it isn't, in my opinion, more capricious than the French. I had wanted to spend the second day of my stay in Paris in visiting the left bank. It was evident, however, that I should have to give up this plan, for I should have been soaked to the skin if I had been unwise enough to go for a long walk in such weather, and I had no wish to catch a cold. Fortunately I was in the very middle of Paris. The entrance of the Louvre was only two hundred yards off, and I was anxious to visit (I held to visit) this celebrated museum.

The old palace of the kings of France, which serves now as a museum, is the most enormous building that one can imagine. Very little remains of the original keep, and the central part of the palace dates from the 16th century, for Catherine de Médicis adopted the Louvre as a royal residence and had the Little Gallery constructed, finished later in the reign of Henry IV. Louis XIV took little interest in the Louvre. He established himself at Versailles, 15 kilometres (10 miles) from Paris, and the Louvre, which already housed the French Academy, gave shelter to a crowd of parasites whose hovels encumbered the courtyard. Seized upon during the Revolution by journalists and Stock Exchange speculators, the Louvre was restored during the First Empire and transformed into a Palace of Arts.

During the course of centuries many things of great interest have happened at the Louvre. It was from there that Coligny was coming when he was shot with an arquebus ball by Maurevert two days before the Massacre of St. Bartholomew, which took place on August 24th, 1572.

It was in the former guard-room that Molière played for the first time before the king. He presented a tragedy of Corneille, which had a moderate reception, and a farce of his own composition with which the monarch, then aged twenty, was delighted.

Opposite the Louvre is the Church of St. Germain l'Auxerrois, founded in the 7th century, destroyed by the Normans and rebuilt. It was from the present belfry that the tocsin was rung which gave the signal for the massacre to which I have referred above. It is one of the most interesting churches in Paris.

Exercise 26(a)

1. Let us suppose that he will succeed. 2. It is important that you should keep this secret. 3. It follows from that that you are wrong. 4. He wishes me to come. 5. I was not aware that she was mad. 6. England expects every man to do his duty. 7. I see nothing there to hurt you. 8. I am the only one who knows you. 9. It is the youngest who won a prize. 10. He is the youngest (of all those who have gained prizes) who has gained a prize. 11. I shall do nothing unless you pay me in advance. 12. You have taken my watch in order that you may use it yourself. 13. Is it not fair that we should defend our rights ? 14. Do you think he will come ? 15. I doubt if you will bring this affair to a successful conclusion. 16. Eloquent as that orator is, he is not heeded because he is not respected. 17. Poets must have been very rare in your century. 18. It is possible that she will be late. 19. It is certain that we shall arrive in time. 20. God be praised !

Exercise 26(b)

1. Si deux et deux font quatre, quatre et dix font quatorze. 2. Il ne savait (pas) si elle était morte. 3. Le premier qui entrera dans cette chambre trouvera la montre. 4. Je dois aller chez lui.[1] 5. Il faut que cet homme aille

[1] Note special meanings of *devoir*. *Je dois* = I am to, have to, must. *Je devais* = I was to, had to. *Je devrai* = I shall have to. *Je devrais* = I ought to, I should have to. *J'ai dû* = I (have) had to. *J'aurais dû* = I ought to have. This verb is not as forcible as *falloir* = to be necessary.

G

se coucher. 6. Il se mit à boire pour qu'il oubliât son anxiété. 7. Il travaille quoiqu'il soit las. 8. Est-il évident qu'il ait parlé? 9. Il est évident qu'il a parlé (Note the doubt in 8, the certainty in 9). 10. Il est venu afin de vendre la viande. 11. Qu'il soit puni. 12. Elle venait de cacher l'argent de peur que le voleur n'arrivât. 13. Quoique je sois pauvre je travaillerai jusqu'à ce que je sois riche. 14. Je cherche un homme qui sache le français.[1] 15. Qu'elle reste ici jusqu'à ce que ses amis soient arrivés. 16. Je ne veux pas que vous lui parliez. 17. Selon les journaux, beaucoup de soldats auraient été tués. 18. Quoique nous nous soyons levés de bonne heure nous serons en retard. 19. Est-il possible qu'elle ne soit pas morte? 20. Il fallait que l'homme partît aussitôt pour ne pas manquer le train.

Translation XII

This passage is written in a more colloquial style than the earlier ones :—

On my return to the hotel I asked for my mail, and among the letters which the hall-porter handed me was one bearing a French stamp. The address was written in a hand I knew well. It was the writing of a friend of mine who, some months before, had found a post in a big business house, the head office of which was situated in the Boulevard Haussmann. In this letter he invited me to come and see him the next morning, and begged me to telephone to him as soon as I had received his note.

On entering the hotel telephone box, it was with a certain hesitation that I unhooked the receiver, for it was my first attempt at using a telephone in France.

At first I heard nothing but a terrific crackling, which

[1] *Qui sache le français.* This implies that I am not certain of finding such a person. If the sentence ran : *qui sait le français*, it would mean I was searching for a certain individual who, to my knowledge, spoke French.

gave way to a comparative silence, broken by the operator, who said in a funereal tone : " I am listening."

I glanced at the letter I had just received to verify the number I wanted to ask for.

" Please give me," I said, addressing the invisible girl, " Tait-bout 05-32."

But she remained relentless.

" Kindly repeat the number. Speak nearer the instrument."

Without allowing myself to be disconcerted, I asked for the number again. This time she seemed better pleased with me, but I was not yet at the end of my troubles. The " number engaged " signal sounded, and I had to hang up.

After a few minutes I tried again. This time everything went well, and I asked to be put through to my friend. He came to the telephone at once and, recognising his voice, I gave a sigh of relief.

" Hallo ! Is that you, John ? "

" Yes. Speaking. I had a bit of trouble in getting you, you know. Still, no matter. All's well that ends well. How goes it ? "

" Not too bad. So you got my note ? "

" Yes. Just now. And we shall see one another to-morrow."

" Certainly. Come about eleven. I've heaps of things to tell you. I hope we shall be able to lunch together. And I'll show you the wireless sets we make here. If I remember aright, you're interested in wireless."

" Yes. I think I'm a judge of anything to do with broadcasting."

" Good. But I'm very busy just now and——"

" And I'm disturbing you, eh? All right, old son. Until to-morrow."

NOTES. The formal way of saying " How are you ? " is *Comment vous portez-vous ?* *Comment allez-vous ?* is less stiff and *Comment ça va ?* is more familiar still.

Exercise 27(a)

1. My old (former) teacher has given me something to do. 2. A common soldier is not always a plain (simple) man. 3. He is nothing but a downright scoundrel. 4. King Harold was at once a great man and a tall one. 5. It is a true story. 6. It is a downright story (lie). 7. There is a tiresome story-teller. 8. That is a dark deed. 9. Nero was a cruel emperor. 10. He has made a mistake there. 11. She has sent me a miserable (paltry) present. 12. We have only one bottle full of wine. 13. He has had a new suit made (for himself). 14. The sad boy drank what you left him. 15. He spoke to me of certain affairs in which he is interested. 16. In the depth of winter he always washes with cold water. 17. A great man is sometimes a little man but never a petty one. (Note that *petit* reverses the rule and has its literal meaning when it comes first.) 18. It is the result of pure accident. 19. There is a poor (indifferent) actor who has plenty of money. 20. My dear friend is always complaining of the cost of living.

Exercise 27(b)

1. Ils lui faisaient suivre le long chemin. 2. J'irai voir comment il se porte. 3. Il lui a envoyé un livre cher. 4. Une maison humide n'est pas assez bonne pour moi. (Note that *assez* always comes before the adjective.) 5. Ils lui feront couper du pain. 6. Cet orateur honnête et éloquent parlera pour les soldats français. 7. Je laisserai faire ce qu'elle voudra à la vieille femme. 8. Le savant docteur (*médecin* is confined to medical doctors) a écrit un livre long, important et ennuyeux. 9. Où la faites-vous aller? 10. Il faut faire faire un chapeau pour le garçon. 11. Je vais faire bâtir une maison. 12. Je viendrai aussitôt que j'aurai fini mon travail. (Note the logical use of the future in French when futurity is implied.) 13. Je ferai faire ce que je veux au garçon. 14. Pensez-

vous qu'il essaye de vous tromper? 15. Le roi fit tuer le voleur. 16. Vous devriez aller chez vous. 17. Vous m'avez fait attendre une heure. 18. C'est une affaire qui vous intéressera, j'en suis sûr. (Note that "he is," "she is," "it is," etc. are translated in French by *c'est* before a noun, not by *il est* or *elle est*.) 19. Il faut que vous soyez au théâtre à sept heures. 20. Il a laissé tomber la lettre.

Translation XIII

It is needless to say that my friend gave me a most cordial welcome the next morning, and, for my part, I was delighted to see my old school friend again. In fact for some moments it was a question of which of us talked the most (it was to whom should talk the best). But at last he cut me short.

"That's enough," he said with a smile. "It seems that we both have the gift of the gab (the tongue well hung). At lunch we shall have time to talk. Meanwhile I should like to show you some of the sets I told you about yesterday. They're really magnificent. Look, here is one of our latest models."

He pointed with his forefinger to a six-valve set, adorned with two broad strips of chromium-plated metal with feet to match.

"This set will give you America, and you will get absolutely clear reception. I listened myself to the time signal and the news bulletin broadcast yesterday by the Schenectady station."

"But this set must be pretty dear."

"On the contrary. This set can't be equalled by any other of a price anywhere near it. This model only costs 2,800 francs, or you can get it by instalments for 150 francs a month. It's an absurd price, you know. With this set one can laugh at atmospherics and heterodyning. The Morse which comes in under your favourite station when you're trying to listen to a first-class (choice) programme, that continuous whistling which accompanies the transmissions from certain stations—by using this set you will not have to complain of the nuisances which sometimes disturb a whole wave-band.

" Moreover, look at this control which makes the tuning of the set so easy. Its luminous indicator and indirect lighting allow you to read clearly and exactly the wave-length or the station that you want (the station sought)."

" That's too bad," I said. " Take pity on me, I beg you. You know that I only have a wretched portable at home, and you're making my mouth water, talking like that. Besides, you're wasting your time. To hear you talk, one would think that you're trying to make me buy one of these models. Evidently you think me richer than I am. If you were really nice, you would make me a present of it ! "

" And you're trying to get me sacked (thrown to the door). Come and have lunch, you ass ! "

Exercise 28

1. Quoi ! Répétez-vous ce qu'il a dit ? 2. Il jette toujours ses fardeaux sur moi. 3. Ils mènent les chevaux à l'eau. 4. Il faut que je répète l'histoire que vous venez de me raconter. 5. Il nageait avec ses amis. 6. A quoi pensez-vous ? 7. Qu'est-ce que vous dites ? 8. Qu'en pensez-vous ? 9. Quel homme pourrait le faire ? 10. Il faut oublier ce qui est fait (*or* : ce qu'on a fait). 11. En avançant vers la maison il pensait à ce qu'il fallait dire. 12. Qu'elle répète ce qu'elle a dit. 13. Il n'avait que deux ans mais il commençait à parler. 14. Je vais chez lui pour que je reçoive le cadeau qu'il m'a acheté. 15. Laquelle de ces dames avez-vous vue ce matin ? (Note agreement of past participle because object, *laquelle*, comes before the verb.) 16. De quelles dames est-ce que vous parlez ? 17. Je mangeais des fruits tous les jours. Mais j'y ai renoncé. 18. Je l'emploie depuis six mois (il y a six mois que je l'emploie) : c'est un habile ouvrier. 19. Si je

reçois l'argent que j'attends je vous paierai (payerai) aussitôt. 20. Je ne me fie pas à cet homme-là. Il s'appelait Dupont. Maintenant il s'appelle Simon.

Translation XIV

I fancy I have already said something about the Café de la Régence. Since my first visit I returned there several times, and I ended by wanting to have more extensive information about it. One evening a gentleman, sitting near me, asked me for a light (some fire) for his cigarette and, after handing him my lighter, I took advantage of the opportunity to broach the subject of the Café, asking him to tell me something of its history. He needed no second bidding (he did not make himself prayed). For more than half an hour he talked to me about the Paris cafés, a subject of which he appeared to have a profound knowledge. He was, as the saying is, a walking encyclopædia.

"Do you know," he said to me, "that Jean-Jacques Rousseau frequented the café, and when he appeared there the police were obliged to forbid him to show himself in public places, because his presence attracted a huge crowd. It was Grimm who noted this fact in one of the seventeen volumes of his 'Literary Correspondence.' Nowadays a philosopher passes unnoticed. It needs a film star to make the people gather in crowds.

"But of all the 18th-century cafés," he continued, "the most famous was the Procope, the customers of which consisted mainly of literary men. There also Rousseau was acclaimed. Voltaire went to the Procope sometimes. Once he disguised himself as an ecclesiastic and hid himself in an obscure corner of the café in order to learn the opinion of the frequenters of one of his tragedies which had just had its first performance. Dramatists of to-day would not endure so patiently the judgments of too outspoken critics!

"On the eve of the Revolution literary discussions gradually gave way (yielded the place) to political disputes. The Procope was infested with spies, which caused Voltaire to keep away (which was to remove Voltaire). Having spent some months in prison in his youth, he had no desire to find himself arrested again."

" And does the Procope still exist ? "

My companion shook his head.

"No. Under the Second Empire gas-light had been installed, but the younger generation preferred newer and more noisy cafés. It lost its vogue. Then "—he shrugged his shoulders—" that is another bit of old Paris which has disappeared."

He emptied his glass, gave me a friendly little nod and went out.

NOTES. *Je crois avoir dit déjà.* Note this use of the infinitive after *croire*, possible only when the subject of the second verb is the same as that of the tense *croire*. I think I saw him = *Je crois l'avoir vu.* I think he saw me = *Je crois qu'il m'a vu.*

J'ai fini par. By followed by an English participle is seldom translated in French by *par. En* is the usual preposition except with verbs of beginning or ending—e.g. *En forgeant, on devient forgeron* = by forging one becomes a smith, *i.e.* practice makes perfect. But : He began by laughing = *il commença par rire.*

Après. Note perfect, not present infinitive after *après.*

Sujet. The article in French is frequently left out in apposition. Charles (the) king of England. *Charles, Roi d'Angleterre.*

Exercise 29

1. Il le fait mal. 2. Ils étaient déjà près de la maison paternelle (de la maison de leur père—but the other rendering is better). 3. Vous le ferez vite au moins. 4. Il me demanda aussitôt de l'accompagner. 5. Après avoir arrêté un voleur l'agent de police se mit aussitôt à chercher

l'autre (or, better, à la recherche de l'autre). 6. J'ai marché quelquefois jusqu'à Paris. 7. Ayant perdu beaucoup d'argent il commença par vendre sa maison. 8. Je crois avoir déjà lu ce livre. 9. Je crois qu'elle nous a vus. 10. Je le vois de temps en temps, mais il va souvent à Londres. 11. Il se dirigeait lentement vers le château. 12. Vous me posez toujours des questions ridicules. 13. Il portait un chapeau jaunâtre. 14. Montez vite dans le train, de peur qu'il ne parte. 15. Je voudrais beaucoup y aller en bateau. 16. Combien de fois vous ai-je dit de ne pas marcher si vite? 17. Je devrai couper demain le poirier (or, Demain je devrai, etc.). 18. Je profiterai du beau temps pour venir vous voir. 19. Si vous vous déguisez en ouvrier, personne ne vous reconnaîtra. 20. Il secoua tristement la [1] tête.

Translation XV

On coming down to the lounge the next morning, I stopped for a moment at the hotel office.

" I'm short of French money," I said to the clerk; " will you change £5 for me into French money? "

" Certainly, sir. To-day's rate of exchange is 146 francs. I charge one franc commission, which makes 145. Here, then, is one 500-franc note, two 100-franc notes, a 20-franc piece and one of 5 francs."

" Thank you. But couldn't you give me some small change? I should be very glad of it, for I have some quite small purchases to make."

" Very well. I will take back the 20-franc piece and here are 10 two-franc pieces. Does that suit you? "

" Perfectly. And I also want some stamps. Would you please give me (be so kind as to give me) two one-franc-fifty stamps? "

[1] When there is no ambiguity the definite article is generally used in French instead of the possessive, with parts of the body, etc.

" Unfortunately I have absolutely none left, sir. But I can give you six fifty-centime stamps. That will do you equally well, won't it ? "

" Thanks very much."

" Is that all, sir ? "

" Yes. Oh, by the way, I want some cigarettes. Would you be good enough to tell me if there is a tobacconist near here ? "

" Certainly, sir. There's one two minutes from the hotel. You have only to turn to the left as you go out, and you will see it opposite."

" Good morning, sir. What can I do for you ? " said the tobacconist politely, as soon as I had crossed the threshold of his shop.

" Do you sell English cigarettes ? "

" Yes, sir. We have all the best brands."

" Good ! Then give me a packet of twenty Gold Flake. What does that cost ? "

" Eight francs seventy-five, sir."

" Heavens ! That's dear. I see that I shall have to get used to smoking French cigarettes."

" You will easily acquire a taste for them, sir. Very good cigarettes are made in France now. Here are some Gitanes. It's a brand I can recommend, and they sell at three francs fifty a packet."

" Very well, I will take two."

" Thank you, sir. And in the way of tobacco——"

" No, thanks. I don't smoke a pipe."

I went next to a shirt-maker's to buy some turn-down soft collars.

" What size collar do you take, sir ? " the assistant asked.

That was an awkward question, and I didn't know how to get out of a difficult position (to draw myself from the predicament).

" I don't know the French measure," I said at length. " But in England I wear 15-inch collars."

" To find the French measure one must divide by two and multiply by five. Let's see "—he made a rapid calculation—" Yes. That gives us 38 centimetres."

" Good! I want white cotton cambric collars."

" Very well, sir. I have exactly what you want. How many do you need? "

" I will take three. That will be enough, seeing that I have to return to London on Saturday."

" And you want nothing else, sir? "

" No, thanks. I have all I require."

NOTES. *Veuillez.* The imperative of *vouloir.* More polite and formal than *voulez-vous ?*=will you? Remember not to use the future of a verb when "will" has no idea of futurity, but merely expresses willingness—*e.g.* Will you have some more tea? = *Voulez-vous* (not *aurez-vous) encore du thé ?*

N'est-ce pas ? A most useful expression. Meaning, literally, *is it not so?*, it can be used when in English we put: *isn't he ? wasn't it ? don't they ?* etc.

Dès que j'eus franchi. After *dès que* and *aussitôt que* (as soon as) and *quand* and *lorsque* (when) the past anterior is used instead of the pluperfect in French. Also after *après que*—e.g. *J'étais allé* = I had gone; but *Quand je fus allé* = when I had gone. *Il avait vu* = he had seen; but *dès qu'il m'eut vu*=as soon as he had seen me.

Exercise 30(a)

27 PATERNOSTER ROW,
                          LONDRES, *le 14 mars,* 1937.

MESSRS. JARGEAU ET CIE.

MESSIEURS,

J'espère que vous avez reçu le livre que je vous ai envoyé samedi. J'ai quelques boîtes chez moi que je puis vous donner afin que vous me renvoyiez les autres. Quelques doutes que vous ayez je vous assure qu'on vous payera l'argent quand vous le demanderez. C'est mon père qui l'a promis, et quelque fâché qu'il soit il ne manquera pas de payer.

> Agréez, messieurs, mes salutations sincères,
> JOHN SMITH.

NOTE. *Cie* is the contraction for *compagnie* = company. Save in the case of a place so well known as London (Londres), the English form of the name of a town should be used, so that a foreigner, in replying, should copy the address just as it stands.

Exercise 30(b)

1. Quelque habile qu'il soit il ne réussira pas à moins qu'il ne travaille bien. 2. Dès que les soldats furent entrés dans le château ils tuèrent le roi. 3. Il vint nous voir mais nous étions sortis. 4. Quelques lettres qu'il reçoive il les montre à son frère. 5. Quand il eut vendu son automobile il en acheta une autre. 6. Il a perdu tout son argent, n'est-ce pas? Oui, il a fait faillite. 7. Je l'ai vu il y a quelque temps. 8. Voulez-vous me couper du pain, s'il vous plaît? 9. Veuillez ouvrir la fenêtre. Il fait très chaud. 10. Qu'est-ce que vous avez (Qu'avez-vous) en fait de fruits ce matin?

Translation XVI

Paris is so full of interest that I could scarcely make up my mind to leave the city for a few hours in order to visit the surroundings. But before my departure from London, my former French master had begged me not to fail to make an excursion to Versailles. I had promised to do what he asked me, and I didn't want to break my word to him. Besides, after visiting this sumptuous palace I understood why he was anxious that I should go there. For Versailles is one of the wonders of the world.

At the beginning of the 17th century Versailles was only

a small village. In 1624 Louis XIII, a great lover of hunting, had built for himself on the summit of the mound dominating the village an unpretentious castle of stone and brick. His successor, who felt ill at ease in the Louvre, thought of transferring the seat of the court and the government to Versailles. He commissioned the best architects in the kingdom to refashion and embellish the original building, and the total expenses of the work amounted to more than 60 million livres,[1] or about £20,000,000.

Under Louis XIV, whose reign lasted seventy-two years, the castle of Versailles was at the zenith of its glory. But the great days passed.

In 1789 the mob invaded the castle, massacred the guards and brought back the king, Louis XVI, the queen, Marie Antoinette, and their children to Paris. This event marked the close of the old régime.

During the war of 1870 the Germans made Versailles the centre of their operations against Paris, and it was in the Hall of Mirrors that King William was proclaimed Emperor of Germany. In this same gallery was signed, forty-eight years later, the Treaty of Versailles, which restored to France the provinces lost in 1871.

I tried to get to know the history of the castle, by consulting my guide-book before taking the tram which does the journey between Paris and Versailles. But the castle is too big for one to be able, at a single visit, to form a good idea of its splendour. I am longing to go there again. Unfortunately it's not possible, for my stay in Paris is drawing to its close.

[1] Not the pound sterling, but an old French coin, now obsolete. Note that *sterling* does not take an *s* in the plural.

Exercise 31(a)

HÔTEL DE L'UNIVERS,
PLACE DU PALAIS ROYAL,
PARIS, *le* 15 *septembre*, 1937.

MON CHER EDOUARD,

Avant de traverser la Manche j'avais promis de vous mettre au courant de tout ce qui m'arriverait pendant mon séjour à Paris. Je ne sais que trop bien que j'ai manqué de parole, car je serai de retour samedi à Londres et voici la première lettre que je vous adresse. Cependant je vous prie de ne pas me tenir rigueur de ma négligence. J'ai été tellement occupé dès le moment de mon arrivée que c'est à peine si j'ai eu le temps d'écrire à mon père et à ma mère.

Bien à regret j'ai passé ce matin chez l'Agence Cook pour réserver ma place dans le train qui part tous les jours à midi de la Gare du Nord. J'espère que j'aurai une belle traversée, car je n'ai pas le pied marin. Je vous donnerai un coup de téléphone samedi soir vers les huit heures. Vous pouvez compter là-dessus, car il me tarde de vous revoir. A propos, j'ai déjeuné avant hier avec Pierre. Il m'a prié de vous dire bien des choses de sa part.

Eh bien, en voilà assez de

Votre ami bien dévoué
JEAN.

Exercise 31(b)

1. Ne lui prêtez pas ces livres. Il ne vous les rendra jamais. 2. Je n'aime pas ce livre-là. J'espère que vous n'en parlerez plus. 3. Allez-vous-en, si vous ne voulez pas qu'on vous tue. 4. Ne le lui donnez pas, donnez-le-moi. 5. Vous dites qu'il n'est pas allé à la gare, mais je l'y ai vu moi-même (better : *de mes propres yeux*—with my own eyes). 6. Il a beaucoup d'argent, mais il ne m'en donne jamais. 7. Cette affaire est ennuyeuse : n'y pensons plus.

8. Si j'avais su que vous aviez perdu votre montre je ne vous l'aurais jamais demandée. 9. Ce garçon cherche mon père depuis une heure. Menez-le-lui. 10. Si vous n'avez pas de montre, je vous en achèterai une.

Translation of Passage on p. 142

It was necessary to follow this painful way to break branches and to gather in them the fire which my hands caused to spring from (the) pebbles. From the snows, with which winter whitened that shore, I painfully pressed out a dreary draught. Finally that cave and my deadly bow and fire, the kindly preserver of life, have at least alleviated the wants that I endure, but nothing has been able to cure my lamentable wound.

Translation XVII

The day fixed for my departure arrived. Having had breakfast, I went to have a last little walk through the streets of the quarter. Going along the Rue de Rivoli, I looked anxiously at the trees in the Tuileries gardens. Not a branch was stirring, and I heaved a sigh of relief. The sea would be calm. I went as far as the Place de la Concorde, but time was passing quickly, and I soon had to retrace my steps. I paid the bill, and the porter had my luggage brought down while the page-boy went to look for a taxi.

Twenty minutes later I got out at the Gare du Nord. The train started on the stroke of 12, and at ten minutes to five I disembarked at Dover.

I was thirsty. There were still a few minutes before the express started, so I went to the station buffet.

" What ! Beer ? At this hour ? " said the attendant in a reproachful tone.

" Ah, I beg your pardon," I said. " I was thinking I was still in France. But I see clearly now that I am in my native country ! "

Moral

We do not complain at having many children when they are all handsome, well-made, big and of prepossessing exterior; but if one of them is weak we say nothing, we despise him, we ridicule him, we attack him; sometimes, however, it is this little urchin who will make the fortune of the whole family.

LIST OF THE MORE COMMON IRREGULAR VERBS

	Pres. Part.	Past Part.	Pres. Ind.	Preterite	Future	Pres. Subj.
H						
absoudre = to absolve	absolvant	absous (m.) absoute (f.)	j'absous	—	—	—
abstraire = to abstract	See *traire*					
acquérir = to acquire	acquérant	acquis	j'acquiers acquérant	j'acquis	acquerrai	j'acquière acquièrent
aller = to go [s'en aller = to go away]	allant	allé	je vais | allons vas | allez va | vont	j'allai	irai	aille, aillent
assaillir = to assault	assaillant	assailli	j'assaille	j'assaillis	—	—
asseoir = to set (s'asseoir = to sit down)	asseyant	assis	j'assieds | asseyons assied | asseyent	j'assis	assiérai *or* asseoirai	asseie, asseyent
avoir = to have	ayant	eu	j'ai	j'eus	—	aie aient
battre = to beat	battant	battu	je bats	je battis	—	batte
boire = to drink	buvant	bu	je bois ils boivent	je bus	—	boive, boivent
bouillir = to boil	bouillant	bouilli	je bous	je bouillis	—	—
clore = to close	—	clos	je clos	—	—	—
conclure = to conclude	concluant	conclu	je conclus	je conclus	—	—
confire = to pickle	confisant	confit	je confis	je confis	—	—
connaître = to know	connaissant	connu	je connais	je connus	—	—
coudre = to sew	cousant	cousu	je couds	je cousis	—	—
courir = to run	courant	couru	je cours	je courus	courrai	coure
croire = to believe	croyant	cru	je crois	je crus	—	—
croître = to increase	croissant	crû	je crois	je crûs	—	—
cueillir = to gather	cueillant	cueilli	je cueille	je cueillis	—	—

	Pres. Part.	Past Part.	Pres. Ind.	Preterite.	Future.	Pres. Subj.
devoir = to owe	devant	dû	je dois / doivent	je dus	devrai	doive / doivent
dire = to say }	disant	dit	je dis	je dis	dirai	—
maudire = to curse }	dissant	—	—	—	—	—
dormir = to sleep	dormant	dormi	je dors	je dormis	—	—
écrire = to write	écrivant	écrit	j'écris	j'écrivis	—	—
échoir = to fall due, expire	échéant	échu	il échoit	il échut	il écherra	échoie
envoyer = to send	envoyant	envoyé	j'envoie / envoyons	j'envoyai	enverrai	envoie / envoient
être = to be	étant	été	je suis	je fus	serai	sois / so-yons, -yez, -ient
faire = to make or do	faisant	fait	je fais faisons faites font	je fis	ferai	fasse
faillir = to fail	faillant	failli	je faux	je faillis	faudrai	—
falloir = to be necessary	—	fallu	il faut	il fallut	il faudra	qu'il faille
fleurir = to flourish	fleurissant } florissant }	fleuri	je fleuris	je fleuris	—	—
frire = to fry	—	frit	je fris	—	—	fuie
fuir = to flee	fuyant	fui	je fuis	je fuis	—	fuie / fuient
haïr = to hate	haïssant	haï	je hais	je hais	—	—
joindre = to join	joignant	joint	je joins	je joignis	—	—
lire = to read	lisant	lu	je lis	je lus	—	—
luire = to shine	luisant	lui	je luis	—	—	—
mettre = to put	mettant	mis	je mets	je mis	—	—
mourir = to die	mourant	mort	je meurs / meurent	je mourus	mourrai	meure / meurent
mouvoir = to move	mouvant	mû	je meus / meuvent	je mus	mouvrai	meuve / meuvent

Infinitive	Pres. participle	Past participle	Present	Past historic	Future	Subjunctive
moudre = to grind	moulant	moulu	je mouds	je moulus	—	—
naître = to be born	naissant	né	je nais	je naquis	—	—
nuire = to injure	nuisant	nui	je nuis	je nuisis	—	—
ouïr = to hear	—	ouï	j'ois oyons oyez oient	j'ouïs	oirai	—
ouvrir = to open	ouvrant	ouvert	j'ouvre	j'ouvris	—	—
paître = to graze	paissant	pu	je pais	—	—	—
paraître = to appear	paraissant	paru	je parais	je parus	—	—
partir = to set out	partant	parti	je pars	je partis	—	—
plaire = to please	plaisant	plu	je plais	je plus	—	—
pleuvoir = to rain	pleuvant	plu	il pleut	il plut	il pleuvra	qu'il pleuve
poindre = to dawn	—	—	il point	—	il poindra	—
pourvoir = to provide	pourvoyant	pourvu	je pourvois	je pourvus	—	pourvoie pourvoient
pouvoir = to be able	pouvant	pu	je puis peux peut peuvent	je pus	pourrai	puisse puissions puissiez puissent
prendre = to take	prenant	pris	je prends	je pris	—	prenne, prennent
réduire = to reduce	réduisant	réduit	je réduis	je réduisis	—	—
résoudre = to resolve	résolvant	résolu (résous)	je résous	je résolus	—	—
rire = to laugh	riant	ri	je ris	je ris	—	—
rompre = to break	rompant	rompu	je romps rompt	je rompis	—	—
savoir = to know	sachant	su	je sais savons savez savent	je sus	saurai	—

	Pres. Part.	Past Part.	Pres. Ind.	Preterite.	Future.	Pres. Subj.
sentir = to feel	sentant	senti	je sens	je sentis	—	—
seoir = to become, to befit	seyant	—	il sied / ils siéent	—	il siéra / ils siéront	qu'il siée / qu'ils siéent
servir = to serve	servant	servi	je sers	je servis		
sortir = to go out	sortant	sorti	je sors	je sortis		
suffire = to suffice	suffisant	suffi	je suffis	je suffis		
suivre = to follow	suivant	suivi	je suis	je suivis		
taire = to conceal	taisant	tu	je tais	je tus		
tenir = to hold	tenant	tenu	je tiens / tiennent	je tins	tiendrai	tienne / tiennent
traire = to milk	trayant	trait	je trais	—	—	traie / traient
valoir = to be worth	valant	valu	je vaux	je valus	vaudrai	vaille / vaillent
vaincre = to conquer	vainquant	vaincu	je vaincs	je vainquis		—
venir = to come	venant	venu	je viens	je vins	viendrai	vienne / viennent
vêtir = to clothe	vêtant	vêtu	je vêts	je vêtis		
vivre = to live	vivant	vécu	je vis	je vécus		—
voir = to see	voyant	vu	je vois	je vis	verrai	voie / voient
vouloir = to wish	voulant	voulu	je veux / veulent	je voulus	voudrai	veuille / veuillent

VOCABULARY

VOCABULARY

A.

à	.	.	.	to, at.
d'abord	.	.	.	at first.
aborder	.	.	.	to broach.
s'absenter	.	.	.	to absent oneself.
absolument	.	.	.	absolutely.
accaparer	.	.	.	to seize upon, monopolise.
acclamer	.	.	.	to acclaim.
accompagner	.	.	.	to accompany.
accomplir	.	.	.	to accomplish, execute.
accoutumer	.	.	.	to accustom (s'accoutumer à = to get used to).
accroissement, *m.*	.	.	.	inflation.
accueil, *m.*	.	.	.	welcome, reception.
acheter	.	.	.	to buy.
achever	.	.	.	to finish, complete.
acte, *m.*	.	.	.	act.
actuel	.	.	.	present.
adresse, *f.*	.	.	.	address, skill.
affaire, *f.*	.	.	.	affair, matter (affaires = business).
affluence, *f.*	.	.	.	multitude, plenty.
agent de police, *m.*	.	.	.	policeman.
agir	.	.	.	to act (s'agir de = to be a question of).
agréable	.	.	.	nice, pleasant.
ailleurs	.	.	.	elsewhere (d'ailleurs = besides).
aimer	.	.	.	to love, like.
aîné	.	.	.	elder.
ainsi	.	.	.	thus, so.
air, *m.*	.	.	.	air.
aise	.	.	.	glad.
aise, *f.*	.	.	.	ease, comfort.
ajouter	.	.	.	to add.
Allemagne	.	.	.	Germany.
allemand	.	.	.	German.
aller	.	.	.	to go (s'en aller = to go away).
allumer	.	.	.	to light.

allusion, *f.*	. . .	allusion, reference.
alouette, *f.*	. . .	lark.
amateur, *m.*	. . .	lover, enthusiast.
ami, *m.*	. . .	friend.
amical	. . .	friendly.
amoureux	. . .	amorous, in love.
ample	. . .	ample.
amusant	. . .	amusing.
amuser	. . .	to amuse (s'amuser = to amuse, enjoy oneself).
an, *m.*	. . .	year.
anglais	. . .	English.
Angleterre	. . .	England.
animal, *m.*	. . .	animal.
animation, *f.*	. . .	animation, liveliness.
animé	. . .	animated, lively.
année, *f.*	. . .	year.
apercevoir	. . .	to perceive.
apéritif, *m.*	. . .	appetiser.
apogée, *m.*	. . .	apogee, zenith.
appareil, *m.*	. . .	apparatus, instrument.
appeler	. . .	to call (s'appeler = to call oneself, be called).
applaudissement, *m.*	.	applause.
approcher	. . .	to approach, put near (s'approcher de = to approach).
approfondi	. . .	profound.
après	. . .	after (prep.) (après que = after (conj.)).
après-midi, *m.* or *f.*	.	afternoon.
argent, *m.*	. . .	money, silver.
armée, *f.*	. . .	army.
arquebuser	. . .	to shoot with an arquebus.
arracher	. . .	to tear (s'arracher à = to tear oneself from).
arrêt, *m.*	. . .	stopping-place.
arrêter	. . .	to arrest (s'arrêter = to stop).
arrivée, *f.*	. . .	arrival.
arriver	. . .	to arrive, happen.
arrondissement, *m.*	.	administrative area of Paris, quarter.
art, *m.*	. . .	art.
article, *m.*	. . .	article.
ascenseur, *m.*	. . .	lift.
asile, *m.*	. . .	shelter.
aspect, *m.*	. . .	aspect, appearance.
s'asseoir	. . .	to sit down (assis = seated, sitting).

assez	enough, sufficient.
assistance, *f.* . .	audience.
assister (à) . .	to be present (at).
s'assombrir . .	to grow dark.
assorti . . .	matched.
atelier, *m.* . .	studio.
atteindre . .	to attain, afflict.
attendre . .	to wait (for) (en attendant = meanwhile).
attirer . . .	to attract.
attrouper . .	to collect, mass.
aucun . . .	any (obsolete) (ne . . . aucun = no one, none, no).
au-dessous . .	below.
au-dessus . .	above.
audition, *f.* . .	audition, reception.
augmenter . .	to increase, enlarge.
aujourd'hui . .	to-day.
auparavant . .	before.
auprès . . .	near.
aussi . . .	also, so as (aussi . . . que = as . . . as).
aussitôt . . .	at once (aussitôt que = as soon as).
autant . . .	as much, as many.
autobus, *m.* . .	motor-bus, bus.
automobile, *f.* .	motor-car, car.
autre . . .	other.
s'avancer . .	to advance.
avant . . .	before (of time).
avantage, *m.* . .	advantage.
avec . . .	with.
avenir, *m.* . .	future.
avion, *m.* . .	aeroplane.
avis, *m.* . .	opinion, notice.
avoir . . .	to have (avoir lieu = to take place).
avouer . . .	to admit, confess.

B.

bagages, *m. pl.* .	luggage. (In singular the word also means a writer's literary output).
bande, *f.* . .	band, wave-band (wireless).
baraque, *f.* . .	booth, stall.
barre, *f.* . .	bar.
barrière, *f.* . .	barrier.
bas . . .	low.

bas, *m.*	.	stocking.
basilique, *f.*	.	basilica.
bateau, *m.*	.	boat.
bâtir	.	to build.
battre	.	to beat (se battre = to fight).
beaucoup	.	much, many, very much.
besoin, *m.*	.	need (avoir besoin de = to have need of, need).
beurre, *m.*	.	butter.
billet, *m.*	.	ticket.
bien	.	well, very, indeed.
bientôt	.	soon.
bière, *f.*	.	beer.
blanc	.	white.
se blottir	.	to crouch, hide.
boire	.	to drink (boire à petits coups = to sip).
bois, *m.*	.	wood.
boîte, *f.*	.	box (boîte de nuit = night-club, " dive ").
bondé	.	packed.
bonheur, *m.*	.	happiness.
bonté, *f.*	.	goodness, kindness.
bouche, *f.*	.	mouth.
boulevard, *m.*	.	boulevard.
bourgeois	.	middle-class.
boursier, *m.*	.	Stock Exchange speculator.
bousculer	.	to jostle.
bout, *m.*	.	end (être à bout de = to be at the end of).
bouteille, *f.*	.	bottle.
bref	.	brief (adj.), in a word (adverb).
briller	.	to shine.
brique, *f.*	.	brick.
briquet, *m.*	.	lighter.
brise, *f.*	.	breeze.
bruyant	.	noisy.
bulletin, *m.*	.	bulletin, list.
bureau, *m.*	.	office.
butte, *f.*	.	hill, mound.
byzantin	.	Byzantine.

C.

ça et là	.	here and there.
cabaret, *m.*	.	cabaret, tavern.
cabine, *f.*	.	cabin, booth.

cacher	.	.	.	to hide (se cacher = to hide oneself).
cadeau, *m.*	.	.	.	present.
café, *m.*	.	.	.	café, coffee.
calcul, *m.*	.	.	.	calculation.
campagne, *f.*	.	.	.	country (as opposed to town), campaign.
capitale, *f.*	.	.	.	capital.
capricieux	.	.	.	capricious.
capter	.	.	.	to pick up, get (wireless).
car	.	.	.	for (conj.).
caractère, *m.*	.	.	.	character.
carnet, *m.*	.	.	.	booklet.
cas, *m.*	.	.	.	case.
casser	.	.	.	to break.
causer	.	.	.	to chat.
céder	.	.	.	to yield.
cent	.	.	.	hundred.
centime, *m.*	.	.	.	centime.
central	.	.	.	central.
centre, *m.*	.	.	.	centre.
cependant	.	.	.	however, meanwhile.
cesser (de)	.	.	.	to cease (to).
chagriner	.	.	.	to annoy, vex.
chaise, *f.*	.	.	.	chair.
chambre, *f.*	.	.	.	room, bedroom.
champ, *m.*	.	.	.	field.
chance, *f.*	.	.	.	luck.
change, *m.*	.	.	.	exchange.
changer	.	.	.	to change (changer de place = to change one's place).
chanter	.	.	.	to sing.
chapeau, *m.*	.	.	.	hat.
charger	.	.	.	to charge, load.
charme, *m.*	.	.	.	charm, spell.
chasse, *f.*	.	.	.	hunting.
chasseur, *m.*	.	.	.	hunter, page-boy.
chat, *m.*	.	.	.	cat.
château, *m.*	.	.	.	castle.
chauffage, *m.*	.	.	.	heating.
chaussette, *f.*	.	.	.	sock.
chef d'œuvre, *m.*	.	.	.	masterpiece.
chemin, *m.*	.	.	.	way, road.
chemisier, *m.*	.	.	.	shirt-maker.
cher	.	.	.	dear, expensive.
chercher	.	.	.	to look for, seek.
cheval, *m.*	.	.	.	horse.
chez	.	.	.	at the house of.

chien, *m.*	. . .	dog.
choisir	. . .	to choose.
choix, *m.*	. . .	choice.
chose, *f.*	. . .	thing.
ci-dessus	. . .	here above, above.
ciel, *m.*	. . .	sky, heaven.
cigarette, *f.*	. . .	cigarette.
circulation, *f.*	. . .	circulation (circulation fiduciaire = paper money).
clair de lune, *m.*	. .	moonlight.
clairement	. . .	clearly, distinctly.
classe, *f.*	. . .	class.
client, *m.*	. . .	customer, client.
clientèle, *f.*	. . .	clientèle, custom.
climat, *m.*	. . .	climate.
clocher, *m.*	. . .	belfry.
clouté	. . .	nailed, studded.
cœur, *m.*	. . .	heart.
coin, *m.*	. . .	corner.
colonne, *f.*	. . .	column.
combien	. . .	how much, how many.
comédie, *f.*	. . .	comedy.
commander	. . .	to order.
comme	. . .	as, how.
comment	. . .	how.
commerce, *m.*	. . .	business, trade.
commission, *f.*	. . .	commission.
communément.	. .	commonly, ordinarily.
compagnon, *m.*	. .	companion.
compliqué	. . .	complicated, involved.
comporter	. . .	to entail.
se composer (de)	. .	to consist (of).
comprendre	. . .	to understand, include.
compter	. . .	to count.
concierge, *m.*	. . .	hall-porter.
conduire	. . .	to lead, conduct.
confort, *m.*	. . .	comfort.
connaissance, *f.*	. .	knowledge, acquaintance.
connaître	. . .	to know (se connaître en = to be a judge of).
conseil, *m.*	. . .	advice.
conseiller	. . .	to advise.
consister (en)	. . .	to consist (of).
consommateur, *m.*	.	consumer, customer.
constater	. . .	to note.
construire	. . .	to construct.
construction, *f.*	. .	building.

consultation, *f.*	. .	consultation.
consulter	. .	to consult.
content	. .	content, satisfied.
(au) contraire	. .	(on the) contrary.
contrôle, *m.*	. .	control.
convaincre	. .	to convince.
convenir	. .	to suit.
correspondant	. .	connecting.
côté, *m.*	. .	side.
côte, *f.*	. .	coast.
se coucher	. .	to go to bed.
coup, *m.*	. .	blow (coup d'œil = glance).
couper	. .	to cut.
cour, *f.*	. .	court, courtyard.
courir	. .	to run.
courrier, *m.*	. .	letters, mail.
cours, *m.*	. .	course, rate.
court	. .	short (être à court de = to be short of).
cousin, *m.*	. .	cousin.
couteau, *m.*	. .	knife.
coûter	. .	to cost.
(à) crédit	. .	(on) credit.
crème, *f.*	. .	cream.
critique, *m.*	. .	critic.
crouler	. .	to shake, totter.

D.

dame, *f.*	. .	lady.
dater	. .	to date.
débarquer	. .	to disembark.
débit, *m.*	. .	shop (tobacconist's, etc.).
déception, *f.*	. .	disappointment.
déchirer	. .	to tear.
décider (de), se decider (à)		to decide to.
déconcerter	. .	to disconcert.
décrocher	. .	to unhook.
dédaigneux	. .	scornful.
défendre	. .	to forbid, defend.
se déguiser (en)	. .	to disguise oneself (as).
déguster	. .	to savour, sip.
dehors	. .	outside.
déjeuner, *m.*	. .	lunch.
déjeuner	. .	to have lunch.
délicieux	. .	delicious, delightful.
demain	. .	to-morrow.

demander	. . .	to ask (for).
demeurer	. . .	to live, dwell.
demoiselle, *f.*	. .	girl, damsel.
dent, *f.*	. . .	tooth.
départ, *m.*	. .	departure.
dépasser	. . .	to pass.
dépendre (de)	. .	to depend (on).
dépenser	. . .	to spend (money).
dépense, *f.*	. .	expense.
déplaire	. . .	to displease.
depuis	. . .	since.
déranger	. . .	to disturb.
dérisoire	. . .	absurd.
dernier	. . .	last.
se dérouler	. .	to unroll.
dès	. . .	from (since) (dès que = as soon as).
descendre	. .	to descend, bring down.
désirer	. . .	to desire, want.
dessein, *m.*	. .	design, plan.
dessous (en—de)	.	below, under.
détacher	. . .	to detach, tear off.
détail, *m.*	. .	detail.
détruire	. . .	to destroy.
devant	. . .	before, in front of (of position).
devenir	. . .	to become.
deviner	. . .	to guess.
devoir	. . .	to owe, have to.
devoir, *m.*	. .	duty.
difficile	. .	difficult.
difficulté, *f.*	. .	difficulty.
diffusion, *f.*	. .	broadcast(ing).
dire	. . .	to say.
diriger	. . .	to direct (se diriger = to make one's way).
disparaître	. .	to disappear.
se disposer (à)	. .	to get ready (to).
diviser	. . .	to divide.
dizaine, *f.*	. .	ten, about ten.
dominer	. . .	to dominate.
donjon, *m.*	. .	keep.
donner	. . .	to give.
doucement	. . .	gently, softly.
doute, *m.*	. . .	doubt.
douzaine, *f.*	. .	dozen.
dramaturge, *m.*	. .	dramatist.
se dresser	. . .	to stand.
droit, *m.*	. . .	right.

droit	. . . .	right (adj.).
drôle	. . . .	funny, comic.
durer	. . . .	to last.

E.

eau, *f.* . . .	water.
éblouir	. . .	to dazzle.
échecs, *m. pl.*	. .	chess.
éclairage, *m.*	. .	lighting.
éclairé	. . .	lighted.
école, *f.* . .	school.
économie, *f.*	. .	economy.
écouter	. . .	to listen (to).
écrire	. . .	to write.
écriture, *f.* .	.	writing.
écureuil, *m.* .	.	squirrel.
édifice, *m.* .	.	building.
effet, *m.* . .	effect (en effet = indeed).
s'efforcer (de)	.	to endeavour (to).
également	. .	equally.
égaler . . .	to equal.
s'égarer . .	.	to lose one's way.
église, *f.* . .	church.
élégant	. . .	elegant, fashionable.
s'élever . .	.	to amount.
éloigner	. . .	to remove.
embellir	. . .	to beautify, embellish.
émission, *f.* .	.	broadcast, transmission.
empereur, *m.*	.	emperor.
empirer	. . .	to grow worse.
emplette, *f.* .	.	purchase.
emploi, *m.* .	.	post, employment.
employé. *m.*	.	employee.
employer	. .	to employ, use.
emprunter	. .	to borrow.
encolure, *f.* .	.	size in collars.
encombrer	. .	to encumber, clutter.
encore	. . .	still, yet, again.
encre, *f.* . .	ink.
endroit, *m.* .	.	place.
enfant, *m.* or *f.*	.	child.
enfin	. . . .	at last.
s'ennuyer	. .	to be bored.
s'enrhumer	. .	to catch a cold.
s'enrichir	. .	to grow rich.
enseigne, *f.* .	.	sign.

ensemble	.	.	together.
entendre	.	.	to hear.
enthousiasmé	.	.	enthusiastic.
entourer	.	.	to surround.
entr'acte, *m.*	.	.	interval.
entrée, *f.*	.	.	entrance.
entrer (dans)	.	.	to enter, go (into).
entretenir	.	.	to converse with, talk to.
envahir	.	.	to invade.
envie, *f.*	.	.	desire.
environ	.	.	about.
environs, *m. pl.*	.	.	surroundings.
épaule, *f.*	.	.	shoulder.
époque, *f.*	.	.	epoch, period, time.
éprouver	.	.	to experience.
escalier, *m.*	.	.	stairway.
espérer	.	.	to hope.
espion, *m.*	.	.	spy.
essayer (de)	.	.	to try (to).
est, *m.*	.	.	east.
s'établir	.	.	to settle.
établissement, *m.*	.	.	establishment.
état, *m.*	.	.	state.
étendre	.	.	to stretch, extend.
étoile, *f.*	.	.	star.
étonner	.	.	to astonish.
être	.	.	to be.
étroit	.	.	narrow.
étranger	.	.	foreign (à l'étranger = abroad).
éveiller	.	.	to awake (s'éveiller = to wake up).
événement, *m.*	.	.	event.
évidemment	.	.	evidently.
évident	.	.	evident.
éviter	.	.	to avoid.
exemple, *m.*	.	.	example (par exemple = for instance).
explication, *f.*	.	.	explanation.
expliquer	.	.	to explain.
exposition, *f.*	.	.	exhibition.

F.

fabriquer	.	.	to make, manufacture.
en face	.	.	opposite.
facile	.	.	easy.
facilement	.	.	easily.
façon	.	.	fashion, manner.
faim, *f.*	.	.	hunger (avoir faim = to be hungry).

faire	.	.	.	to make, do.
fait, *m.*	.	.	.	deed, fact (en fait de = in the way of).
falloir	.	.	.	to be necessary.
farce, *f.*	.	.	.	farce.
fardeau, *m.*	.	.	.	burden.
faux-col, *m.*	.	.	.	(detachable) collar.
se féliciter (de)	.	.	.	to congratulate oneself (on).
femme, *f.*	.	.	.	woman.
fenêtre, *f.*	.	.	.	window.
fermer	.	.	.	to shut.
feu, *m.*	.	.	.	fire.
se fier (à)	.	.	.	to trust.
fille, *f.*	.	.	.	daughter, girl.
fils, *m.*	.	.	.	son.
fin, *f.*	.	.	.	end.
finir	.	.	.	to finish.
flâner	.	.	.	to stroll.
flâneur	.	.	.	stroller, loiterer.
flanquer	.	.	.	to throw, chuck.
fleuve, *m.*	.	.	.	river.
foire, *f.*	.	.	.	fair.
fois, *f.*	.	.	.	time.
fondation, *f*	.	.	.	foundation.
fonder	.	.	.	to found.
formidable	.	.	.	formidable, frightful.
fort	.	.	.	strong (c'est trop fort = it's too bad).
foule, *f.*	.	.	.	crowd.
foyer, *m.*	.	.	.	vestibule, foyer.
franc	.	.	.	frank.
franchir	.	.	.	to cross.
frapper	.	.	.	to strike, hit, knock.
fréquenter	.	.	.	to frequent.
frère, *m.*	.	.	.	brother.
friture, *f.*	.	.	.	crackling.
froid	.	.	.	cold.
fruit, *m.*	.	.	.	fruit.
fumer	.	.	.	to smoke.
funèbre	.	.	.	funereal.

G.

gaffe, *f.*	.	.	.	mistake (familiar).
gagner	.	.	.	to gain, earn, reach.
galerie, *f.*	.	.	.	gallery.
garçon, *m.*	.	.	.	boy, waiter.
garde, *m.*	.	.	.	guard.

gare, *f.*	. . .	station.
gauche	. . .	left.
gaz, *m.*	. . .	gas.
général, *m.*	. . .	general.
gens, *m. pl.*	. . .	people (gens de lettres = men of letters).
glace, *f.*	. . .	mirror.
glisser	. . .	to slip (se glisser = to slip).
gloire, *f.*	. . .	glory.
goût, *m.*	. . .	taste.
goûter	. . .	to taste, relish.
gouvernement, *m.*	. .	government.
grand	. . .	great, big, large.
gratuit	. . .	free, gratuitous.
guerre, *f.*	. . .	war.
guichet, *m.*	. . .	grill, booking-office.
guide, *m.*	. . .	guide-book.
Guillaume	. . .	William.

H.

habile	. . .	clever.
habiller	. . .	to dress (s'habiller = to dress oneself).
habit, *m.*	. . .	coat.
habitué, *m.*	. . .	frequenter.
s'habituer (à)	. . .	to get used (to).
se hâter	. . .	to make haste.
hausser	. . .	to shrug.
haut	. . .	high, loud.
hauteur, *f.*	. . .	height.
hein ?	. . .	eh ?
hétérodynage, *m.*	. .	heterodyning.
heure, *f.*	. . .	hour, time (of day) (tout à l'heure = just now, presently).
heureusement	. .	happily.
heureux	. .	happy.
hier	. . .	yesterday.
histoire, *f.*	. . .	history, story.
hiver, *m.*	. . .	winter.
homme, *m.*	. . .	man.
honneur, *m.*	. . .	honour.
hôtel, *m.*	. . .	hotel (hôtel de ville = town hall).

I.

ici	. . .	here.
idée, *f.*	. . .	idea.

île, *f.*	. . . .	island.
n'importe	. . .	no matter (n'importe quel = no matter what, any you please).
impressionner	. . .	to impress.
imprimer	. . .	to print.
inaperçu	. . .	unnoticed.
inconvénient, *m.*	. .	inconvenience.
index, *m.*	. . .	fore-finger, indicator.
indiquer	. . .	to indicate, point out.
indispensable	. .	essential.
innombrable	. .	innumerable.
inquiet	. . .	uneasy, anxious.
installer	. . .	to install (s'installer = to install oneself).
interdire	. . .	to forbid.
intéressant	. . .	interesting.
s'intéresser (à)	. .	to be interested (in).
intérêt, *m.*	. . .	interest.
interrompre	. .	to interrupt.
intervenir	. .	to intervene, interfere.
intrigue, *f.*	. .	plot.
inviter	. . .	to invite.

J.

jaser	. . .	to chatter.
jaunâtre	. . .	yellowish.
jaune	. . .	yellow.
Jean	. . .	John.
jeter	. . .	to throw, cast.
jeune	. . .	young.
jeunesse, *f.*	. .	youth.
jouer	. . .	to play, jouer de (instrument), jouer à (game).
jouir (de)	. . .	to enjoy.
jour, *m.*	. . .	day.
journal, *m.*	. .	newspaper (journal parlé = news bulletin (wireless)).
journaliste, *m.*	. .	journalist.
jugement, *m.*	. .	judgment.
juger	. . .	to judge.
jusque	. .	up to, as far as, until.
juste	. . .	just, exact (au juste = exactly).
justement	. .	exactly.

K.

kilomètre, *m.*	.	kilometer (about ⅝ of a mile).

L.

là	.	.	there (là-dessus = thereupon, on it).
laisser	.	.	to leave, let, allow.
lait, *m.*	.	.	milk.
lampe, *f.*	.	.	lamp, valve (wireless).
langue, *f.*	.	.	tongue, language.
lapin, *m.*	.	.	rabbit.
large	.	.	wide, broad.
largeur, *f.*	.	.	breadth.
las	.	.	weary, tired.
se lasser	.	.	to grow weary.
laver	.	.	to wash (se laver = to wash one-self).
léger	.	.	light.
légume, *m.*	.	.	vegetable.
lendemain, *m.*	.	.	the next day, to-morrow.
lever, *m.*	.	.	rise.
se lever	.	.	to get up.
libre	.	.	free.
ligne, *f.*	.	.	line.
lire	.	.	to read.
livre, *m.*	.	.	book.
livre, *f.*	.	.	pound.
loger	.	.	to lodge.
loin	.	.	far.
loisir, *m.*	.	.	leisure.
long	.	.	long (le long de = along).
longer	.	.	to walk along.
longtemps	.	.	long (adv.) (for) a long time.
longueur, *f.*	.	.	length.
loterie, *f.*	.	.	lottery.
lourd	.	.	heavy.
lumière, *f.*	.	.	light.

M.

magasin, *m.*	.	.	shop.
magistral	.	.	masterly.
magnifique	.	.	magnificent.
main, *f.*	.	.	hand.
maintenant	.	.	now.
mais	.	.	but.
maison, *f.*	.	.	house.
mal	.	.	badly, ill (adv.).
malgré	.	.	in spite of.
malheureusement	.	unfortunately.

Manche, *f.*		English Channel.
manche, *f.*		sleeve.
manquer		to miss, lack.
marchand, *m.*		merchant, dealer.
marchandise, *f.*		merchandise, wares.
marché, *m.*		market.
marcher		to walk, march.
marque, *f.*		mark, make, brand.
marquer		to mark.
maternel		motherly.
matin		morning.
méchant		wicked, wretched.
médecin, *m.*		doctor.
méfiance, *f.*		mistrust.
même		even (adv.) (le même = the same).
mener		to lead, take.
mer, *f.*		sea.
mère, *f.*		mother.
merveille, *f.*		marvel, wonder.
merveilleux		marvellous.
métal chromé, *m.*		chromium plate.
Métropolitain, *m.*		Paris Underground Railway.
mettre		to put (se mettre à = to begin, set to work to).
midi		midday.
milieu, *m.*		middle.
minuit		midnight.
minute, *f.*		minute.
modèle, *m.*		model.
modéré		moderate.
moderne		modern.
modeste		modest, unassuming.
moins		less (au moins = at least (as a minimum), du moins = at least (at all events)).
mois, *m.*		month.
moment, *m.*		moment.
monarque, *m.*		monarch.
monde, *m.*		world, people (tout le monde = everybody).
monnaie, *f.*		change, small coinage.
monsieur, *m.*		sir, gentleman, Mr.
mont, *m.*		mount, mountain.
monter		to mount, get (into).
montre, *f.*		watch (montre-bracelet = wrist watch).
montrer		to show.

se moquer (de)	. . .	to laugh (at).
morse, *m.*	. . .	Morse (code).
mort, *f.*	. . .	death.
mot, *m.*	. . .	word.
mou	. . .	soft.
mouchoir, *m.*	. . .	handkerchief.
moyen, *m.*	. . .	means.
moyennant	. . .	in consideration of.
multiplier	. . .	to multiply.
munir (de)	. . .	to supply, provide (with).
musée, *m.*	. . .	museum.

N.

natal	. . .	native.
naturellement	. . .	naturally.
ne . . . guère	. . .	scarcely.
ne . . . personne	. . .	nobody.
ne . . . plus	. . .	no more, no longer.
ne . . . que	. . .	only, nothing but.
ne . . . rien	. . .	nothing.
ni . . . ni	. . .	neither . . . nor.
nom, *m.*	. . .	name.
nombre, *m.*	. . .	number (collective).
nombre d'appel, *m.*	. . .	telephone number.
nord, *m.*	. . .	north.
note, *f.*	. . .	note, bill.
nouveau	. . .	new (de nouveau = again).
numéro, *m.*	. . .	number.
numéroté	. . .	numbered.

O.

obliger	. . .	to oblige, compel.
obscurité, *f.*	. . .	darkness.
s'obstiner (à)	. . .	to persist (in).
obtenir	. . .	to get, obtain.
occasion, *f.*	. . .	opportunity, occasion.
occuper	. . .	to occupy.
œil, *m.* (plur. yeux)	. . .	eye.
œuf, *m.*	. . .	egg.
officier, *m.*	. . .	officer.
offrir	. . .	to offer.
oiseau, *m.*	. . .	bird.
oncle, *m.*	. . .	uncle.
onde, *f.*	. . .	wave.
or, *m.*	. . .	gold.

oreille, *f.*	. . .	ear.
s'orienter	. . .	to get one's bearings.
orner (de)	. . .	to adorn (with).
os, *m.*	. . .	bone.
ou	. . .	or.
oublier	. . .	to forget.
outre	. . .	besides, in addition to.
ouvreuse, *f.*	. . .	girl usher, attendant.
ouvrier, *m.*	. . .	workman.

P.

pain, *m.*	. . .	bread.
palais, *m.*	. . .	palace.
papeterie, *f.*	. . .	stationer's shop.
papier, *m.*	. . .	paper.
paquebot, *m.*	. . .	liner, packet-steamer.
paquet, *m.*	. . .	packet.
par	. . .	through, by.
parasite, *m.*	. . .	parasite, *m. pl.* atmospherics (wireless).
paraître	. . .	to appear, seem.
parce que	. . .	because.
parcourir	. . .	to traverse.
parcours, *m.*	. . .	trip, journey, ride.
pareil	. . .	like.
parisien	. . .	Parisian.
parfait	. . .	perfect.
parfaitement	. . .	perfectly.
parler	. . .	to speak.
parole, *f.*	. . .	word, word of honour.
parterre, *m.*	. . .	pit.
partie, *f.*	. . .	part.
parti, *m.*	. . .	party (prendre son (le) parti = to make up one's mind).
pas, *m.*	. . .	step, pace.
passage, *m.*	. . .	passage.
passant, *m.*	. . .	passer-by.
passer	. . .	to pass, spend (of time) (se passer = to happen.)
payer	. . .	to pay, pay for.
pays, *m.*	. . .	country, district.
pédant	. . .	pedantic.
peine, *f.*	. . .	trouble, difficulty (à peine = hardly).
pendant	. . .	during (pendant que = while).
pendre	. . .	to hang.

penser	.	.	to think.
percale, *f.*	.	.	cotton cambric.
perdre	.	.	to lose, ruin.
père	.	.	father.
permettre	.	.	to permit, allow.
personne, *f.*	.	.	person (ne . . . personne = **no** one).
petit	.	.	little, small (adj.).
peu	.	.	little (adv.).
peur, *f.*	.	.	fear (avoir peur = to be afraid).
pièce, *f.*	.	.	piece.
pied, *m.*	.	.	foot (à pied = on foot).
piéton, *m.*	.	.	pedestrian.
pipe, *f.*	.	.	pipe.
pierre, *f.*	.	.	stone (Pierre = Peter).
pitié, *f.*	.	.	pity.
pittoresque	.	.	picturesque.
place, *f.*	.	.	place, seat, square.
plaindre	.	.	to pity (se plaindre = to complain).
plaire	.	.	to please (s'il vous plaît = **(if you) please**).
plaisir, *m.*	.	.	pleasure.
plan, *m.*	.	.	plan, map.
plein	.	.	full.
pleuvoir	.	.	to rain.
pluie, *f.*	.	.	rain.
plume, *f.*	.	.	pen.
(la) plupart	.	.	most.
plus	.	.	more (de plus = moreover).
plusieurs	.	.	several.
plutôt	.	.	sooner, rather.
poche, *f.*	.	.	pocket.
poli	.	.	polite.
poliment	.	.	politely.
polir	.	.	to polish.
politesse, *f.*	.	.	politeness.
pont, *m.*	.	.	bridge, deck (of ship).
populace, *f.*	.	.	populace, rabble.
portatif	.	.	portable.
porte, *f.*	.	.	door.
porter	.	.	to carry, wear.
porteur, *m.*	.	.	porter, bearer.
poser	.	.	to put.
poste, *m.*	.	.	wireless-set.
pour	.	.	for, in order to.
pouce, *m.*	.	.	thumb, inch.
pourquoi	.	.	why.

pousser	. . .	to grow, utter.
pratique	. . .	practical.
précision, *f.*	. .	precision, exactitude.
préférer	. . .	to prefer.
prélever	. . .	to deduct.
premier	. . .	first.
(la) première	. .	first performance.
prendre	. . .	to take (se prendre à = to set about).
présenter	. .	to present.
presque	. . .	almost.
prestidigitateur, *m.*	.	conjurer, juggler.
prêter .	. .	to lend.
prier .	. .	to beg, pray.
prix, *m.*	. .	prize, price.
problème, *m.*	. .	problem.
proche	. . .	near.
proclamer	. .	to proclaim.
prodiguer	. .	to lavish.
profiter (de)	. .	to profit (by), take advantage (of).
profondeur, *f.*	. .	depth.
proie, *f.*	. .	prey.
promenade, *f.*	. .	walk.
se promener	. .	to walk.
propriétaire, *m.*	. .	landlord, owner.
province, f.	. .	province.
public, *m.*	. .	public, audience.
punir .	. .	to punish.

Q.

qualité, *f.*	. .	quality.
quand	. . .	when.
quant à	. . .	as for.
quartier, *m.*	. .	quarter, district.
que .	. .	that (conj.), whom, which, that (rel. pronoun).
quelque	. . .	some.
quelquefois	. .	sometimes.
quelqu'un(e)	. .	someone.

R.

raccrocher	. .	to hang up (telephone).
raconter	. .	to relate, tell.
radio-diffusion, *f.*	.	broadcasting.
raison, *f.*	. .	reason (avoir raison = to be right).

ramasser	. . .	to pick up, gather.
ramener	. . .	to bring back, lead back.
rapide	. . .	fast, rapid.
rapide, *m.*	. . .	express train.
rang, *m.*	. . .	row, rank.
se rappeler	. . .	to recall, remember.
ravir	. . .	to delight.
receveur, *m.*	. . .	conductor.
récepteur, *m.*	. . .	receiver.
recevoir	. . .	to receive.
rechercher	. . .	to look for (à la recherche de = in search of).
reconnaissant	. . .	grateful.
reconnaître	. . .	to recognise.
redouter	. . .	to dread.
réel	. . .	real.
réflexion, *f.*	. . .	reflection.
regarder	. . .	to look at.
régime, *m.*	. . .	régime, diet.
réglage, *m.*	. . .	tuning.
règlement, *m.*	. . .	regulation.
régler	. . .	to pay (bill).
règne, *m.*	. . .	reign.
reine, *f.*	. . .	queen.
relatif	. . .	relative, comparative.
relation, *f.*	. . .	relation, connection.
remarquer	. . .	to notice.
remède, *m.*	. . .	remedy.
remercier	. . .	to thank.
remettre	. . .	to hand, put back.
remonter	. . .	to mount again, go back to.
remplir	. . .	to fill.
remuer	. . .	to move, stir.
rendez-vous, *m.*	. . .	meeting-place.
rendre	. . .	to render, give up (se rendre = to betake oneself).
renoncer (à)	. . .	to give up, abandon.
renseignement, *m.*	. .	information.
se renseigner	. . .	to get information.
rentrer	. . .	to return.
répandre	. . .	to spread.
repas, *m.*	. . .	meal.
répéter	. . .	to repeat.
répondre	. . .	to answer.
reprendre	. . .	to take back, resume.
représentation, *f.*	. .	performance.
représenter	. . .	to perform.

reproche, *m.*	.	.	.	reproach.
résonner	.	.	.	to (re)sound.
résoudre	.	.	.	to solve, resolve.
restaurer	.	.	.	to restore.
rester .	.	.	.	to remain.
restituer	.	.	.	to restore.
résultat, *m.* .	.	.	.	result.
retenir	.	.	.	to retain, book.
retour, *m.*	.	.	.	return.
réussir (à)	.	.	.	to succeed (in).
revenir	.	.	.	to come back.
réverbère, *m.*	.	.	.	street lamp.
revers, *m.*	.	.	.	back, reverse.
revoir .	.	.	.	to see again.
riche .	.	.	.	rich.
rideau, *m.*	.	.	.	curtain.
ridicule	.	.	.	absurd, ridiculous.
rire .	.	.	.	to laugh.
rive, *f.*	.	.	.	bank.
roi, *m.*	.	.	.	king.
rôle, *m.*	.	.	.	part (theat).
route, *f.*	.	.	.	road, route, way.
royaume, *m.*	.	.	.	kingdom.
rougir .	.	.	.	to blush.
rue, *f.* .	.	.	.	street.

S.

sacré .	.	.	.	sacred.
sacrifier	.	.	.	to sacrifice.
sage .	.	.	.	wise.
saisir .	.	.	.	to seize, grasp.
saison, *f.*	.	.	.	season.
salle, *f.*	.	.	.	hall, auditorium.
salon, *m.*	.	.	.	lounge, drawing-room.
sans .	.	.	.	without.
sauver	.	.	.	to save (se sauver = to escape).
savoir .	.	.	.	to know.
scène, *f.*	.	.	.	scene, stage.
secouer	.	.	.	to shake.
secret, *m.*	.	.	.	secret.
séduire	.	.	.	to seduce, charm.
séjour, *m.*	.	.	.	stay.
selon .	.	.	.	according to.
semaine, *f.*	.	.	.	week.
sembler	.	.	.	to seem.
sens, *m.*	.	.	.	sense, direction.

sentinelle, *f.*		sentry.
sentir		to feel.
serein		clear, serene.
serrer		to press, squeeze.
servir		to serve (servir de = to serve as; se servir de = to make use of).
seuil, *m.*		threshold.
seul		alone.
si		if (conj.), so (adv.).
siècle, *m.*		century.
siège, *m.*		seat, siege (siège social = head office).
sifflement, *m.*		whistling.
signal, *m.*		signal (signal horaire = time signal).
situé		situated.
soi-disant		self-styled.
soie, *f.*		silk.
soin, *m.*		care.
soir, *m.*		evening.
soirée, *f.*		evening, evening party.
soit		either—or.
soldat, *m.*		soldier.
sombre		dark.
somme, *f.*		sum.
sommet, *m.*		summit.
somptueux		sumptuous.
songer		to think.
sonner		to ring.
sorte, *f.*		sort, kind.
sortir		to go out.
souffler		to blow.
soulagement, *m.*		relief.
soupir, *m.*		sigh.
sourire		to smile.
sous		under.
souterrain		underground.
spectacle, *m.*		show, sight.
station, *f.*		station (underground or wireless).
style, *m.*		style.
subventionner		to subsidise.
succéder		to succeed, follow.
suffire		to suffice.
suivre		to follow.
sujet, *m.*		subject.
supérieur		superior, upper.
supporter		to endure, bear.

sur	.	.	.	on.
sûr	.	.	.	sure.

T.

tabac, *m.*	.	.	.	tobacco.
table, *f.*	.	.	.	table.
tant	.	.	.	so much, so many.
tante, *f.*	.	.	.	aunt.
tapis, *m.*	.	.	.	carpet.
tard	.	.	.	late.
tarder (impersonal)	.	.	.	to long.
tas, *m.*	.	.	.	heap (tasse = cup).
téléphone, *m.*	.	.	.	telephone.
téléphoner	.	.	.	to telephone.
téléphonie sans fil (T.S.F.), *f.*	.	.	.	wireless.
temps, *m.*	.	.	.	time, weather (il fait beau (temps) = it is fine).
tendre	.	.	.	to hand.
tenir	.	.	.	to hold (tenir (à) = to be anxious (to)).
terminer	.	.	.	to end, finish.
terrasse, *f.*	.	.	.	terrace.
tête, *f.*	.	.	.	head.
théâtre, *m.*	.	.	.	theatre.
Tiens !	.	.	.	Look !
timbre-poste, *m.*	.	.	.	postage stamp.
tirer	.	.	.	to draw, pull, fire.
titre, *m.*	.	.	.	title.
tocsin, *m.*	.	.	.	tocsin, alarm-bell.
toilette, *f.*	.	.	.	dress.
tomber	.	.	.	to fall.
ton, *m.*	.	.	.	tone.
tonner	.	.	.	to thunder.
torturer	.	.	.	to torture, torment.
toucher	.	.	.	to touch.
toujours	.	.	.	always.
tour, *m.*	.	.	.	round, tour, walk, trip.
touriste, *m.*	.	.	.	tourist.
tourner	.	.	.	to turn.
tout	.	.	.	all, every (adj.), quite (adv.).
tout à fait	.	.	.	quite.
tragédie, *f.*	.	.	.	tragedy.
trahir	.	.	.	to betray.
train, *m.*	.	.	.	train (en train de = in the act of).
traité, *m.*	.	.	.	treaty.

trajet, *m.*	. . .	crossing, journey, trip.
travail, *m.*	. . .	work.
travailler	. . .	to work.
traverser	. . .	to cross.
tremper	. . .	to soak.
très	. . .	very.
triste	. . .	sad, wretched.
tromper	. . .	to deceive (se tromper = to make a mistake).
troubler	. . .	to trouble, worry.
trouver	. . .	to find (se trouver = to find one-oneself, to be).
tuer	. . .	to kill.

U.

unique	. . .	unique, only.
utile	. . .	useful.

V.

vache, *f.*	. . .	cow.
valable	. . .	valid.
varier	. . .	to vary.
véhicule, *m.*	. . .	vehicle.
veille, *f.*	. . .	eve, day before.
vendeur, *m.*	. . .	vendor, shop-assistant.
vendre	. . .	to sell.
venir	. . .	to come.
vérifier	. . .	to verify, confirm.
verre, *m.*	. . .	glass.
vers	. . .	towards, about.
à verse	. . .	in torrents.
viande, *f.*	. . .	meat.
vider	. . .	to empty.
vie, *f.*	. . .	life, living.
vieux	. . .	old.
village, *m.*	. . .	village.
ville, *f.*	. . .	town, city.
vingtaine, *f.*	. . .	score, twenty.
visiter	. . .	to visit, examine.
visiteur, *m.*	. . .	visitor.
vite	. . .	quickly.
vivre	. . .	to live.
vocabulaire, *m.*	. . .	vocabulary.
vogue, *f.*	. . .	vogue, fashion.
voie, *f.*	. . .	track, railway line.

voir	.	.	.	to see.
voisin .	.	.	.	neighbouring.
voiture, *f.*	.	.	.	carriage, motor-car, coach.
voix, *f.*	.	.	.	voice.
volontiers	.	.	.	willingly.
voyage, *m.* .	.	.	.	journey.
voyager	.	.	.	to travel.
vrai	.	.	.	true.
vraiment	.	.	.	truly, really.
vu . . . que	.	.	.	seeing that.
vue, *f.*	.	.	.	sight.

IMPORTANT NOTE

If you have worked steadily through this book and feel that you have mastered its contents, you will now be eager to go further. Perhaps it is French conversation that interests you; or you may want to qualify yourself to assist with the French correspondence of your firm; or you want to read the great French writers. Whatever you need, we think you will find it in the sequel to TEACH YOURSELF FRENCH which Mr. Scarlyn Wilson has produced under the title of EVERYDAY FRENCH. It is a really original and lively book, planned for the home student in just the same way as TEACH YOURSELF FRENCH, but greatly extending the range of your knowledge. Each lesson consists of three sections : (*a*) Conversational and Idiomatic; (*b*) Commercial; (*c*) Literary. The conversational passages make a continuous ' story ' through the book. The literary passages for translation are all taken from famous writers and are arranged in backward chronological order—that is, starting with modern writers and working back to the earlier classics—so that, with the accompanying notes, this section forms a miniature survey of French Literature. There is a complete key to the Exercises, a large Bibliography and a list of Military Terms.

B

ADVERTISING & PUBLICITY   ALGEBRA   AMATEUR ACTING   ANATO
OOK-KEEPING   BRICKWORK   BRINGING UP CHILDREN   BUSINESS
CHESS   CHINESE   COMMERCIAL ARITHMETIC   COMMERCIAL ART
COMPOSE MUSIC   CONSTRUCTIONAL DETAILS   CONTRACT BRIDGE
PEEDWORDS   ECONOMIC GEOGRAPHY   ECONOMICS   ELECTRI
NGLISH GRAMMAR   LITERARY APPRECIATION   ENGLISH RENASCE
EVIVAL   VICTORIAN AGE   CONTEMPORARY LITERATURE   ETCHIN
REELANCE WRITING   FRENCH   FRENCH DICTIONARY   FRENCH
IVING THINGS   GEOLOGY   GEOMETRY   GERMAN   GERMAN
GOOD CONTROL OF INSECT PESTS   GOOD CONTROL OF PLANT DISEA
GOOD FARMING BY MACHINE   GOOD FARM WORKMANSHIP   GOOD
GOOD MARKET GARDENING   GOOD MILK FARMING   GOOD PIG KEE
GOOD ENGLISH   GREEK   GREGG SHORTHAND   GUIDEBOOK TO TH
GREAT   BOLIVAR   BOTHA   CATHERINE THE GREAT   CHATHAM   CLEM
IBERALISM   HENRY V   JOAN OF ARC   JOHN WYCLIFFE   LENIN   LOUIS X
ROBES   HASTINGS
HOUS   REPAIRS
WRITI   ND TOOL
MECH   LCRAFT
MOTO   FICIENCY
PHYSI   DESIGN
ADMI   NG   RE
PHRA   OOK   SAILING   SALESMANSHIP   SECRETA   ACTICE
EBATE   SPELLING   STAMP COLLECTING   STUDE   DE   ST
YPEWRITING   USE OF GEOGRAPHY   WAY TO POETR   WRIT
COOKERY FOR GIRLS   DOGS AS PETS FOR BOYS AND GIRLS   KNIT
HOTOGRAPHY FOR BOYS AND GIRLS   RADIO FOR BOYS   RIDING F
OCCER FOR BOYS   STAMP COLLECTING FOR BOYS AND GIRLS   WO
ACTING   ANATOMY   ARABIC   ASTRONOMY   BANKING   BEE
CHILDREN   BUSINESS ORGANISATION   CALCULUS   CANASTA   C
COMMERCIAL ART   COMMERCIAL CORRESPONDENCE   COMMERC
CONTRACT BRIDGE   COOKING   CRICKET   DRAWING   DRESS
ECONOMICS   ELECTRICITY   ELECTRICITY IN THE HOUSE   ELOCU
NGLISH RENASCENCE   ENGLISH RENASCENCE TO THE ROMANTIC
ITERATURE   ETCHING   EVERYDAY FRENCH   TO EXPRESS YOURS
ICTIONARY   FRENCH PHRASE BOOK   GARDENING   GAS IN TH
GERMAN   GERMAN DICTIONARY   GERMAN GRAMMAR   GERMAN
CONTROL OF PLANT DISEASES   GOOD FARM ACCOUNTING   GO
GOOD FARM WORKMANSHIP   GOOD FRUIT FARMING   GOOD GRA
GOOD MILK FARMING   GOOD PIG KEEPING   GOOD POULTRY KEE
GREGG SHORTHAND   GUIDEBOOK TO THE BIBLE   HINDUSTANI
CATHERINE THE GREAT   CHATHAM   CLEMENCEAU   CONSTANTINE   COC
ARC   JOHN WYCLIFFE   LENIN   LOUIS XIV   MILTON   PERICLES   PETER TH
USE OF HISTORY   WARREN HASTINGS   WOODROW WILSON   HOCKE
HOUSEHOLD ELECTRICITY   HOUSE REPAIRS   ITALIAN   JOINERY
MANAGEMENT   MATHEMATICS   HAND TOOLS   ENGINEERING
DRAUGHTSMANSHIP   METEOROLOGY   MODELCRAFT   MODERN DAN
MUSIC   NORWEGIAN   PERSONAL EFFICIENCY   PHILOSOPHY   PHO
SHORTHAND   PLANNING AND DESIGN   PLUMBING   POLISH   PO

GIVE INSTRUCTION
TO A WISE MAN···